BUSINESS ETHOS AND VALUES

BUSINESS ETHOS AND VALUES

R. Joseph

ANMOL PUBLICATIONS PVT. LTD.
NEW DELHI - 110 002 (INDIA)

ANMOL PUBLICATIONS PVT. LTD.
H.O.: 4374/4B, Ansari Road, Daryaganj
New Delhi - 110 002
Ph.: 23261597, 23278000
B.O.: No. 1015, Ist Main Road, BSK III Stage
III Phase, III Block
Bangalore - 560 085 (India)
Visit us at: www.anmolpublications.com

Business Ethos and Values

First Published, 2006

Reprint, 2009

PRINTED IN INDIA

Published by J.L. Kumar for Anmol Publications Pvt. Ltd., New Delhi - 110 002 and Printed at Mehra Offset Press, Delhi.

Contents

1

An Introduction to Business Ethos

The simplest definition of business ethos is to view it as the application of ordinary human ethical values or principles in the conduct of business. In this respect business ethos is no different from other branches of applied ethics, such as medical ethics or social ethics or sexual ethics, which all submit various fields of human behaviour to ethical and moral analysis and evaluation. (For most practical purposes the terms ethical and moral have exactly the same meaning and differ only in their origin, 'ethos' deriving from ancient Greek and 'morals' from classical Latin. Occasionally, however, ethos is considered the more scientific and systematic term.)

Yet it would be over simplifying to consider business ethos as just routinely applying general ethical or moral values or rules to different business activities such as voting on a particular company policy, marketing a new product, securing a contract or making a sale. Frequently, general ethics can be led to develop its thinking by considering various business activities and recognising that experience of real-life situations can lead us to refine or deveiop our understanding and appreciation of moral values or principles. For isntance, considering the various ethical or moral issues which can arise in advertising or in negotiations can throw light on human communication and lead to the realisation that what ethically counts as telling the truth or telling a lie will often vary according to circumstances or conventions. Giving ethical attention to marketing can help to clarify our understanding of the different types of human needs, how these may differ from desires, wishes and wants, and how the satisfaction (or creation) of such needs may be evaluated from a moral or ethical point of view. Again, the whole issue of bribery not only demands that ethical significance be attached to differences of culture and social convention. Its analysis can also produce important distinctions with differing ethical evaluations, including the difference between bribing someone to do their ordinary job (facilitating payments) and bribing someone to abuse their position (corruption), and between volunteering a bribe on the one hand and being compelled to pay extortion on the other. Considering corporate behaviour forces us to look closely at ideas about collective responsibility and dispersed responsibility, or responsibility spread thin, as well as taking into account the force of corporate pressures and influences (the corporate culture) in determining the degree of accountability of individual members of a firm in wrongful business behaviour.

It follows from these preliminary considerations that business ethos is not the unvarying imposition of ethical standards on the gamut of business situations. It is more of a dialogue between the science of ethics and the conduct of business. The values and principles which come into play are what have been termed the ordinary human decencies, which are obviously not limited solely to business behaviour; yet the types of actions and the ways of behaving in which these human and social values are applied are unique to business and have varied through the ages. The interplay of these values and situations provides the material of modern business ethos.

Future Research and Developments

Research in the field of business ethos covers both empirical study of what is actually going on and normative study of what business ethically might or ought to be doing. As the academic discipline of modem business ethos has been evolving through several stages, each has influenced the directions which research has been following. In a seminial article, De George (1987) pointed out that the rise of business ethos as an emerging field of intellectual activity in the 1970s was due in large measure to the entry of a significant number of philosophers who brought ethical theory and

Preface

"Business Ethos and Values" as a paper is being taught at post graduate, M.B.A. and other management courses at various universities and institutions. This book is designed as an introductory text to the above paper, encompassing vital information on all pertinent aspects. Thus the material presented here would be of interest as well as of great use to the students, teachers and professionals of management. This book will provide complete knowledge of the business ethos, global e-business, corporate structure of planning environment, ethical leadership, ethical marketing, ethics and social responsibility, administration and social ethics, globalisation etc. to the students.

The major topics dealt in this book are—An Introduction to Business Ethos; Indian Ethos for Management; Global E-Business; Corporate Structure in Business; Corporate Planning and Environment; Ethical Leadership in Business; Market Economy in Business; Corporate Code of Ethics; Strategy Implementation in Business Ethos; Value of Management Ethics; Ethical Marketing in Business; Case Study Methodology of Business Ethos; Ethics and Social Responsibility; Administration and Social Ethics; Globalisation in Business Ethos; Business Concept in Constitution.

It is hoped that all those will benefit from the contents of this book for whom it is meant. The author will feel amply rewarded, if motive is achieved.

Author

philosophical analysis to bear on the subject and thus helped form the structure of what developed into business ethos. Given this strong injection of philosophical reflection and analysis into business ethics, following the earlier paradigm of medical ethics, it is not surprising if the predominant line of research at the time was normative rather than empirical. At the same time, however, philosophers were not universally welcomed on to the business playing field, and were indeed quite often the target of resentment if not outright hostility as trespassers in an area with which they were not professionally conversant. Hence, it would not be surprising if there arose among professional ethicists who ventured into the field of business ethos around that time a sense of inadequacy both of their approach to business and of their expertise by comparison with the scientific rigour and empirical confidence of business academics as these addressed the same field of business activity.

Another reason for an increasing amount of empirical research in business ethics in recent years may be found in the way in which entry of practitioners into the field has changed. On the whole, the subject of business ethics was not developed by business academics but by a variety of individuals whose primary qualification was in some other discipline, usually at first connected with philosophy or theology. In the circumstances they tended to approach business ethics less as a branch of business studies and more as an area of applied ethics comparable to the areas of medical ethics, nuclear ethics, political ethics and the like. Very few experts even today in business ethos are also qualified business academics and generally speaking business ethos is not yet a career track in business or management studies, nor is it yet universally accepted as an integral branch of such studies.

Nevertheless interest in business ethos has begun to grow in recent years also among business academics, and it is not surprising if their favoured lines of research in ethos echo the mainly empirical approach with which they are professionally at home. Thus, ethical issues related to the workplace were initially developed by scholars interested in organizational behaviour and only later have issues to do with the marketplace begun to be explored by marketing researchers (Robertson 1993). To this might now be added the increasing influence of social science academics in the field and the consequent growing awareness of the need to be aware of the social or structural contexts, pressures and constraints under which individuals in a company behave.

A third reason for the modem increase in empirical by contrast with normative research in business ethos may arise from a certain loss of confidence in modern society in any fixed or reasonably recognisable ethical markers. One of the most debated issues in business ethics at all levels of activity concerns cultural relativism and the danger of incurring charges of ethical imperialism if one asserts the existence and accessibility of any absolute or trans cultural moral values or norms (Donaldson 1989). The studied decision not to espouse any clear ethical aposition is a noticeable feature of many standard textbooks on business ethos today, and this seems to be more than an avoidance by the author of appearing to dogmatize or to indoctrinate readers, especially undergraduate readers. It may stem from the prevailing overriding respect for tolerance and pluralism as the outstanding ethical, values in modern society, which leads to reluctance or inability to do more than record in empirical fashion the sorts of moral attitudes, behaviour and arguments which mayor may not appeal to managers or staff or business students.

In the words of Rogene A Buchholz, "Business ethos refers to right or wrong behaviour in business decisions".

In the words of Peter F. Drucker, "Ethos deals with the right actions of individuals."

In the words Thomas M. Garrett, "Business ethos is concerned primarily with the relationship of business goals and techniques to specifically human ends".

Thus, business ethos are the principles, practics and philosophies that guides the business people in their day to day business decisions. It relates to the behaviour of a businessman in a business situation. They are concerned primarily with the impacts of decisions of the society, within and outside the business organisation or other groups who keep interest in the business activities.

Albert Z. Carr is of view that the business ethos are different from the ethics of society at large. He argues that the ethos of business is game ethics, which is different from the ethics of religion and society. Business has the impersonal characteristics that demands both a special strategy and an understanding of its special ethos. The basic rules of game ethics are set by the government and the country, which makes effort to detect and punish the fraudulent behaviour of business.

Ethos and Related Concepts

Many concepts are linked with the term 'ethos'; namely ethos and morality; ethos and moral theology or religious morality; ethos and law, etc.

Ethos and Morality. The terms 'ethos' and 'morality' are not synonymous terms. Ethos is the principle that guide the human behaviour. Morals are related with the traditional believes, norms, moral judgments, ideas and existing social formalities by which the man regulates and guides his social behaviour. Ethos do not accept these things. In other words, customs, conventions and the accepted courtsies of a society are not the foundations of ethos though they may provide valuable guidance to the man. In brief ethos is the code of conduct developed by proper testing to guide the human behaviour, whereas morality is concerned with generally accepted conducts and conventions of the society.

Ethos and Moral Theology. Ethos is not synonymous to religious morality or moral theology. Thomas M. Garrett writes "The religions derive their moral percepts not only from human experience but from devine relevation. It must rely on the unaided human reason. Because of this, the conclusions of ethos often fall far short of the ethical imperatives found in both Judaism and Christianity. Ethos admits its incompleteness and sends the religious men to his faith for the completion of his moral equipment." Really speaking, moral theology is the source for development of ethics. Ethos gets ideas and values from moral theology and through the experiments, it approves them as "Code of Conduct". This way the economic life of man is activated on the basis of religious principles. The development of ethos could be possible only through religious morality. For example: there are certain saying like "Honesty is the best policy"; "Customer is the King".; "Social satisfaction is our motto", etc. are developed from religious morality only, but are used by the business.

Ethos and Law. There are differences between ethos and law also. It may be accepted by everyone that law is enacted by the government. Law is concerned with the minimum regulation necessary for public order while ethos examines both the individual and the social good in all dimensions. Social customs and traditional beliefs cannot get a place in the law. The government gives shape to only those minimum social obligations, customs or traditions which are essential to be complied with by the people. On the other hand, ethos contains all those social obligations, customs and traditions which are argumentally essential to be implemented in the society.

Some people believe that ethos, particularly honesty provides the moral foundation for a free enterprise. According to this view, ethos involves more than being honest, but honesty is the beginning point of ethos and it is a basic social principle. Ethos may be equated with fairness and justice as well as honesty, but the conditions for fairness and justice derive from honesty.

Interrelationship between Ethos, Morality and Law

From the foregoing description it is clear that morality gives birth to religious theology. The society gets values, traditions and customs from the morality which is called moral values. When the society lays down certain guiding principles and regulations for public compliance after testing the moral values, customs and traditions; ethos takes shape. On the other hand, when certain minimum social customs, traditions and moral values are codified and implemented by a socail institution, it is called the law.

CHARACTERISTICS OF BUSINESS ETHOS

For understanding business ethos, it is necessary to know its important characteristics. Which are as follows:

1. It is Art and Science, Both. Business ethos lays down the principles of business behaviour, standards, moral values, decisions etc. It is an ideal science because business ethos presents the base for differentiating good or evil, proper or improper, just or unjust actions of business. It is an art because it emphasis practical use of behavioural standards and principles.

2. A Discipline. Business ethos are the guiding principles of business functions. It is the knowledge through which human behaviour is learnt in a business situation.

3. Dynamic Philosophy. It is a dynamic philosophy. It continuously test the rules, dynamic moral standards and behaviour of the society.

4. Different from Social Morality. Ethos is different from social morality. The business ethos does not accept the customs and traditions of the society. But, where the customs, traditions and social values are tested practically, they are accepted as principles of business ethos.

5. Not based on Emotions. Business ethos is not based on emotions but is based on the reality and social customs prevailing in business environment. Really speaking business ethos is developed after testing the requirements of business environment, social customs and traditions, and the rules of its conducts.

6. Study of Goals and Means. Business ethos is the study of goals and means for the rational selection of sacred objects and their fulfilment. It accepts the principles of "Pure goals inspire for pure means" and "Means justifies the end".

7. Recognition to Moral Responsibility. Business ethos has the moral responsibility to accept proper and improper things where it has not legal binding. The business accepts the moral responsibility only by its own will, and not by any force.

8. Theology is the Base of Business Ethos. The base of business ethos is theology. The development of business ethos became possible due the theological principles such as sincerity, human welfare, service, good behaviour, etc.

9. Business Ethos is not Affected by Social Approval or Disapproval. Business ethos is not affected by the social approval or disapproval. Decisions taken by the business on the principles of ethos may sometimes be criticised by the society, but such decisions have their own importance in the business point of view.

10. Different from Social Responsibility. Social responsibility mainly relates to the policies and functions of an enterprise, whereas the business ethos to the conduct and behaviour of businessmen but it is a fact that social responsibility of business and its policies are influenced by the business ethos.

11. More Greater than Law. Although the law approves various social decisions, the law is not so greater than ethos. Law is usually related to the minimum control of social customs whereas ethos gives importance to individual and social welfare actions.

12. Good Intention. The inner contents of business ethos is good wishes, good opinion, and good expectations. It is a moral science which differentiates between good and evil, right and wrong actions of business.

13. Relating to Human Aspects. Business ethos studies those activities, decisions and behaviours which are concerned with human aspect. It is the function of the business ethos to notify those decisions to customers, owners of business, government, society, competitors and others on, good or bad, proper or improper conducts of business.

14. A Universal Philosophy. Business ethics is a universal philosophy. Wherever there are business functions, there it would become necessary to consider the questions relating to business ethos.

Arguments in Favour of Business Ethos

Once Robert Day has said that good ethics not only promotes professionalism in management, but it purify the inner mind of every businessman. It brings advantages of mutual dealings or transactions in case both the parties follow the principles of good ethics. Some of the important arguments are as follows:

1. Satisfaction of Sub-conscious Mind. Certain people consider only good ethics can promote good business as the ethical conducts give satisfaction to their sub conscious mind. Really speaking a businessman is first a member of the society, a businessman later. Many businessmen first behave like individuals and then work for satisfaction to their inner subconscious mind. A person may not take any decision which does not give him mental satisfaction.

2. It Increases Mutual Trust and Confidence. Prof. Robert Day writes, "when ethical conduct is displayed, it puts some kind of trust and confidence in relationship". Because of this reason, people deal with a businessman.

3. Goodwill of Business and Businessman. Ethical conduct of business increases the goodwill of business and the businessman, both. It is a known fact that nobody likes to deal with a mischievous or fraudulent businessman. At the same time, people do like to deal with a good businessman, but introduce him with others also, for regularity in dealings. This way good ethical behaviour increases the goodwill of both, the business and the businesman.

4. Helps in Professionalization of Management. Prof. Day writes that management cannot become a profession so far as it does not follow good ethics. Really speaking, an important feature of a profession is that it has a laid down code of conduct, which remains on the principle of "Service to Humanity". Therefore, it is the first condition for professionalisation to develop and follow ethos.

5. Releases from Tensions. A businessman who follows the ethical principles in the conduct of business, releases himself form tensions or worries. He needs not have the fear of legal action or social boycott. He need not worry about the security of his property as he gets legal protection.

6. Protects Each Other. Prof. Robert Day further adds, "Good ethos is sound business insurance". It protects people in dealing with each other. In reality, businessmen act more sincerely with each other.

7. Perpetual Succession. Ethical conduct of business leads to development and perpetual succession of success. The business may prosper in the shadow of ethics. Learned writes that a sincere person who does hard work becomes ethical and always succeed in his efforts, but an unethical person cannot.

8. Greater Zeal and Productivity. There will be greater zeal of a person who follows the ethical principles in business. This will increase his creative capability and be success in achieving his objets. Learned and associates write that an unethical person is of deceiving nature and never be able to face the creative zeal of a sincere person.

PRINCIPLES OF BUSINESS ETHOS

The various wellknown authorities on the subject have contributed much to establish the principles of business ethics. They include the name of Cantt, J.S. Mill, herbert Spencer, Plato, Thomas Garrett, Woodrad Wilson, etc. The principles of business ethos developed by them are given below:

1. Principle of Sacredness of Ends and Means. This is the first and foremost principle of business ethos. It emphasises that the means and techniques adopted to secure the business ends must be sacred and pure. A good objective should not be obtained by evil means. Therefore, both the end and the means must be sacred.

2. Principle of Proportional Judgement. In practice, there arise a situation (while achieving the ends through means) where the business gives some losses to others. In order to avoid such a situation, the principle of proportional judgement must be observed. This principle suggests that one should make proper judgement before doing anything so that others do not suffer from any loss or risk of evils by the conduct of business. A proportionate judgement is said to be present where ends and means equals or exceeds bad effects.

3. Principle of Not to do Evil. This is another important principle of ethics that not to do any evil or to desire any evil for others. Gararett writes that it is unethical to expect evil against oneself or against anybody else, irrespective of the fact that such expectation is in the form of ends or means. All the functions of business and the society are symbol of their expectations.

4. Principle of Publicity. This one of the principles of business ethos given by W. Wilson. This principle suggests that anything that is being done or to be done, should be brought to the knowledge of everyone. When everything or any decision is in the knowledge of all concerned, none gets any opportunity to do unethical act.

5. Principle of Equivalent Price. According to Woodrad Wilson, the people are entitled to get goods equivalent to the value of money they pay. Businessmen are responsible to ensure the principle of equivalent price.

6. Principle of Non-cooperation in Evils. This principle suggest that it is unethical to cooperate with evil or to do evil as a means to an end. Therefore, one should not cooperate with anyone for doing evil acts. *e.g.*, giving bribe to any government employee for getting any work done is unethical and this act is a cooperation for doing evil.

7. Principle of Satisfaction. The conduct of business should be such that it must produce satisfacation. One should make efforts by his own actions to keep others more satisfied.

8. Principle of Universal Value. This principle suggests that the conduct of business should be based on universal values. He should act with sincerity, mutual good and confidence. All his acts should be based on the accepted principles of ethics.

9. Principle of Cooperation with Others. This is another important principle of business ethics; to cooperate with others in doing good work. It should not cooperate with those who do not deserve it or to those who do evils.

10. Principle of Consciousness on Business. This principle states that a businessmen should give importance to his inner voice coming out from his sub-conscious mind. He should not play the game of business like other games. He should have an interest above the level of winning of losing.

11. Principle of Due Process. This principle of business ethos suggests that the businessmen/managers should follow due process in their decisions so that the interests of others will not be overlooked. This will help to give justice to all and get an opportunity to differentiate between good and evil, right and wrong, proper and improper conducts.

12. Principle of Aspirit of Service. This principle suggests that a businessmen should be guided by the 'service motto' in all his acts and decisions.

13. Principle of Human Dignity. Professor Sturdivant has correctly stated that it is the basic principle of ethos to keep the human dignity up. In other words, man should not be treated as a factor of production, but his satisfaction should be one of the objects of business.

14. Principle of Exemplary Conduct. For the purpose of establishing high quality of ethos, the managers and officers should present exemplary conducts before their subordinates. Simply by quoting examples/ideals, the subordinates cannot be motivated towards ethical behaviour/conducts.

15. Principle of Expectations. This principle suggests that a businessman should give attention to those who keep reasonable expectations from the business and are affected by the functions and decisions of business. He should give priority to the expectations of customers and employees.

16. Principle of Autonomy. This principle suggests that there should be autonomy in conduct of business. One should not be bound to act under any pressure from statutory provisions, but he should act voluntarily on ethical principles.

ETHICAL STANDARD AND ISSUES IN BUSINESS

The ethical standards and issues or the scope of business ethos are dynamic. It is so because these standards and issues are based on the existing social-political and economic systems which are dynamic in nature. There was a time when the ethical issues were set by the state or law, but since the beginning of 20th century, religious institutions and government felt difficulty in understanding the changing complexities of business. Business itself, therefore, has started developing its moral philosophy, keeping in view of the state policies, rules, regulations and social needs. The ethical quandary in business today stems partly from the fact that a company is in a sense a social system, and as such reflects social values. Furthermore, the expectations of society, for instance, with respect to the social responsibilities are placing a heavier responsibility on the business community to meet ethical values.

Ethical standards and issues as given by Prof. Bowen are:

1. The Question Regarding Distribution of Income

This issue involves the problem relating to distribution of income, long run costs and distribution of net profits.

2. Other Ethical Issues Such as:

— Honesty and legal provisions.

— Working conditions and labour profit.

— Social costs and values.

— Advertising and sources of public relations.

— Economic stability.

— Relations with government and

— Others

Samuel B. Shapero, has suggested four general problems of ethos that typically concerning to executives, such as:

(a) What is the limit of our job responsibility?

(b) Do we make the decisions or do we involve our clients?

(c) Shall we manipulate the people for their own good?

(d) What is more important? The system or the individual.

ISSUES IN BUSINESS ETHOS

The scope of business ethos or the issues in business ethos are briefly stated below:

1. Issues Relating to Objectives of Business. Business ethos includes all such matters which are concerned with business objects. It is necessary for the businessmen to consider ethical values in setting business objectives. Whether to achieve maximum profits or a reasonable profits; is a matter of ethical issue. The social, human and national objectives must also be set on business ethos.

2. Issues Relating to Owners of Business. The role of investors in business is very important. They are the owners of business. Although there are a number of laws and regulatory provisions to safeguard the interests of investors, there is need to consider this issue in view of ethical principles. Some of such issues may be relating to:

(a) investment of capital on profitable schemes/projects.

(b) quantum of risks involved in establishing new business.

(c) safeguards to the interest of minority shareholders.

(d) notice of information to every member of the progress and profitability of business.

(e) new issues of shares and debentures, and priority of allotment.

(f) notices of meetings to all members of the company use and misuse of company property.

(g) speculation in shares known from confidential report.

All these issues are concerned with interests and rights of share-holders. Day to day managerial decisions may influence anyone or more of these issues. All the managerial decisions must be weighed on ethical standard to ascertain whether they are proper or improper, right or wrong.

3. Issues Relating to Customers. There are a number of issues relating to customers which are also to be considered on ethical grounds. These matters include:

(a) quality, price and usability of the products.

(b) purity and safety.

(c) pricing of goods.

(d) correct measures and weights.

(e) consumer education and protection of consumers rights.

(f) warranty and conditions on sale of goods.

(g) misleading advertising and publicity.

(h) monopolistic and restrictive trade practices, etc.

4. Issues Relating to Employees. Business has certain moral responsibility towards its employees. There are a number of legislative provisions regulating to the conditions of work, appointments, promotions, transfers, security, training and development, wages and salaries, labour welfare and machinery for settlement of disputes. In all these matters, ethical and moral standards must be applied.

5. Issues Relating to Creditors. The issues relating to creditors which need attention on ethical grounds are:

(a) Health, education and living standards.

(b) removal of wastes coming out of manufacturing process.

(c) Social welfare and community development schemes like hospitals, public parks, community centres, etc.

(d) protection of environment.

(e) priority in employment.

9. Issues Relating to National Interest. The business should give top priority to national interests.

The following issues need consideration towards national interest:

(a) Priority in national schemes.

(b) providing of employment.

(c) export policy matters ind ustrial policy and licensing policy.

(d) international cooperation.

(e) upliftment of socially and economically backward people.

(f) decentralisation of economic power.

(g) matters concerned with national reputation.

(h) optimum use of resources and equal distinction of income.

From the foregoing description, it is clear that the scope or the issues in ethos are much larger and dynamic. The areas of business where the human behaviour, individual respect and satisfaction, morality public welfare are involved, needs consideration on ethical ground.

TECHNIQUES TO IMPROVE ETHICAL CONDUCT OF BUSINESS

There is need to motivate the businessmen to follow ethical principles in the everyday conduct of business. There are a number of measures to motivate them for ethical conduct in business. These measure are classified into the following categories:

I. At the Institutional Level

The following measures can be used at the institutional level.

1. Ethical Code of Conduct. An ethical code of conduct is an handbook containing the rules, regulations and procedures to be followed by the employees of an organisation. Now increasing number of business organisations lay down code of conduct to be followed by the employees.

2. Ethics Committees. Ethics committees are formed for influencing the ethical conduct of business on a permanent basis. Usually big business organisations easily formulate such committees; consisting of top executives. This committee evaluates the ethical problems confronting the organisation and advice proper steps for improving ethical standards.

3. Ethical Training. There is need to provide training to the officers and employees to improve the ethical conduct in business.

4. Social Aduit. Social aduit is the audit by which the social costs and benefits from the business are evaluated. This will help to identify the ethical and unethical conducts of business.

5. Ethics Specialists. Some organisations appoint ethics specialists to advice the top management towards the ethical behaviour. The specialists examine the activities of employees and take decisions to improve the ethical behaviour of employees.

6. Penalties. There should be provision for punishment in case of violation of ethical principles and rules. Criminal and monetary punishment may be given to those who neglect the ethical code of conduct.

7. Appointment of Professionals. Ethical standards can easily be followed by appointing professional managers in business organisations. Professional managers are found by the code of conduct of their respective professions. As such, they will enforce the ethical standards in the conduct of business.

8. Transparency in Working. The procedure of functioning, rules and policies, decisions, etc. of a business organisation should not be kept so secret. An open and free communication system should be encouraged. This will help in improving the ethical values.

II. Efforts at the Government level

The government controls and regulates the business activities. It makes efforts through various enactments to improve the moral and ethical values of business in the society. In this efforts the following measures can be suggested:

1. Clear Cut Policies. The government policies and procedures of working, in many cases, are not so clear. Certain business people take advantage of this situation. They adopt corrupt practices, for taking advantage of the situation.

2. Strict Penalty Provisions. Strict penalty provisions may be made in the various Acts controlling the conduct of business. The present penalty provision, especially in the Companies Act, 1956 must be altered so as to give more criminal and monetary punishments.

3. Excessive Control. Excessive controls on business may lead corruption. Where the government introduces economic controls in licensing, allotment of quotas and permits, etc. ethical standards must be kept in mind. As far as possible excessive controls on business must be removed.

4. Political Indiscipline. Political indiscipline is one of causes of unethical condut or business. In every country some sorts of examples are found. In India, the Bofors Scandal is a good example.

5. Enactment and Enforcement of Laws. The government has enacted various laws protecting the interests of consumers, workers, public interest, etc. But their real enforcement could not be made possible. The government should enact special Act for the enforcement of ethical principles by the business.

III. At the Social and Religious Levels

Man is in some way or other attached with the society and the religion he belongs. His behaviour can be certainly improved by social relationship and the religious preachings. The measures to be taken in this respect are:

1. Social Boycott of Unethical Acts. A businessman who follows unethical conduct in business should be socially boycotted by the people. People should not purchase the products of such businessman.

2. Efforts by Social Service Institutions. There are a number of social service organisations in the country working for the welfare of the people. Consumer Guidance Society of India, Consumer Action Forum, etc. are a few which look after the interests of consumers. They should take effective steps to bring in the notice of the authorities of such businessmen who act on unethical grounds.

3. Preaching by Religious Preachers. Religious preachers can put much influence on the business people to follow ethical conduct in business. In India, many businessmen have regular meetings with religious heads and followers, and this is a good sign of improvement in ethical conduct of business.

4. Efforts by the Business Associations. The various associations related with trade and industry formulate code of conducts for their members and the members are bound by strict compliance of such code of conduct. The trade and industrial organisations should take adequate measures for strict adoption of these code of conduct.

In conclusion we may state that business ethics examines carefully the business activities and conducts in the context of moral responsibility and then postulates them in the sense of being proper or improper, right or wrong, fair or unfair. It expresses the moral responsibilities and duties of business and further emphasises the need for executing them.

FACTORS CAUSING ETHICAL BEHAVIOUR IN BUSINESS

Where there are certain causes which led the unethical conduct of business, there are certain factors which led the ethical conduct of business. They are briefly stated below:

1. Public Awareness. People are now well aware about their rights and therefore, the business cannot conduct its activities prejudicial to public interest. Short weights and measures, and other restrictive trade practices are well aware to the common people now.

2. Government Policies. The government of the country is adopting certain policies which prevent the unethical conduct of business activities. The policy of nationalisation of uneconomic units and social control on business, dynamic ind us trial policies, licensing, export import policies, environmental protection policy, labour policy etc. have made to follow ethical conduct of business.

3. Active Role of Communication Medias. Various communication medias like newspapers, radios and televisions, etc. play important role in projecting or bringing in light the unethical behaviour of business through articles, editorials, cartoons, etc. This has forced the business to follow ethical principles.

4. Government Laws and Statutory Controls. Government in the country has enacted various laws; rules and regulations under the provisions of which the business is bound to act honestly. The important among these laws are: M.RT.P. Act; Foreign Exchange Regulation Act; Control of Capital Issues (Regulation and Control) Act; Import-Export Regulation Act, etc. The business is, under the provisions of these Acts, bound to follow the ethical code of conduct.

5. Business Education and Professionalisation. The development of professional institutions have been helpful in producing professional managers; who are very conscious about the fulfilment of social responsibility of business. They put more emphasis on consumer satisfaction and human resource development, rather than the motive of profits.

6. Development of Buyers' Market. Large-scale production by industrial units have been helpful for the development of buyer's market. These industrial units make available goods and services according to the needs and wants of consumers. Situation of shortages of products has been disappearing. Now the buyers have wider choice to select from many items.

7. Birth of Consumerism. The development of consumer movement and consumer organisations have been successful in checking the conducts of business. The Consumer Protection Act, 1986 is a good step taken by the government to protect the interests and rights of the consumers. This Act provides for punishment and monetary compensation for the unethical acts of the business. All these have paved the way for the ethical conduct of business.

8. Awareness of Social Responsibility. Modern business pays much importance to the fulfilment of social responsibility towards the different sections of the society. It gives more emphasis to 'Service' aspect, such as consumer satisfaction, social interest and welfare, etc. in place of maximisation of profits and assets. They voluntarily adopt ethical standards by coming out from the clutches of statutory restrictions.

9. Efforts by Business Associations. Many business associations like Federation of Indian Chamber of Commerce (FICCI), Associated Chamber of Commerce and Industry (ASSOCHEM), Chambers of Commerce in the States, etc. have laid down certain code of conduct for their members and they are forced to follow the code of conduct strictly. This also has led the ethical conduct of business.

10. Inspiration from Leaders. National leaders, economists, educationists, etc. have given inspiration of business from time to time through their public speeches and writings. Mahatma Gandhi, our Father of Nation gave everlasting inspiration to the people and business community. His principle of trusteeship concept is an inspiration to the business.

11. Pressure from Top Executives. The top executives of certain business houses give inspiration to their managers and employees to keep them away from unethical conducts. The top executives themselves present ideals before the subordinates, and the subordinates follow them.

FACTORS CAUSING UNETHICAL CONDUCT OF BUSINESS

The causes of increasing number of unethical conduct of business are summarized below:

1. Increase of Acute Competition. The nature of competition at national and international levels has been increasing day-by-day. Brener and Molander have found in their studies in 1974 that the important cause of decreasing use of ethical conduct in business is the increasing nature of competition.

2. Increasing Indiscipline and Dependence. Indiscipline and dependence are found increasing in today's world. People do not follow the legal permissions. They are dependable to the comforts and amenities available in the modem world.

3. Decline in the Social Values and Customs. Social values and customs are not followed by the new generation.

4. Decreasing Standards of Society. Another reason for increasing the unethical conduct of business is that the standards of the society is declining, according to Brener and Molander. Their study revealed that 34 per cent of the business managers admit this fact.

5. Political Corruption. Almost in all the countries, political corruption is increasing. Today political parties and politicians accepts donations/gifts/contributions from businessmen for their political gain.

6. Information of Unethical acts Through Medias. Unethical acts of business is made known to the people in the society through various medias. Such information may give advantage or disadvantage to some people. Inexperienced businessmen, who lost their ways through misguided advertisements and publicity programmes and are pursueded to do unethical conduct of business for short-run gains.

7. Economic Greed. Greed for money and property are increasing in the minds of the people. They want to become rich in a short while even by doing any unethical acts. Such people consider money/profits are the measurement of efficiency and success. Some businessmen have the same kind of greed and they are directed towards unethical conducts of business.

8. Pressure to Earn More Profits. This also is an important factor of unethical conduct of business. There is again an increasing pressure on the businessmen to maximise profits to cope with enlarged requirements. This is mainly due to the fact that the share holders expect larger returns from money they invested, the managers want higher salaries and benefits, the directors want higher remuneration and perquisites, and similarly all other categories, who have interest in the business directly keep their high expectations from the business.

9. Loss of Personal Character and Integrity. People lose their personal character and integrity by doing unethical acts. They lose sincerity, trust and confidence and do the unethical acts.

TYPES OF SCOPE OF UNETHICAL CONDUCT OF BUSINESS

Walton writes that business ethics is related with truth and justice; and it has various components like expectations of society, healthy competition, advertising, public relations, social responsibility, consumer freedom and good behaviour. People expects that all the business activities and decisions must be aimed at ethical grounds. But in practice, it finds that business is involved in unethical activities. Many of its activities are objectionable, exploitative and loss giving to the people. Many of its decisions are violation to principles of ethos. A few of such unethical conduct of business are:

1. Political Donations and Gifts. Gifts, donations or contributions to political leaders or parties to get any unconstitutional act done, namely sanctioning of any special contracts, issue of licenses, etc.

2. Neglect of Social Interest. Social and consumer interests are neglected by misutilising the national aspects and using the government machinery for private gain.

3. Creation of Cut-throat Competition with other Business Institutions. In addition to the creation of acute-competition, it solicits the consumers and leaks out the business secrets of other institutions.

4. Spreading of Corruption. Giving bribe to government officers and subordinates encourages for the practice of corruption in government offices.

5. Presentation of false Returns of Income and Statement. False income returns and statements of accounts are presented before the various authorities for the purpose of evading taxes, and to have the benefit of various incentives from the government.

6. Production and Distribution of Illegal Items Opposed to Public Policy. It produces and distributes goods of harmful nature to health and security, be conduct of unethical methods.

7. Accumulation of Profits by Illegal Means. It undertakes various unconstitutional activities like hoarding of goods, black marketing, speculation, etc. to maximise profits.

8. Trading with Enemy Countries. For the purpose of acquiring wealth within a short period of time some business people establish relations with people of enemy counties either by leaking out the country's security measures or by supplying information or materials relating to the security/defence of the country.

9. Exploitation of Society. For the purpose having monopoly profits it gives misleading advertisements and publicity, false labelling, use of false trade mark, etc.

10. Encourages Smuggling Activities. It engages in smuggling activities and establishes relations with international gang of smugglers to enter into illegal trading between countries.

❐

2

Indian Ethos for Management

Business need not be regarded evil, tainted and unethical. Business is sacred. It is a matter of attitude, approach and level of management consciousness. One can do business, make money, earn profit, build up property and even then it can be managed with due recognition to human and ethical values and respecting all persons in the enterprise and in the society as human beings. Indian ethos demands subjective management system.

(1) Management Attitude

Top management must have firm belief in values oriented holistic management of business. The management is called upon to meet expectation of all stakeholders, *e.g.* employees, customers, citizens and shareholders and fulfil the social responsibility. Profit is earned through service and satisfaction of all these interested parties. No one can calculate statistically the gains made through mental peace, harmony, self-contentment and consolation. No amount of profit acquired through unfair business and trade practices can guarantee health, happiness and harmony of all members of the organisation and the community.

(2) Humanising the Organisation

There are three aspects of humane organisation.

(a) Inter-personal relations;

(b) man-machine equation; and

(c) inner management—mental and spiritual.

The core of an organisation is worker. Any person is a human being and then he may play any role in life. As a human being, he/she is a complex personality with changing psychology. Hence, whole-person approach is necessary to manage human resources and their multiple needs. Management must develop human touch and humanised managerial style. An organisation can create best inter-personal relations based on promotion from within equality, autonomy, selfesteem and fraternal affection. Hierarchy should show greater human concern in the entire life of the subordinate and operator. Unity, harmony and effective communication can assure team spirit and team work in an organisation.

(3) Interiorising Management

Self Management. The manager is first a man and then a manager. The manager should first learn to manage and control himself. Without self management and control, how can he manage and control others? The first need is understand and know himself. This is a course in the subjective system of management. Western management is based on objective system of management. Indian insights want first system of subjective management and then only management in objective terms can be perceived and practised.

Management of self brings about harmony and integration among the five members of your total being body, vital, mind, intellect and soul. Now instead of mind and ego leading other members, your phychic being, *i.e.* soul will act as the manager or leader of all members. Thus conflict among the other four members can be resolved. This is called management by consciousness or self-management. To manage your self is a difficult and challenging job. But with determination and self-effort it is feasible. To co-ordinate and harmonise body mind intellect complex is the essence of self-management. Once your manage and control yourself, to your own satisfaction, you will be able to manage and control effectively your subordinates and workers. In fact they will also be tempted to follow your example and would motivate themselves to develop self-discipline and self control in their life.

4. Self-introspection

We have to embark upon self-study, selfanalysis and self-criticism to locate areas of friction and disharmony. We should prepare a balance sheet of our own strengths and weaknesses. Our mind and heart may indicate weak spots. By regular introspection we would find out solution to problems so that the concerned parts of our being can be persuaded and guided to play the desired role. We have to reduce or subdue our ego. Of course, it would require patience and perseverance to tame the members of our being. Introspection involves self examination of your own thoughts, feelings, emotions, sensations and passions.

5. Brain-Stilling (Decision-making in Silence)

The Western managment resorts to brain storming, *i.e.*, loud thinking by managers for decisions to solve management problems. The Indian insight advocates a better alternative in the form of brain-stilling. For rational and enduring decisions, silent mind is a much more effective medium to get sound and lasting solution to all management problems.

A perfect Mounum (calm mind enjoying tranquility) is necessary. It indicates absence of any thought flow in the mind. Preferably manager should have a small room of silence attached to his office where he may retire from busy life to meditate in silence over the burning problems in case of need. Such facilities may also be provided to the employees to retire in silence and seek solutions to their problems. By this method the manager and his employees come into contact with the inner mind or higher consciousness for arriving at proper solutions to their problems. They should be receptive to receive the guidance through intuitive mind (immediate insight). Intuition means immediate mental apprehension without reasoning, usually through inspiration.

Based on consciousness, management is developed from within to without *i.e.* management of your own self and then management of others. The consciousness or Chetana has two elements, awareness of self and things, a will or force that makes the consciousness effective. Awareness and will power are always one movement.

(6) Stepping Back (For a While)

The stepping back or drawing back into yourself is another device of learning to go deep within and look; you can remain quiet and call on the inner consciousness force and wait for a while for an answer. Then you know exactly what to do. Remember, therefore, that you cannot receive the answer before you are very peaceful. Practise that inner silence, make at least a small beginning and go on in your practice until it becomes a habit with you. Once you enter into inner consciousness, you will know what true behaviour would be, what true solution to a problem is, what true action is. The stepping back from a situation for a while enables you to control and even master the situation. Such withdrawing from involvement helps you to receive right guidance or intimation from within from your inner-self.

When your have a problem to solve, when you are ought in a difficulty, try this method, instead of becoming agitated, turning over all the ideas and actively seeking solutions of worrying, fretting, running here and there inside your head I do not mean externally—remain quiet, implore the light and wait for a few moments for it to come. In silence, the solution comes very quickly and in silence you are able to hear it.

(7) Self-dynamising Meditation

A dynamic meditation is meditation of transformation of lower consciousness into higher consciousness. Hence, we call it transforming meditation. It opens the third eye of wisdom through insight.

You may meditate to open yourself to the Divine Force to receive its guidance to discover the points to be transformed, *viz.* baser or evil elements in your nature, *i.e.* your weaknesses and to trace out the line of progress.

You may meditate to reject your ordinary consciousness (your selfish and egoistic traits). You may meditate for practical reasons; you have a difficulty to clear up, a solution to find, a solution to a problem, you want help in some action or other, you want to know how to face a crisis, a sudden change you want to reduce stress and strain which is inevitable in the current hectic life. Meditation helps to solve many complex problems of management and organisation demanding higher consciousness. Behind our outer and lower consciousness, we have our true inner being, the centre of consciousness. Through meditation, in a silent and calm mind, you are able to contact this centre or higher consciousness, refer all problems of your life and when your mind is open and receptive to this higher consciousness, you receive intimations in the form of intuitions guiding you to form your right decisions and to solve your problems and difficulties. This is called consciousness approach to management, a process of Within-to-Without management. The management and workers must have absolute faith or trust on the Supreme's Infinite Power.

(8) Role of Intuition in Management

Intuition is the act of coming to direct knowledge or certainly without reasoning or inferring. It is immediate cognition by inner mind through inspiration, instant awareness the little voice, within you which you hear when your mind is silent, *i.e.*, thoughtless. Intuitive skills enable a manager to cope with confidence the fluctuating environment and rapid changes. Firstly we must have faith in the power of intuition. What we, firmly believe, we can do. Faith is the pre-requisite in decision-making based on intuition. People do not know how important faith is, how faith is miracle, creator of miracles.

Secondly practice leads to perfection. By consistent practice we can develop our capacity of decision-making by intuition. We all possess intuitive capacity to the fullest. Dynamic meditation transforms our lower-consciousness into higher consciousness, *i.e.* in the inner mind where we have silence. In the silent mind you have flashes of intuition. New skills like intuitive abilities are in great demand in complex and fast changing environment. Intuitive mind reflecting quality of mind is much more important than mere data or information for decisions on strategic matters. Intuition has the veto power. Intuition is more powerful than reason. Feelings are born with us. Reason is developed later. In the 21st century, manager will face extremely complex and turbulent environment. He will have to deal with changing world and a world force demanding increasing use of intuition in strategic planning and strategic decision-making.

Till 1990, management approach relief on left brain style, *i.e.*, logical analytical style and deductive reasoning based on case studies and information. A new model ort combination of left train (analysis and deduction) and right brain (contemplation, luition and induction) is now popular. It is a blending of Western and Eastern management concepts.

Management development programmes are how giving more emphasis on the training of intuitive right brain skill, alongwith usual deductive analytical left brain skills relying totally on data for solving management problems. The best mix of brain types and the personality types would provide the effective team work and team spirit. Managers with higher intuitive ability can be very suitable in management areas, *e.g.* personnel, health public relations advertising, marketing and crisis management. These fields demand creativity, imagination and other right brain skills.

Those who possess higher intuitive ability and potential should actively develop right brain skills and market their intuitive ability for improving their career and rise quickly to the higher managerial jobs in the organisation. Top management members must have intuitive faculty. Exercise of mind stilling and meditation must be an integral part of management development programmes. These will have double benefit: *(1)* reduction of stress and strain, *(2)* development of right brain skills.

The aforesaid Indian insights should evoke a good response in a manager to the existence of a master-key within functioning in a human being which can resolve all problems of management. Even in a computerised age, human being is necessary in decision-making.

Essential Features of Indian Ethos and Insight

1. The divinity of a human being is not merely a notion but a truth which can be expereinced by a person in the stillness of mind, *i.e.*, in absence of any thought. Hence, potentially one is divine or a perfect being.

2. Balance or equilibrium is the keynote of Indian thought. We have synthesis, harmony between the dual concepts, *e.g.*, desire and desirelessness, material discontent and divine discontent. Such opposites are thought and worked out harmoniously. Spiritual and secular or worldly life are duly recognised. Even a king can be the knower of the reality and lead both worldly and spiritual life.

3. The individual is taken as the central focus by Indian Ethos. He/she both are regarded as the foundation. If you are good, the world is good. Such a thought ensures the wholesome quality of work life.

4. The divine element in the individual (as a core or substratum) is only a portion of the universal or cosmic consciousness (pure consciousness). The sublime Indian concept offers a secure base for mutual trust, co-operation, team work, living and working for the public benefit (and not exclusively for personal benefit) and such noble smoothening ideas of organisational and societal life.

5. Indian ethos is based on the Indian scripture: (a) Sruties (*e.g.* Upanishads, Gita) and Smrutis (the Puranas). Indian thought provides eternal knowledge of creation, cosmos and man and recognises close interrelation between spiritual and worldly life of a human being. This is called whole-man approach.

6. The Indian ethos gives much greater emphasis on values, human and ethical. Knowledge is not power. Character is the real power and wealth. Values must be combined with skills. Then only we can have effective and efficient management and we can assure

the quality of work life in the organisation and enriched quality of human life.

7. Indian ethos rarely speaks of rights and privileges of an individual. It emphasizes only duties and responsibilities. Human existence is primarily to pay our debts tó all quarters of the universe. Rightly understood, it implies that in practice nobody's rights are ignored. They are automatically ensured. Thus values, moral and ethical are given status in the human life and activities. Value-based education is needed.

8. As per Indian ethos all work is worthy and honourable. This is called dignity of work. All work is considered as a valuable means for purifying our mind and ego as well as for gaining money, power, fame and name. Ourtlaily life has a unique combination of materialism and spiritualism. Work is worship of the Divine within and without. We are called upon to be constantly conscious of His Presence through all our actions. Shri Aurobindo says: Behave as if the Divine Mother was looking at you (as an observer). Indeed she is always present. "Divine Mother is Divine Power or Shakti."

9. Indian thought deals with two types of knowledge *(a)* knowledge of creation or world, *(b)* knowledge of creator, *i.e.*, Divine. What is one thing by knowing which everything else will be known? The answer to this question is the knowledge of the Creator. This is subjective knowledge. It is known to you only in silence through personal experience. It is not an intellectual knowledge. It is called wisdom. The wisdom is born of contact with the Creator.

Character is based on divine values. The divine values are themselves based on wisdom. Therefore, Indian thought regards wisdom as balance. Inernalisation alone enables you to cultivate moral and ethical values and improve your own character and quality as a human being. Manager with enriched quality of mind and heart can have effective management. Management with proper combination of values and skills can assure the harmony and progress of their own organisation as well as enable the society and the country to enjoy healthy development and growth. This is the unique contribution of Indian ethos. Spiritual elixir in the field of management is necessary to achieve secular or worldly goals without unfavourable consequences for society and The Mother Earth.

Enlightened management thought in big corporate management expressing top management's values and attitudes in the mission or creed even in the U .S.A. and many over countries'in the West can be found. We want this in the management style in all levels of management and we would advocate all employees to be deeply involved in preparing the mission, 'vision, values, plans and policies. Then only corporations or firms will have credibility and character.

Basic Principles of Indian Ethos for Management

1. Immense potential energy and talents for perfection as human being has the spirit within his heart.
2. Holistic approach indicating unity between the Divine, individual self and the universe.
3. Subtle, intangible subject and gross tangible objects are equally important. One must develop one's Third Eye, Jnana Chakshu, the Eye of Wisdom. Vision, insight and foresight. Inner resources are much more powerful than outer resources. Divine virtues are inner resources. Capital materials and plant and machinery are outer resources.
4. Excellence at work through self motivation and self development is the best means of Total Quality Management.
5. Karma Yoga offers double benefit, private benefit, self purification and public benefit.
6. Co-operation is a powerful instrument for team work and success in any enterprise involving collective work.

INDIAN APPROACHES FOR MANAGEMENT

We reproduce here some Indian approaches or concepts for management mentioned by learned Prof. S.A. Sherlekar in his book "Ethics in Management."

(1) Holistic Approach in Management. This is based on spiritual principle that entire humanity is one and there is respect for all human tbeings. Managers to follow whole man approach of combining values and physical aspects of life. Higher consciousness will adopt holistic attitude. It will bring out divine in man which will achieve perfection, and excellence in our work. It will achieve peace, harmony and prosperity within and without. Spiritual and worldly life are equally recognised. Thus, balance or equilibrium is the keynote of Indian thought. There is close relationship between spiritual and worldly life and this is called whole man approach.

(2) Selfless Work (Karma Yoga). Work is worship. Do your duty without ego and without calculation of fruits of action. So pour your heart and soul in the performance of your work. Do your duty better and better. Work is important for personal growth and good of society (public benefit). Work brings inner joy of selfless service. All work is worthy and honourable. The dignity of work is valuable means of purifying our mind and helps in gaining money, power, fame and name.

(3) Excellence at Work. Excellence at work through self-motivation and self development is the best means of total quality management. To conclude, management with proper combination of values and skills can assure the harmony, progress of the organisation and society. Spiritual aspect is necessary to achieve worldly goals.

(4) Each Person is a Potential Divine Human. The divine means perfection in knowledge, wisdom and power. Therefore a human being has immense potential power of energy for self-development. Human being are more important than physical development and must be developed. Your boss gives you challenging work but may not be able to promote you. However, he can make you "promotable" and if you are promotable, somebody will promote you, as the world is much bigger than your present organisation.

(5) Indian Ethos Give Greater Emphasis on Values. Human and Ethical Value-based management is essential to combine subjective (money materials as well as human skills), objective phenomena (inner resources of human beings, *i.e.* wisdom and work ethics). So development of inner potential vision, insight, values are important for wisdom and character.

(6) Cooperation and Team Work. Healthy competition is a powerful motivator for excellence and success in business success.

The Gita says: "By cooperation and mutual help all small achieve the highest human welfare." Cooperation is a powerful instrument for team work and success of any enterprise.

CONCEPTS OF HUMAN RESOURCE DEVELOPMENT FROM INDIAN ETHOS

Swami Tejomayananda quotes examples of Human Resource Development from epics like the Ramayana and Mahabharta as under:

1. Awaken and Empower your People. The role of HRD can be drawn with the striking example of Lord Krishna as a master HRD specialist. Look at him in the roles of a counselor, trainer, friend, philosopher, guide and motivator leading by example. He distinctly earmarked Arjun's role to achieve success. He even chose to become Arjuna's sarathi (driver) and impress upon him to pick up his bow and arrow to fulfil his duties and obligations. Lord Krishna gave Arjuna not only the sermon but also enthused him morally to fight his battle.

2. Love and Inspiration are important to Develop Human Resources. The element of love in leaders enables them to collect and harness fortitudes of ardent and dedicated effort nothing significant can be achieved by mere official authority, post or, position. The Ramayana brings out this point beautifully.

Lord Rama and Ravana were both great, but with a vast difference in their greatness. Ravana tried to become big and great by making other people small. He thought that when others became small his own greatness would shine! On the other hand, Lord Rama's greatness is that He made every small person also great and equal to Himself. He even elevated the restless monkeys to the status of divinity. He achieved "monkey resource development"! It is through the mobilization of the monkey forces that He gained victory over the invincible and well equipped Ravana. This is one of the most fascinating aspects of the Ramayana. The secret of Lord Rama's success was His pure love for all.

3. Respect the Authority of Others. Another interesting aspect of Lord Rama's character was that He did not exercise any kind of authority over others. Sugreeva, the monkey king, offered his services alongwith his army to Lord Rama and awaited His orders. Rama however, declined to give orders and gave Sugreeva the freedom of planning the search for Sita Devi. You are aware of the problems of authority in Management. If the boss gives orders directly to the workers then the Departmental Head resents it and feels that his or her authority has been undermined or by passed. Lord Rama understood this fact, and so He respected the authority of others. Love and regard for others can do wonders. Now look at the character of Ravana. He never listened to anybody's advice. He surrounded himself with sycophants and whoever opposed his views was thrown out, as the American saying goes "Do it my way or hit the highway"! He neither possessed a noble inspiration, nor sincere love or regard for others. It is no wonder that he destroyed himself and others as well. Thus, the study of the Ramayana has teaches us Human Resource Development.

4. Leader and Inspiration are Vital. The Mahabharata too contains many fine examples. We know that the Kauravas had a much larger army than the Pandavas yet, the Pandavas won the war. Why? It was because of Lord Shri Krishna. He was their leader and inspiration. He mobilized them well. The Kauravas had no ,such inspiration on their side. Moreover, the Pandavas were convinced of their righteous cause and were totally devoted to Lord Krishna. This too was lacking in the Kaurava.

5. Surrender Individual for Higher Goals. Lord Krishna saw to it that a person must rise above individual importance for the sake of the totality. Without this sacrifice or higher goal great things cannot be achieved.

6. Right Job for Right Man. In this context it should be noted that the success of a project depends upon whether people are working for themselves or the project and are they capable of doing their jobs efficiently or not. There is a view that people can do all kinds of work. However, experience does not back this theory.

The great Chanakya has said it well, a person should be engaged only in a job that he is capable of doing efficiently.

Yo yasmin karmani kushalash sa tasmin eva yoktavyah

Every person cannot do everything, but every person is capable of doing something. In this sense, all people are equal. As such, the leader will have to really find the capabilities of his workers and assign jobs to them accordingly.

7. Perform Your Work in Perfection. Lastly, keep the advice of your masters in 'mind; having discovered your potential and aptitudes, perform your work as your worship of the Lord. You will be free from all impurities of the mind. Such an act of worship will unfold your personality instead of making you self-centered. The Bhagawad Gita says that man 'attains perfection by worshipping the Lord by his own Karmas:

Swakarmana Tam Abhyarchya Sidhim Vindati Manavah.

ROLE OF GEETA IN MANAGEMENT

Shrimad Bhagawad Geeta is a marvellous book of guidance. Be you a seeker of spiritual enlightenment or a person facing a moral dilemma or a managing director of a multinational company working for success, the Geeta can guide people effectively in achieving your objectives. This article outlines the role of the Geeta in Management Science.

According to Swami Sharoopananda, Lord Krishna gives many useful suggestions for an executive on how to manage his company successfully. The executive must have the following qualifications.

1. Jnanam (Vision). This means a complete vision of the entire organisation, its aims and objectives its place in the country and also in relation to other nations. There may be many functional divisions in the organisation but the head must see unity in all of them. The relationship between the parts and the whole must be understood very well.

2. Buddhi (Ability). The chief should be capable of imparting his vision to all his workers at their own level of understanding and field of work. This ability is Buddhi. While translating this vision into reality there will arise many problems, difficulties and obstacles that may be objective or manmade as well. At such moments what is required is Buddhi—the ability to understand the very cause of such problems and to remove it effectively. Buddhi is required to manage two kinds of people those who have difficulties and those who are difficult people! In order to do all this the Executive must have a good knowledge of the human mind.

3. Dhriti Patience. Dhriti means patience and fortitude. The ability to consistently hold on to your goal is called Dhriti. It is a well known fact that no goal is achieved easily and quickly. We meet with many obstacles which try our patience. Similar is the case when all workers are not able to see the vision and they act strangely enough as to frustrate even an effective leader. On all such occasions the leader must have extreme patience to win them over and achieve the goal. This ability is called Dhriti.

4. Theory of Karma (Result of our Actions). The law of Karma explains the entire phenomena of life. It is precise and comprehensive as the laws of science. Physics states that every action has an equal and opposite reaction. The theory of Karma postulates the universal accounting system in which each individual experience the appropriate result of his actions. What is accumulated in the past life becomes the fate in the present life. So fate is the result of the past Karma and is of our own making. So we have to take the responsibility of the results of our actions. In the Bhagawad Geeta, Bhagwan Sri Krishna convinces Arjuna to shed weakness and act, take the responsibility and fight in the battlefield. The result of the action naturally will depend upon the quality of the action undertaken. (Swami Nikhilananda).

5. Right Person for Right Job. Another important point to be considered is that the success of a project depends on the appointment of right persons for various jobs. There will be diversity in jobs and functions but there should be unity in purpose and total dedication to it. The greater the goal and higher the inspiration, the more spectacular success will be. The way Lord Krishna managed the crisis at the time of war, teaching Arjuna and then leading the Pandavas to victory, is proof of this fact.

6. Meditation. Meditation is concentration. The flow of the same kind of thoughts, all related to the Supreme Truth, uninterrupted by contrary or different thoughts, is meditation. When the mind becomes steady and concentrated and the intellect is redeemed from its wasteful habits of wrong imaginations, then the equipment (body mind and intellect) is ready for higher flights through the path of meditation. Meditation, consists in withdrawing by concentration all the sense organs away from their respective sense objects into the mind, and then withdrawing the mind into the inner intelligence and then contemplating upon the Highest. It is a continuous and unbroken thought flow, like a stream of flowing oil. In order to pursue this path, naturally the individual must have a dynamic head and heart—both minimally disturbed by their own subjective defects.

On what does One meditate? The highest form of meditation consists of steady contemplation on the nature of the Self, the Atman. Other forms of meditation do exists in the vast variety of spiritual practices such as meditating on a form a sound etc.

7. Self Control. Self-control is not self-denial. It is channelising our energies towards a purposeful end. Without disciplining the senses, no higher goals can be achieved in life.

The Bhagawad Gita is a companion for the journey of life. To relegate its study towards the ends of lie is to miss out on living meaningfully.

8. Development of the Intellect. To control and direct one's action is important for success. This is possible through a strong intellect. The intellet acts on reason and judgement. Acting on one's likes and dislikes may give us an immediate sense of pleasure, but it ultimately leads to ruin.

9. Choosing One's Career. One must choose in life a field of activity as per one's swadiharma (one's own nature). To find success and satisfaction, it is important to be in the field of one's interest, a fact often overlooked in choosing a career.

The above are basic requirements in successful management.

The Bhagwad Gita is the repository of the highest knowledge. This time tested and renowned dialogue holds answers to innumerable doubts that plague the human mind. Bhagawad Gita is book of life in everyday living. The Bhagawad Gita is a technique for dynamic living and not a retirement plan, says Vedantin Swami Parthasarathy. Yet most people believe that the study of the Gita should be initiated after one's active life is over. Such a belief has deprived us of the benefits of this glorious message.

The message of the Gita is meant to be a preparation for life. It helps us be productive in life while keeping the mind at rest. The Gita rendered by Lord Krishna, who is an epitome of dynamism. It is given to Arjuna the greatest warrior of his times. The message is given in a battlefield where the two are fighting adharmic forces. The message pulls Arjuna out of a despondent state and enabales him to gain victory and glory. How then can the message of Gita be directed towards inactivity and retirement?

INDIAN WISDOM AND MODERN MANAGEMENT

1. Model of Man. In Indian Wisdom (philosophy, psychology), material and spiritual aspects of human existence or life are given equal emphasis and there is very close interrelationship between worldly life and spiritual life. Both are manifestations or expressions of the divine or pure consciousness.

The holistic approach of Indian wisdom is needed for modern management to integrate matter /spirit or skills/values of object/ subject. Modern management must incorporate Indian ethos to perfect the turncated model of man (stressing only material progress at any cost) and recognise man as a whole man to assure wholesome human progress—spiritual as well as material progress—to satisfy the hunger of mind and soul as well as the hunger of physical and vital human being.

Values based holistic approach to management will assure such all round wholesome human development and prosperity. Western model of man and management could not give rich dividends. It is inadequate in solving all the problems of modern society. Important concepts of Indian wisdom and thought will enrich Western thought and provide a complete set of ideas for the management of organisations.

2. Managerial/Organisational Effectiveness. Managers should liberally draw on Indian wisdom for achieving highest levels of excellence in management and organisations. They can achieve both, the quality of work life and also the quality of output of goods. We will have the excellence in manager's and workers' performance as well as their own spiritual development, because managment and workers would have values orientation and also self management through self-motivation. We will have harmony, happiness, prosperity of managers and workers not only in external life but also in their internal life. The people of the enterprise will also enjoy healthy and enriched life.

3. High Technology. High technology not only accelerates industrialisation but also announces problems of an industrial civilisation. But high technology can be misused in the pursuit of the mindless pleasure of senses in a materialist, high consumption society. In that case it could provide a handy instrument of control and oppression. However, if Indian wisdom is associated with modern management, high technology will give spiritually evolved managers, statesmen and leaders in the society, a golden opportunity for a global dialogue to discover the variety of worlds and bring about higher levels of unity across the human race. High technology can offer assistance to the humanity to pursue its evolution rapidly and effectively under value oriented management.

4. Globalisation. From 1990 onwards the term globalisation has assumed unique significance. It indicates free market economy all over the world. It also points out emergence of global brands with ISO mark under total quality management. Now we have global marketing competition. People in all countries with the help of satellite communication tools would enjoy prompt inter communication even in their daily transactions. This would give us opportunities to discover our basic humanness as well as our cultural differences and heritage. This opportunity can also help to know broader and higher levels of human consciousness. We would achieve harmony and unity between material progress and spiritual evolution in our emerging global economy.

5. Ecology. Ecological crisis for mankind is a burning problem next in importance to corruption and crisis of values. Indian wisdom knows that holistic approach by management alone can restore the ecological balanceas hurnan beings and nature are interdependent and interrelated. They are parts of the universal consciousness. Fortunately marketers and business leaders of the world are coming together under the UNO to bring about sustainable industrial development free from dangers of pollution rather than self destructive, indiscriminate exploitation of nature. Science and technology can help us in this right direction, though progress in this movement is bound to be slow and not so easy. Right minded managers and leaders can adopt Indian wisdom to solve all impending problems with the help of divine grace and blessings.

6. The New Marketing Concept and Total Quality. The customer-citizen satisfaction and total quality requirements are now recognised as desirable means to assure profitability, survival and progess by all marketing companies. These are regarded as secrets of global competitiveness. These would also serve our citizens and society in the best possible way. Incidentally management would reduce its old ego centred world view of profit maximisation at any cost. Fortunately this new trend does not oppose human evolution towards ecological and social concerns in order to achieve unity with spiritual development.

Spiritual growth would certainly enable us to realise great human potential energy and to achieve excellence and extraordinary output without sacrificing quality of life all over the world. Adoption of Indian wisdom in modern management will surely accelerate the positive movements mentioned above. All members of organisation and management would also find out a higher level of sense of achievement and joy much better than short-lived pleasures of senses only.

The present management, based on the Western management theory and practice, refined and sophisticated in the 20th century was dominated by the development of Science and Technology. It adopted the gospel of materialism. Man was ignored and machinery and materials played a dominant role. They expected mechanical efficiency from workers based on financial incentives. Workers were regarded as articles of trade to be bought and sold in the open market. Labour capital conflicts assumed permanent character. Amassing of wealth even at the cost of workers, community and environment became universal. Even with the push button economy management could not achieve good health of human beings, inner and outer harmony. The quantitative progress was amazing but enrichment of the quality of life and quality of environment could not be achieved. The 21st century will have to face the severe crisis of values-spiritual, ethical and human values.

The Indian thought of holistic, value based management approach can achieve harmony, happiness and good health in all countries. We have to give equal attention to both the wings of spirit and science. Then only management would succeed to fulfil the ecological, individual and social welfare. We must recognise holism in our management theory and practice.

❐

3

Global E-Business

The combination of broadband capabilities, connectivity, standard languages, wireless communication and portability have given birth to the digital age and its most pervasive manifestation: the Internet. The Internet is a global network connecting millions of computers across the world, exchanging data, opinions, information and news using a common architecture, the Internet Protocol (IP). The network is also known as the World Wide Web (WWW) or the 'Web'. In essence, the Internet is a global tool since it has abolished physical distance for the transmission of data, images and sounds and it has standardised the transmission protocol as well as the machine software, making it possible for any computer in the world to be part of network and to 'talk' to other computers. Infact, the Internet and its attendant power have made it possible for many companies to conduct global business at a much more discernible and attainable level. New economies and efficiencies of scale have been created. Not too long ago, only a few companies had the resources to compete on a global scale. Now, more than at any time in history, almost any size firm with the vision and ambition to do so can extend its reach globally.

As a result of the Internet and new information technology, many of the myths about globalization can be unmasked. According to one theory, globalization is a conspiracy by big companies against smaller markets. Some companies, of course, are bigger, financially, than others. That's a testimony to the market-based economy that more and more markets are choosing to adopt. But no company or group of companies is calling all the shots. Small and midsize companies are getting in on the act and thriving globally.

What is Global E-Business?

Global e-business is not a simple undertaking. It involves a variety of complex issues. Moreover, failure to adequately address the IT element can alienate entire markets and erode the relationship between a company and the marketplace. A comprehensive global e-business strategy can greatly help to ensure a place in the global economy, thus enabling a business to take advantage of a world of possibilities.

Global e-business strategically uses IT to take apart physical supply chains and reassemble them in better ways, create highly focused communications for specific cultures, and select the parameters needed to support multiple markets.

Global e-business adapts specific IT to a company's products and message to best meet the varied expectations of markets around the world. In addition, global e-business is, in many ways, a complete revolution of how a company perceives distance; time, and location.

Global e-business is the most powerful communications medium the business world has ever known, in large part because of its reach into factories, offices, and homes around the world. The substantially lower cost of communication via the Internet has dramatically lessened the importance of distance: For many products that can be digitized-such as pictures, video, sound, and words-distance will become a nonfactor. The same is true for services. And even for most products, because of the Internet, distance will have much less an effect on overall business costs.

In the physical world, time and season predominate the flow of goods and services around the world. We see this in the hours of operation-activities that occur by time of day and in social and climactic seasons. The virtual marketplace, on the other hand, is always open. The seller need not be awake, or even physically present, for the buyer to be served by the seller. The Internet is independent of season. Time can thus be homogenized-made uniformly consistent for all buyers and for all sellers.

Because any screen-based activity can be operated anywhere on earth, location does not play an important part in most business decisions. Is it even relevant? Does location mean where the firm is officially registered? Is it where most of the people employed by the company work? Or is it where the server is physically located? In most cases, it simply doesn't matter.

Following the recent decade's IT explosion, a world marketplace awaits, with its entire attendant of consumers and competition. An initial presence on the Internet can be relatively easy and inexpensive to establish. And any company that has a presence on the World Wide Web is international by definition, whether it chooses to become a global company or not.

Global e-business exploits the Internet's ability to level the playing field for all participants, regardless of size, especially as it relates to a company's ability to communicate with customers, employers, suppliers, investors, and other targeted groups. No other media can claim this ability. No individual or company has a better right to establish a place on the Web than any other. Mere purchasing of limited physical space in newspapers or magazines, or buying time on radio or TV, cannot achieve such presence. No other medium can even come close to achieving the level of scalability that the Internet can achieve, *i.e.*, the ability to leverage its own power and impact to much higher levels and with a much broader global reach.

Global e-business eliminates the historic rigid hierarchy of business processes. According to leading corporate strategists, individual workers must be given maximum autonomy, and the patterns of communications within a worldwide organization should resemble a knowledge-based ecology more than a flowchart. All of this is irrespective of a company's size and physical location.

The internet would increase the globalisation of markets, reinforce global cost reduction, foster global competition and weaken governments' barriers open trade (See Table-1). The challenge for businesses of all sizes-especially smaller ones-that want to maximize their global presence involves structuring relationships and information flow so that the right parties can obtain the information at the right time. In all these views, IT and e-business initiatives 'play critical roles in the strategy of global competition, especially in regard to their global supply chain application.

TABLE-1

EFFECTS OF THE INTERNET ON GLOBALISA TION

Market globalisation	• Increase global commonality in customer needs and tastes (facilities customised standardisation and strengthen appeal of global brands: Barbie online) • Enables global customers and global channels (facilitates global sourcing) • Supports global marketing (enhances global brands and standardises search) • Makes global products more rapidly visible
Cost reduction	• Exploits differences in country costs and facilitates competition from low-cost small-scale companies from emerging markets • Enhances global sourcing • Speeds up global logistics • Reduces product development costs
Foster global competition	• Makes competitive comparisons easier • Increases the number of potential global suppliers by reverse auctions • Puts new rivals in the global competitive arena
Weaken government barriers to open trade	• Makes it easier for customers to by-pass customs and tax levies • Puts pressures on government to harmonise standards and policies • Gives customers more incentives to lobby their governments to align with more customers • Friendly regulations

Before the advent of the new information and e-business technologies of the past decade and before easy access to global information systems became available to companies, customers and suppliers had to make major decisions with little information on which to base them. With the global e-business solutions, buyers and suppliers of all sizes can now' easily track the status and current location of their orders around the world. Before this proliferation of global e-business capability was available, small and midsize companies, especially, might have found themselves left out of the countless new business opportunities in an exploding global economy.

Obviously, small and midsize companies do not possess the sizable resources usually reserved for the biggest global companies in the world. At the same time, those that will succeed in the future understand that the Internet and e-business technology are invaluable, indispensable business tools that need to be harnessed and crafted into a company's overall strategies. To ensure success on the new global business frontier, business leaders from these companies must do what they've always had to do: formulate and implement ideas, tactics, and strategies. Now, they must do this at a much higher level-at a global level-to enable their companies to survive and prosper in the new global marketplace.

Developing Global E-Business Strategy

The greatest challenge for all businesses that want to truly maximize their global presence centers on structuring relationships and the flow of information so that the right parties-customers, suppliers, employees, etc. can obtain it at the right time and at the right place. In this view, e-business and IT initiatives play critical roles in forging a successful global company. This is especially true for small and midsize businesses.

Many companies, however, large and small, wrongly believe e-business and IT will harvest big rewards by merely overlaying computers on top of traditional work processes. These companies fail to understand that e-business and IT work best when they are used to transform those same traditional processes as well as the entire corporate culture. The most successful companies specifically focus on ways that e-business and IT can add value to existing business systems by gaining improved and increased efficiencies. Such a mind-set and resulting strategy affords a small and midsize company the ability to develop entirely new business capabilities and processes to then forge the company's global presence.

Globally savvy companies and their managers view projects, as well as the business overall, from a global perspective. Striving to overcome cultural challenges, regional, national, and personal differences are subrogated to the overall global good of the company to maximize results for the entire organization. Leaders of these companies realize that success depends on the unrestricted flow of information throughout their global business network, which then comes together in the right place and at the right time. For these companies, this doesn't happen by chance. It's a function of its global company culture, and at its core, it is this culture that drives the global organization and, in turn, its global business success. Now, more than ever, e-business technology is driving culture and this new culture is driving globalization.

E-business Strategy: Manifestly Global

The new digital economy is manifestly global—a global phenomenon, yet truly globalized e-businesses are the exception. Even the largest companies on the planet still have a ways to go before they can claim total globalization. Globalization to a company's e-business processes or its Internet presence is not a simple task. It engages a variety of complex issues, and language translation is just the beginning. Failure to sufficiently tackle e-business globalization can isolate entire markets and jeopardize relationships between a company and the marketplace. Moreover, it has the potential to erode and destroy a company's business on a regional or global scale. A cogent and inclusive e-business globalization strategy can ensure a company's place in the new borderless digital economy, enabling businesses of all sizes to exploit a new world of opportunities.

A global marketplace awaits all business, with all the attendant customers, consumers, competition, and suppliers that this entails. This is an exciting time for business, indeed, but also a potentially dangerous time. Companies of all sizes too often are blinded by the promises of the new global economy. Herein lays the seductive danger of the Internet and its creation of e-business. Harvesting the Internet's potential rewards requires more than just making a company Internet-enabled. Companies that want to offer their products and services to the world and successfully compete in the new global marketplace must fundamentally change the very way they think about doing business. In this new global, digital world, the axiom, "change or die," has never been more appropriate.

Global E-business Strategy: Key Components

Communications. Global business is about adapting a company's products and services to meet the varied expectations of markets around the world. A company must also adapt and customize its communications to customers, consumers, suppliers, and others around the world. There exists no common formula to achieve either of these in business today.

Further complicating matters, developing a successful global e-business strategy demands cautious and thorough consideration of linguistic, cultural, economic, and legislative differences in markets around the world. In the past, only the largest companies attempted to create a truly global presence. Companies incapable of competing at this level simply confined themselves to a domestic market, or to a very limited subset of international markets. The Internet and the advent of e-business fundamentally rewrite the rules by wiping out distance, dramatically reducing the barriers of entry to the electronic marketplace, and inciting an atmosphere of hypercompetition on a global level.

Change or Die. The global companies must discard their previously successful strategies or face real danger. Large and small, new and old businesses similarly must struggle with the challenges of how to best conduct business in the new, global digital world.

In the past, businesses adapted their products simply by translating the language on their packaging and their user instructions or by simply changing electrical connectors and voltage to meet local market requirements. Simple language translation or minimal, basic product modifications are not the solutions today.

Business globalization is likewise not simply including existing local cultural and business nuances into a collective global melting pot. A global e-business strategy with its message streaming along the Internet will have to simultaneously provide localized communications to both internal and external users in dozens of different markets while adhering to exacting performance requirements—all this as it processes real-time content changes. Few companies, if any, have mastered this.

The following information will provide companies of all sizes, and most of all, small and midsize companies, a practical road map or template to use as they develop their own global e-business strategy. This information should serve as a checklist of the most critical activities required to successfully deploy a global e-business strategy for any company. The level and depth to which a company will need to go depends largely on the size of the company, the resources it has available, and its vision and aspirations to become truly global.

Global E-business Strategy and Business Plan Development

Any company's globalization strategy can be tremendously enhanced with an effective e-business strategy. To develop a successful e-business globalization strategy, companies of all sizes must first: clearly articulate their overall business and e-business strategies; Second, possess a keen knowledge of their target markets (countries), considering: geography, demo graphics, economic conditions, internal country politics the political situation between home and target countries, home and target countries legal requirements, and Internet readiness. Third, carefully select target markets (countries), groups of markets, etc. Finally, plan to establish a company and/or brand identity in target markets. Also, regardless of the degree of complexity of the company's global e-business strategy, some common traits typically emerge with most, if not all, e-business sites. Specifically, these include: *(i)* Visitors to multiple-language sites remain on the site almost twice as long as they do with English-only language sites. *(ii)* Business users are three times more likely to buy when the site is in their own local language. *(iii)* Customer service costs decrease when instructions on the site are in the customer's own local language.

Market Selection

A company should prioritize and rank the markets (countries) that may be targeted in its global business strategy. As with all business, developing a global e-business strategy requires that a company know its targeted customer groups very well.

If a company already conducts business in specific markets or if a market is a new high-priority target market; the firm mutest determine if these markets meet a set of strategic screening criteria. Criteria to be considered are as follows:

For Automatic Inclusion:

(i) Markets already accounting for significant company revenue

(ii) Markets where there already is a large e-business presence

(iii) Markets with large physical presences or strategic regional importance (*e.g.*, Brazil in South America, United Kingdom in Europe)

For Automatic Exclusion:

(i) Markets not a significant source of current revenue

(ii) Markets not a significant source of future revenue

(iii) Markets whose local laws do not support the necessary intellectual property rights or copyrights

(iv) Markets that are subject to trade embargoes or other internationally imposed sanctions

For markets that do not clearly fall into either of the categories of automatic inclusion or exclusion, a more detailed analysis should be conducted. A rating and ranking mechanism should be developed to prioritize these remaining markets. Any mechanism that is developed should rate and rank markets based on key economic, strategic, or business criteria. Criteria for detailed analysis should include: First, economic viability: current market size, potential market size, current market penetration, potential market penetration, current market revenue and profit, potential market revenue and profit, presence or absence of local business and/or brand alliances, and the presence or absence of direct and/ or indirect competition; Second, internet preparedness: current Internet penetration, rate of current and forecasted Internet growth, projected Internet penetration, Internet useage (*e.g.*, willingness to conduct business/purchase online), and, internet infrastructure capabilities; finally, the business capability: size of in market business presence, experience with company/ product brand localization, and the existing language translation capabilities.

Establish Localization/Regionalization Parameters

A company must establish a set of cultural expectations regarding how a local e-business and Internet presence should perform for each market that a company selects. Based on these local expectations, parameters should then be selected for each market.

Sometimes, localization parameters need not apply across all selected markets, but rather they may be applied across a common group of markets in a homogeneous region (*e.g.*, the Middle East). In this case, a regional approach to establishing localization parameters may be more appropriate. Parameters to be considered are: company and/ or product/service brand(s), information architecture, visual design, application functionality, content, and the business processes.

Establish Globalization Parameters

Once a company has set its localization and regionalization parameters it can establish its globalization parameters. The firm must consider relevant factors from each market. To the extent that any localization feature can be applied on a globalized level, localized or regionalized parameters may then influence and otherwise determine specific globalization parameters. Also, not all localization or regionalization parameters may need to be addressed in the final set of globalization parameters. In some cases, it may be more cost-effective to localize or regionalize some systems without globalizing them. Parameters that should be globalized include: languages, writing systems, currencies, weights and measurements, calendars, time zones, time measurements, and postal and telephone systems.

Languages and Phonetic Systems. Language is one of the primary differentiators for many cultures. The importance of language clearly makes language-related functions prime targets in implementing global e-business strategy. This is no simple task, however. Languages are extremely diverse, and they change very rapidly.

There are currently 6,700 living languages in the world, but only 435 of these languages are in commercial use. Of all spoken languages, the top 15 in the world together account for 49.5 percent of all the languages spoken by the world's total population.

Writing and Ideogrammatic Systems. Writing systems have a major impact on the way information is presented. Direction of script varies significantly between writing systems. The direction of Latin script is from left to right, top to bottom. The direction of Japanese scripts is generally from top to bottom, right to left, although there can be a mixture of directions on a single page.

Not only does the direction of script vary between systems, but the method used to sort words differs as well. The Latin writing system sorts words and letters using a process based on a fixed sequence called alphabetical order (A to Z). The Japanese hiragana writing system arranges the syllables in the order they appear in a famous Buddhist poem. The Chinese hanzi writing system orders symbols by the number of brush strokes it takes to draw them.

Currencies. Currency is involved in most commerce, and thus is another prime target of global e-business. Many potential customers in markets around the world expect to purchase goods using their own currencies. While offering them this service is desirable, it can also expose an organization to considerable risk if not handled correctly.

Currency conversion rates fluctuate on a very short time scale because of trading in global currency markets. This fluctuation makes setting fixed prices in different markets difficult to coordinate. The Internet makes this form of arbitrage even easier.

Weights and Measurement Systems. Commerce often involves the exchange of fixed quantities of goods or materials that meet certain dimensional specifications. Thus, it is important to consider internationalizing weights and measures. The International System of Units (SI), more commonly referred to as the metric system, is effectively the global standard for measurement. A few markets still cling to old systems: At this time, only three markets-Myanmar, Liberia, and the United States-have not adopted the SI standard as their official system of weights and measures.

The United States is the only industrialized nation that does not mainly use the metric system in its commercial and standards activities, but acceptance is increasing in science, medicine, government, and many sectors of industry in the United States.

Calender Systems. Calendars, especially in a global e-business context, are useful in determining holidays, shipment dates, or the date on which a transaction took place. Calendars, like writing systems, come in several varieties. Each calendar determines the number and names of days and months in the year, including when leap years occur.

Three calendar types and at least ten calendars are in daily use around the world. Following are the three calendar types with examples of each:

1. Solar-based on the yearly solar cycle. Examples: Gregorian, Julian, Ethiopic, Coptic, Modern Hindu
2. Lunar-based on the cycle of the moon. Example: Islamic
3. Lunisolar-that attempt to reconcile the cycles of both the sun and moon. Examples: Chinese, Hebrew, Old Hindu

These differences can lead to significant confusion when converting from one calendar to another is required. With today's information technology, the task of reconciling the different calendar systems can be made simpler.

Time Zones. Specification of time zones is important for standard time measurement, and could be highly relevant in computer transactions. There are 24 international time zones, and markets set their local time according to the time zone they are in and the time zones adopted by their trading partners and neighbours.

All markets define their own local time in terms of hours ahead or behind Greenwich Mean Time (GMT), up to a maximum of 11 hours ahead or behind. The situation is complicated by the fact that many markets observe daylight saving time, usually hours ahead or behind local time. This is determined at the market level, with different markets beginning and ending daylight saving on different dates (*e.g.*, the U.S. and Canada versus Europe). Individual markets may also vary the start and end dates of daylight saving from year to year, further complicating matters.

Time Measurement Systems. For certain types of e-business systems, the measurement of accurate time is crucial. This is especially true when systems comprise multiple components distributed geographically. The management of time can become a significant hurdle. Coordinating multiple clocks and managing time changes to and from daylight saving time across multiple time zones requires considerable planning. While these problems may be new to many commercial organizations, they have been recognized and solved by scientific and military institutions.

An example illustrating the need for highly accurate time coordination is in the financial and commodities markets. Most financial and commodity market maker systems that provide auctions also require accurate time synchronization so auctions can close exactly when required and bids can be "time-stamped" with the correct time. Time stamps are also very useful in many cryptographic protocols, where time is intimately connected with the exchange of messages.

Postal Systems. The Universal Postal Union (UPU), with headquarters in Bern, Switzerland, is a specialized institution of the United Nations that regulates the postal services of its member countries. The postal addressing systems outline the elements that form the basis for proper postal addressing. These elements ensure the correct wording of addresses and guarantee the quick and efficient handling of letter-post items.

Postcodes can also be used to validate text addresses. Software systems are available that can derive a postcode from a text address and a text address from a postcode. These systems are usually only available with delivery code systems. They require large supporting databases and must be updated frequently to account for new addresses and codes.

Telephone dialing systems. Telephone dialing codes are another means for geographic location; they are quite useful for communication as well. From the standpoint of globalization, it is important to understand the relevant international standards for telecommunications, and also the degree of local variation in the way countries handle telephone numbers.

Key Attributes of A Successful Global E-Business Strategy

Irrespective of any individual company-specific parameters (globalization localization/ regionalization), company size, industry or markets targeted, a successful global e-business strategy should possess three key attributes: flexibility, adaptability and controllability.

Flexibility. Localization/regionalization parameters that may apply in one market may not apply in another. Globalization parameters that are critical to support a single major market may undermine the overall strategy and render it cost-ineffective. Typically, most companies find there is no single, correct solution, and that any global e-business strategy will have its tradeoffs. In the end, any viable globalization strategy chosen must be flexible across targeted markets.

Adaptability. Everything in the world of business and financial markets changes. International and national politics and laws change, sometimes daily. So, too does the Internet; and changes seem to be accelerating each year. Any chosen global e-business strategy must be able to adapt to the many changes that have become part of everyday business life, especially on a global level.

Controllability. To ensure the success of any global e-business strategy, a company must exert a high degree of control to implement a stable and manageable global business organization and its resulting structures. This is especially critical when localizing business processes, for local management will likely be charged with implementing and managing market-specific e-business functions.

Cost-Benefit Analysis

Once a company has determined all the criteria with which to establish its global e-business strategies, it must then conduct a cost-benefit analysis to determine the economic viability of the chosen strategies. When analyzing costs, companies must consider both the implementation costs as well as the costs of re-engineering any business processes, ongoing systems maintenance costs, training costs, etc. Once these costs are determined, they can then be weighed against the strategic and economic benefits offered by extending the company's global reach into targeted markets.

Strategy and Business Plan Optimization

If the cost-benefit analysis reveals anything in the global e-business strategy that may be economically viable, a company should consider either adding or removing markets from the mix, modifying some market-specific localization parameters, or adjusting some of its globalization parameters. For example, the cost of globalizing language and writing systems for the Chinese market may be too high, while localization or regionalization is more viable.

Depending on what parameters will be adjusted, added, or removed, it will likely be necessary to review both sets of localized/ regionalized and globalized parameters. Following each series of adjustments, a new cost-benefit analysis should be conducted and the viability of the global e-business strategy reassessed.

Once optimized, the cost-benefit analysis should yield a global e-business strategy that will include: prioritized list of markets to be targeted; parameters to be localized within the targeted markets; requirements mapping of localization and/or regionalization of selected business processes that may be necessary; parameters to be globalized within various business systems; and estimation of costs and benefits of the global e-business strategy. Table-2 lists the organisational requirement for e-business.

Global E-Business Strategy Implementation

Once a company has successfully developed and optimized its global e-business strategy, it must develop and execute an implementation plan. Key components of any such implementation plan should include the following:

(i) Localization/regionalization of business processes as required

(ii) Globalization of business processes as required

(iii) Globalization of appropriate global parameters as required

(iv) Localize globalized parameters within selected markets

(v) Localize nonglobalized parameters within selected markets

TABLE-2

ORGANISATIONAL REQUIREMENTS FOR E-BUSINESS

Transparency	• Integrity and consistency of information • Clear data and procedures
Sharing Culture	• Horizontal as well as vertical exchange of information • External partners have access to data-bases • No 'silos'
Process Integration	• All management processes are compatible with each other to facilitate information flow
Pooled co-ordination	• Ability to have different department working together instantaneously instead of sequentially • Ability to bundle different parameters in real time • Sequential co-ordination too time-consuming
Real-time commitment	• Ability to make decisions quickly • No time for hierarchical checking
Horizontal processes	• Hierarchical communication and decision processes inefficient

Typically, a phased approach is taken regarding these implementations, with the most strategic markets being implemented first. At the same time, some implementation tasks may be undertaken concurrently with others in selected markets. The ultimate methodology selected by a company will depend on its chosen strategy and the specific challenges presented in each case.

Cultural Adaptability of Global Technology Implementation

Standardized technologies alone won't guarantee successful global e-business operations. The most successful global organizations properly manage multilingual and multicultural implementations of applications and data. Because every successful global e-business implementation must employ components of the technology that require these multilingual and multicultural services and support, companies that specialize in translation, localization, and cultural practices are thriving as part of the global e-business solution. A rudimentary search on the Internet will yield scores of such companies prepared and ready to assist any size company to achieve the desired level of multilingual and multicultural needs that any company may have.

The need to translate and localize foretells that the true challenges in implementing global e-business systems still center on culture, not in the deployment of new technology. In short, everyone can be given the same applications, but ensuring that those applications are used consistently to benefit the company is much more difficult.

By drastically reducing the importance of proximity, the new technologies change people's perceptions of community. The Internet connects people and companies across borders with exponentially growing ease, while separating them from natural and historical associations with nations. Doing business globally filters through many levels of the information technology, local practices, and corporate culture. The more sensitive corporate leadership is toward language and cultural differences, the more an organization is able to improve and add value to its global e-business initiatives. Overall company cultures, particularly in local company offices around the world deeply influenced by their individual market cultures, will need to change their mind sets to make that shift.

Culture-the amalgam of tradition, relationships, and values-shapes business practices and processes in widely varying ways. Cultural differences often make it hard to obtain consensus and collaboration, and not what the "technology of the day" is. The divide between culture, technology, and knowledge can be enormous. To close this divide, successful global organizations of all sizes and cultures realize that a clear understanding of their own company and its home market culture as well as the culture of others is urgently needed.

Cultural Communications in Global E-business Strategy

Cultural differences can make a large impact on the interpretation of tation of visual design. What is considered a cutting-edge design in one culture can appear rude and unprofessional in another. Common interpretations of visual design simply cannot be assumed when working internationally. By their nature, visual messages are often more ambiguous and open to interpretation than is the written word.

Colours. Colours are a part of most people's everyday worlds. We attach a great deal of significance to them, whether we realize it or not. The meanings attached, however, and even the words we use to describe them, vary between cultures. For example, Japanese do not differentiate between green and blue. In the Netherlands, blue connotes quality, and in China, red has negative connotations. Different interpretations of colour abound throughout the world.

Image. Images are also interpreted differently across cultures and locations. It is very difficult for a central organization to make appropriate choices about local imagery. Apart from the obvious case where images include text, images themselves often contain cultural assumptions. Images must be made locally appropriate; what appears as an innocuous pictogram of the thumbs-up signal (representing approval) is, in fact, an offensive gesture in some cultures. A car shown driving down the right side of the road would contradict experience in several markets, thus disrupting the intent of a carefully built design.

Colours, images, and text combine to create a graphical interface, and changes to any one of these elements can impact the entire visual design. Text translation can cause significant expansion in the length of text that, in turn, may create a negative impact on a visual design. Substantial modification of text can disrupt the flow of information and qualitatively change the look and feel of an interface. Careful localization of text helps preserve the original intent and spirit of a visual design.

Cultural assumptions affect function in a way similar to information architecture and visual design. As a result, the function of a system may have to be localized to meet cultural requirements.

For instance, the concept of the shopping cart on a commercial Web site does not translate for all cultures. The supermarket as a standard for a commercial experience is justified only when most customers experience supermarkets as a regular part of their daily life. Only then will they know what to expect when confronted with the Internet shopping cart.

If an application offers a negative or confusing experience to a user with a different set of cultural expectations, it is no longer useful and thus fails in its intent. Before creating any content (words, images, audio, or video), a company with an Internet presence must first develop a content strategy that articulates the voice and tone of its brand. This strategy ensures that the content is consistent and compelling, and that it properly communicates the message of the brand.

As is the case with information architecture and visual design, the local focus of content must account for subtle and not-so-subtle cultural variations. For example, localizing the audio portions of a Web site requires not only translating the audio into the appropriate language, but accounting for dialect and pronunciation differences. The localization of text requires a similar attention-to idiomatic expressions, differences in usage, and culturally specific grammatical conventions.

Language. Language translation is an art, not a science. Literal translation is almost never sufficient. At best, it can produce stilted approximations of the original and, at worst, it can erode a brand's credibility by being unintentionally amusing or even insulting to the target audience and others.

Ensuring text is carefully reviewed by a native speaker is essential even when the text is not ostensibly being translated into another language. In Spain the verb to take is perfectly acceptable, while in Mexico it is considered crude. At first glance, a manufacturer may believe that the American version of a product catalog can be reused in all English-speaking markets. This may be the case; the catalog would probably still be understandable. If local language usage is not taken into account, however, it might also cause serious brand erosion. In effect, this means that language and market are inseparable. For example, American, British, Australian, Canadian, and South African English should be treated as separate languages. Each market has its own language variation that must be handled individually.

Another factor to consider when localizing text is that translation can have a significant, even damaging, effect on visual design and information architectures. When text is translated, the amount of space required to hold that contiguous block of text can change dramatically. On the average, English increases by 30 percent when it is translated to other European languages, and can increase by 400 percent in extreme cases.

Finally, the organisational attributes may sometimes conflict with local cultures. Table-3 contrasts Internet cultural requirements with typical Asian corporate culture. The challenge for the global firm is to overcome these culture differences among their employees, suppliers, customers and partners to make Web transactions effective.

TABLE-3

INTERNET MANAGERIAL CULTURE VERSUS MANAGERIAL CULTURE

Transparency	● Partial, and multiple information ● Lack of clear procedures
Sharing culture	● Vertical information sharing ● Clannicretention
Process integration	● 'Siloed' processes
Pooled co-ordination	● Top-down processes, otherwise sequential processes
Real-time commitment	● Several checks, vertically organised
Horizontal processes	● Hierarchical

❐

4

Coporate Structure in Business

The concept of corporate planning has in recent years gained wide currency in management literature. Its connotation is somewhat overlapping with the concept of strategic planning. It is, therefore, necessary that the scope of corporate planning and strategic planning should be clearly understood.

Simply stated, corporate planning is comprehensive planning process which involves continued formulation of objectives and the guidance of affairs towards their attainment. It is a systematic and disciplined exercise designed to help identification of the objectives of an organisation or corporate body, determination of appropriate targets, and formulation of practical plans by which the objective could be achieved. It is undertaken by higher management for the firm as whole on a continuous basis for making entrepreneurial decisions systematically and with the best possible knowledge of their probable outcome and effects, organising systematically the efforts and resources needed to carry out the decisions, and measuring the results of these decisions against the expectations though systematic feedback.

The object of corporate planing is to identify new areas of investment and marketing. Initiating new projects, new courses of action, and analysing past experience are the subject-matter of corporate planning. Thus, it plies *(a)* the imposition of a planning discipline on the present operations of the business, and *(b)* a reappraisal of the business and of the direction in which it should be heading. The essence of corporate planning lies in the application of the company's resources and competencies to the most profitable uses. Innovation is the core of such planning. At the same time it ensures that managers are continually measuring their performance against the company's long-term profit and market objectives, evaluating alternative methods of reaching the goals, and keeping in touch with changes in the market and in technology.

The comprehensive nature of the corporate planning process lies in that operational planning, project planning and strategic planning are its constituents. These are now examined as follows.

It is essential for every business firm to manage its ongoing operations efficiently to keep the business afloat in the market with which it is familiar. Operational planning is necessary so as to ensure that changes in the market situation for the existing product line do not adversely affect the earnings for the firm. Thus, operational planning involves study of the market conditions for the existing range of products to maintain and improve the position of the form in the face of competition. It is essentially a short-term exercise and deals with the existing product, market and facilities. The degree of uncertainty in operational planning is of a low order; the time span of discretion is short; choice of alternatives is relatively simple. But the firm can ill afford to ignore long-term changes in the product markets. It has to look for new markets for the existing product, develop new products, create a market for the same and utilise the existing facilities and expertise to meet new requirements. Considerations such as these characterise project planning, which is a forward looking exercise concerned with new markets, new products and new facilities. Project planning is, therefore, to deal with a greater degree of uncertainty, and demands a high order of judgment on the part of strategist due to the risks involved.

Strategic planning refers to the formulation of a unified, comprehensive and integrated plan aimed at relating the strategic advantages of the firm to the challenges of the environment. It is concerned with appraising the environment in relation to the company, identifying the strategies to obtain sanction for one of the alternatives to be interpreted and communicated in an operationally useful manner. Thus, strategic planning provides the framework within which future activities of the company are expected to be carried out. Compared with project planning, the time span of discretion in strategic planning is much longer, the degree of uncertainty and corresponding risks involved are much greater, and judgement to be exercised is of more importance.

In as much as strategic planning determines the future direction of a company, corporate planning is essentially based on strategic planning, and at the same time takes care of project planning and operational planning. Thus, corporate planning is described as a formal systematic managerial process, organised by responsibility, time and information, to ensure that operational planning, project planning and strategic planning are carried out regularly to enable top management to direct and control the future of the enterprise. It follows that corporate planning is not synonymous with long-range planning. Corporate planning is concerned with determination of objectives and developing means to achieve the objectives. It may encompass both short periods as well as long periods. The tune span depends on how far ahead a company wants to forecast and to plan, which, in turn, depends upon the nature of business that the company wants to be in and commitment of resources required for it. For instance, in the modern heavy engineering industry, commitment of resources is generally required for a fairly long period to 15 or 20 years.

Thus corporate planning in an engineering enterprise will involve tong-term considerations regarding market demand, technology and such other factors. It will have a short time horizon in the case of garment industry. Long-range planning, however, necessarily connotes planning with a long-term horizon in view, generally five years or more. Corporate planning in capital intensive industries is always associated with long-range planning. Besides, corporate planning is concerned with the existing products in existing markets as well as new products and new markets.

Strategic Planning and Operational Planning

When comprehensive corporate planning is divided into strategic and operational planning, the sphere of activities is deemed on the basis of their objectives and scope in the total management process.

From this point of view the examples of strategic planning in an organisation may be: planned growth rate in sales, consideration of how much growth is to be achieved by internal development as opposed to mergers and acquisitions; planned diversification by technologies, types of products, customers and geographical areas; comparatively important planning activities in the areas of organising, staffing, finance, etc. which affect all major functions. As against strategic planning, operational planning can be defined as follows:

Operational planning is the process of deciding the most effective use of the resources already allocated and to develop a control mechanism to assure effective implementation of the actions so that organisational objectives are achieved. Operational planning taken in this way may include: adjustment of production, marketing and financial capacity of the organisation to the expected level of operations, in both the short term and long term; increasing the efficiency of operating activities through analysing past performance/budgeting future costs, developing control over costs and efficiency; programming the comprehensive and specific details of future short term operations. On the basis of the explanation of strategic and operational planning, following is the distinction between strategic planning & operational planning:

1. The type of environment between two types of planning is different. Strategic planning takes into account the external environment and tries to relate the organisation with it. It usually encampasses all the functional areas of the organisation and is effected within the existing and long term framework of economic, social, technical, and political factors. Operational planning focusses on internal organisational environment so as to make the effective use of given resources.
2. Strategic planning is usually conducted by top level management and other specified planning staff in the organisation. At this level, people can take overall view of the organisation and have necessary capability to relate the organisation with the external environment. Operational

planning is usually spread over a wide range within the organisation and is generally performed by operating managers with the help of the subordinate staff. Since two planning groups are widely separated in the organisation, some incompatibility may exist between two types of planning. Therefore, there is need for integrating these two in order to have better planning effects.

3. Strategic planning guides the choice among the broad directions in which the organisation seeks to move and cope the general planned allocations of its managerial, financial physical resources over future specified period of time. Operational planning, on the of the hand, focusses on the ways and means by which each of the individual functions may be programmed so that process may be made towards the attainment of organisational objectives. In performing a function, operational planning puts questions:
   (i) what objectives and conditions must be met? Within the framework of these questions, operational plans are-formulated. Usually the answers of operational planning tries to achieve the results and actions suggested by the strategic planning.
   (ii) why is the action required?
   (iii) what are the results of the action required?
   (iv) where will the action accomplish?
   (v) what action is to be taken?
4. Strategic planning precedes the operational planning since the later is primarily the implementation of the former. Since strategic planning sets trends and direction for managerial actions, its time horizon is usually quite large say five years or so. Operational planning is heavily concerned with short term programmes implementing step by step progress towards basic organisational goals, organisational depth and tiancial resources. These restrictions

on the organisation's potential accomplishment are more prevalent in the short .term than over a long term; therefore, strategic planning must recognise the limits of what operational planning can realistically be undertaken in given time periods. Thus strategic planning is restricted by the practical limitations under which operational planning operates.

DIFFERENT PLANNING SYSTEMS

Management literature is replete with references to planning. It is discussed as function of management, categorised into different types and considered as a major set of techniques. Here, we direct our attention to a few types of planning systems relevant to business policy. Among these, we briefly discuss operational, project, management by objectives, contingency, short-range, long-range, corporate, and strategic planning.

Operational Planning

Operational planning is lower-level planning and is based on sub-goals derived from organisational objectives. The focus is on managing the day-to-day affairs of the company. The primary responsibility for implementation of operational plans rests on the operating level of management; middle-level executives or line managers, who are guided by the senior management with regard to the formulation of strategies. In managing the day-to-day affairs, operating managers are guided by a set of policies, procedures, rules, forecasts, targets and budgets. In this manner, all operating managers, in different functional areas, implement their respective plans. Operational plans, therefore, are parts of the overall organisational plan and work in tandem with each other. Operating plans and operating managers are to be distinguished from operations plans (which relate to the production function) and operations managers (who look after the production activities).

Management by Objectives

Management by objectives, *per se*, is not a type of planning system; it is a systems approach to managing by emphasising the role of objectives. Operationally, it facilitates planning and the implementation and control of plans. The organisational objectives are divided into divisional or departmental objectives which are further subdivided into individual objectives. Such an inter-locking system of the objectives serves as the basis for managing, evaluation and control of performance. Thus, management is concerned with setting of objectives, goals and targets which are a part of the planning function.

Project Planning

In a broader sense, project planning relates to planning for a clearly identified programme or a set of tasks such as construction project. Within organisations, and in a narrow sense, project planning refers to planning done for a specific task like product development. The nature of each project is unique and planning is done for each project individually. The emphasis in project planning is on working within set time and resource constraints. The form of organisation used is a temporary structure known as matrix organisation. Project planning derives its goals from the organisational objectives. An organisational strategy, for implementation, may require many plans and programmes; each programme includes several projects.

Short-term (Short Range) Planning

Deciding about the planning period-the number of years ahead for which planning is done is an important decision. There is no definite planning period on the basis of which plans could be classified as being of a short or long duration. It would depend, among other factors, on the uncertainty present in the future or the nature cut products. For companies in the oil exploration business, the planning period would be long-up to 20 years or more-while a fashion garments manufacturer may not plan for more than a year. A basis on which plans could be termed as short-or long-range is the commitment principle: "a period of time in the future necessary to foresee, as well as possible, the fulfillment or commitments involved in decisions made today." Ordinarily, plans for less than one year are termed as short-range and those for 3 to 5 years are long-range plans. Short-range planning involves making plans which are based on current data. These are the immediate goals to be achieved, present commitment of resources minor changes in schedules, policies and requirements, and midterm appraisals. Short-range plans operate within the framework of long-range plans. Sometimes, medium-range planning can also be undertaken which froms a linkage between the short and long-range plans.

Long-terms (Long Range) Planning

Long-range planning as the name indicates, deals with planning for a future period of time. The planning process involves a systematic identification of opportunities and threats so that managers may use the date to make current decisions in order to use the opportunities and avoid the threats. By consideration of the future developments, as manager can assess the futurity of current decisions-the likely impact that a decision taken now is going to make in the future-and make current decisions accordingly. In this manner, long-range planning deals with issues which are of the vital significance and have a long-term impact. There are many other terms used to planning which is for a long term is of vital significance, and is concerned with the futurity of current decisions.

Contingency Planning

The contingency approach rests on the premise that there is no one best way to solve a problem, the right approach depends on the situation. Environmental conditions, on which much of long-term planning rests, change so rapidly that policy makers are often constrained in making tenable assumptions regarding future developments. Too much formal planning does not seem to work under such conditions. A realistic approach, to contain these problems, is to adopt contingency planning. This involves taking action in incremental steps, reassessing strategies at each stage and reformulating plans in order to reach a predetermined goal.

For example, a company manufacturing refrigerators faces competition in the market as a result of which it modernises its operations. In the next stage, it raises capacity levels to take advantages of economics of scale. Further, in order to offset seasonal fluctuations, it starts making watches and, thus, diversifies into a new area. The three steps of modernisation, expansion and diversification, show that the company has reviewed its strategies at each stage and tries to ensure survival and profitability by adopting contingency planning. Had the conditions been different at any of the three stages, the company would have adopted a different approach. Such an approach would have been contingent on that situation.

Strategic Planning

Strategic planning is a process which, through an examination of external and internal factors for an organisation, results in a set of mission, purpose, objectives, policies, plans and programmes for implementation. In this manner, strategic planning results in action designed to implement a strategy. A view of strategic planning is that the objectives and goals, and the strategies designed to achieve them, give rise to two types of plans. These are the operating and strategic plans. The operating plans are implemented by the different units in an organisation while strategic plans are implemented through projects. Strategic planning is considered a part of wider system of managing through strategy *i.e.* strategic management.

Comprehensive or Systematic or Corporate Planning

Corporate planning is a term to denote a formal, comprehensive, and systematic appraisal of environmental and internal factors in order to evolve strategies to achieve organisational objectives. It is formal as it requires formulation of plans, strategies, and policies on the basis of documents and figures. It is comprehensive as it deals with all types of plans: short and long-range, corporate, divisional and functional, and strategic and operational plans. It is systematic as it covers the whole planning process in a logic and sequential manner. Due to its nature, corporate planning is also known as comprehensive corporate planning, comprehensive planning or systematic planning.

In practice, a team of corporate planners assists the senior managers in determining objectives and goals to be achieved, strengths and weaknesses of the company, the opportunities and threats operating in the environment, and the strategies and action plans to be adopted. The corporate planners are also involved in continuous monitoring of the implementation process of plans and the process taking place. On the basis of such an evaluation, the strategies and action plans are reviewed and reformulated, if necessary.

Corporate planning is a term often used synonymously with long-range planning and strategic planning. It is also a term rarely found in American, literature pertaining to business policy. But others including India books, often use the term 'corporate planning'. Some of the earlier books published in the area of business policy in India carried the title of Corporate Planning.

The term 'corporate planning' is also used extensively in management journals, popular business magazines, and in industry. Management courses in the area of business policy offered by institutions and Universities in India are also known as corporate planning courses. Notwithstanding the popular use of the term 'corporate planning', normally, it is taken to be synonymous with long-range planning and strategic planning.

Problem of Semantics in Terminology: Planning Terms

As in Section, we deal with the problem of semantics in terminology related to various planning terms that have been used above. For this purpose, we take up the following combinations of terms as examples.

(1) Long-range Planning—Corporate Planning—Strategic Planning. These three terms, in groups of two each at one time, have been considered above. Much of what has been stated is also valid for these three terms jointly. Individually, these terms do mean different things to different people. Historically, they have emerged at different times. Each of these terms has come to signify planning systems that have been invented in response a unique set of environmental factors. With regard to the literature in the area of business policy, writers have extolled the virtues of one planning system while treating the others as secondary. But the differences between them, as of today, are at best, academic.

Practitioners do not view them differently, many authors also adopt an approach of using them interchangeably. A reasonable approach, in our opinion, could be to consider the nature of planning involved. If the planning is done at a senior level of management, is sufficiently long-range, is valid for the company as a whole, and is of vital, pervasive or continuing importance, it can either be called long-range, corporate or strategic planning. The basic thrust in such planning has to be on the process of identification of opportunities and threats in the environment and their matching with the strengths and weaknesses of the company in order to formulate strategies to achieve the objectives, purpose and mission of the organisation.

(2) **Long-range Planning—Strategic Planning.** Ansoff differentiates long range planning ("Where future is expected to be predictable through extrapolation of the historical growth") and strategic planning ("...future is not necessarily expected to be an improvement over the past nor is assumed to be extrapolable") Steiner, Miner and Gray do not differentiate long-range (also corporate) planning and strategic planning stating that "strategic planning is the phrase most widely used today." Sometimes, strategic planning is considered an emerging term for corporate planning, which itself is thought to be a successor to long-range planning. For all practical purposes, however, both the terms are considered to be synonymous.

(3) **Corpprate Planning—Strategic Planning.** These terms are also mostly taken as being synonymous. But there of different view. "Although corporate planning and strategic planning are closely linked", says Argenti, "they are not synonymous either". Corporate planning can be divided into two parts, according to Agrenti. The first relates to decided the corporate objectives and the second to the determination of corporate strategies. So, "strategic planning is the second part of corporate planning". The present

trend is exemplified to consider both these terms, as well as long-range learning to be synonymous for all practice purposes.

(4) **Long-range Planning—Corporate Planning.** Some authors, specially the earlier ones, differentiate between these two terms. Argenti is of the opinion that not all long-range plans are corporate all corporate plans are necessarily long-range. Ansoff equates both and says that long-range planning is "sometimes called corporate planing." Sometimes, corporate planning is taken as learning for the whole company as contrasted with functional plans. Others do not consider corporate plans as simple aggregates of functional plans. Occasionally, corporate planning is thought to be a combination of long and short-range plans. However, the most accepted approach presently is to consider both long-range planning and corporate planning as synonymous for all practical purposes.

(5) **From Strategic Planning to Strategic Management.** While strategic planning helps to resolve the problem of strategy formulation on the basis of mission and objective-setting and the analysis of environmental and internal factors it falls short of taking into account a few relevant aspects. Asnoff *et al.* deal with these shortcomings in terms of three variables. First, with regard to managerial problems strategic planning considers there external linkages with the environment "under a basic assumption that the internal configuration will remain essentially unchanged". Second dealing with process of resolving managerial problems it covers only problem-solving (or planning) while assuming that implementation and control will follow. Thirdly the variables included in strategic planning analysis are exclusively "technological-economic informational while social and political dynamics both within and outside the organisation are assumed to be irrelevant and unaffected".

The sub-variablest which have been excluded from consideration have a major impact on resolving strategic problems. For instance it is essential to consider the impact that formulation of strategy, and changes in it, have on the organisation. Again-the solution of managerial problems can only be done through a comprehesive approach that not only considers formation but also implementation and control of strategy. Factors like psychosociological and political dimensions of policy-making are essential for diagnosing the myriad of problems faced by managers.

Strategic management a newer and broader concept of managing organisation straregically takes into account all the aspects of managerial.

RANGE OF STRATEGIC PLANNING

1. Following reasons may justify business policy formulation or strategic planning. One justification is that it has been found useful in practice. Research studies, based on the experience of companies and executive viewpoints, have indicated that strategic planning contributes positively to the performance of enterprises.
2. Different Studies reveal that companies which had undertaken formal strategic planning not only out performed the non-planners on most measures of sources (return on equity growth of sales, earning for shares, and value of the firms), but significantly outperformed their own past results/ as well; besides, the companies that used strategic planning were able to predict the outcome of planning much better than others.
3. Researches have shown that strategic planning can isolate the key factors in an industry and thus help companies plan their strategies more effectively.
4. With changing environment of business of product-market conditions technology, economic, climate—strategic planning is the only means by which future opportunities and problems can be anticipated by company executives.

5. It enables executives to provide necessary direction for the enterprise, take full advantage of new opportunities and minimise the attendant risks.
6. Strategic planning is beneficial particularly in organisations when there is a long time lag between managerial decisions and the results thereof.
7. Strategic planning enables management to improve the chances of making decisions which will stand the test of time and revising the strategy on the basis of monitoring the progress of R & D and the changes in product-market conditions.
8. With clear goals and direction provided for the future, employees in general and managers in particular can better perceive the ways of achieving the corporate objectives consistently with the individual and group aspirations. This is conducive to greater harmony and goal congruence.
9. Formal strategic planning focuses on problems of the total enterprise, not just functional problems in the marketing, finance or personnel areas. Persons exposed to strategy formation thus develop a breadth of understanding and undergo change of attitudes in the process.

LIMITATIONS OF STRATEGIC PLANNING

Strategic Planning in management is essential but there are practical limitations to its use. The reasons why people fall in strategic planning emphasise the practical difficulties encountered in planning.

A number of limits within which planning has to operate make this undertaking difficult. Following are the limitations:

(1) Problems of Change. The above factor works more as limiting factor in the light of changes in future conditions. In a complex and rapidly changing environment, the succession of new problems is often magnified by implications that make planning most difficult. The problem of change is more complex in long-range planning. Present conditions tend to weigh heavily in planning, and by overshadowing future needs, may sometimes results in error of judgment. Such factors as changing technology, consumer tastes and desires, business conditions, and many others change rapidly and often unpredically. In such conditions, planning activities taken in one period may not be relevant for another period because the conditions in two periods are quite different.

(2) Failure of People. There are many reasons why people fail in planning, both at the formulation level as well as implementation level. Some of the major failures are lack of commitment to planning, failure to develop, sound strategies, lack of clear and meaningful objectives, tendency to overlook planning premises, failure to see the scope of the plan, failure to see planning as a rational approach, excessive reliance on the past experience, failure to use the principles of limiting factors, lack of top management support lack of delegation of authority, lack of adequate control techniques, and resistance to change. These factors are responsible for either inadequate planning or wrong planning in the organisations concerned.

(3) Lack of Accurate Information. The first basic limitation of strategic planning is the lack of accurate information and facts relating to future., Planning concerns future activity and its quality will be determined by the quality of forecast of future events. As no manager can predict completely and accurately the events of future, the planning may pose problems in operation. This problem is further, increased by lack of formulating accurate premises. Many times, managers may not be aware about the various conditions within which they have to formulate their planning activities.

(4) Inflexibilities. Manager while going through the strategic planning process have to work in a set of given variables. These variables may be more in terms of organisational or external. These often provide considerably less flexibility in planning action.

(A) ***Internal.*** Major internal inflexibilities that may limit planning are related to the an psychology. Organisatonal policies and procedures, and long-term capital investment. The first internal inflexibility is in the form of human psychology in that most of the people have regard for the present rather

than for future. The present is not only more certain than future, it is also more desirable, and more real. Thus, resistance to change is a basic factor which works against planning because planning often depends on the changes. People may have feelings that if planning is soft-pedalled, the changes and the possible danger of future will be minimised. For them, planning tends to accelerate change and unrest.

Second type of internal inflexibility emerges because of organisationnal policies and procedures once these are established, they are difficult to change. Though these policies, procedures, and, rules are meant to facilitate managerial functions by, providing guidelines, they often are too numerous and exacting that they leave very little scope for managerial initiative and flexibility. Since managers have to plan for future which is not static but changing, they often find themselves in great constraints. Such problems are more common in bureaucratic organisations where rules and procedures are the matters of prime concerns.

Third type of internal inflexibility comes because of long-term capital investment. Long-term planning is not a process of making future decisions, but a means of reflecting the future in todays decisions. If the organisation has taken a long-term investment, it is committed by that and future actions have to be takin in the light of the investment. Thus managerial planning is limited to that extent.

(B) External. Beside the internal inflexibilities, managers are contronted with many external inflexibilities and they do not have control over these. These factors may be social, technological, legal, labour union, geographically and economic. The managers have to formulate their plans keeping in view the demand of these factors. Thus their scope of action is limited making planning in effective in many cases.

(5) Time and Cost. While going 'through the strategic planning process managers should also take into account both time and cost factors. The various steps of planning may go as for as possible because there is no limit of precision in planning tools. But planning suffers because of time and cost factors. Time is a limiting factor for every manager in the organisation on, and if they are busy in preparing elaborate reports and instructions beyond certain level, they are risking their effectiveness. Excessive time spent on securing information and trying to fit all of it into a compact plans is dysfunctional in the organisation.

(6) Rigidity. Often people feel that planning provides rigidity in managerial action. Many types of internal inflexibilities, discussed above, may be results of planning itself. The planning stifles employee initiative and forces managers into rigid or straitjacket mode of executing their work. In fact, rigidity may make managerial work more difficult than it need be. This may result in it delay in work performance, lack of intiative, and lack of adjustment with changing environment. Many people feel that planning is limited in value because best results can be obtained by a muddling through types of operation in which each situation is tackled when and if it appears pertinent to the immediate problem. Though this factor of rigidity of planning is limiting factor but without planning, it is really difficult to operate particularly in large organisations.

The planning also involves cost on the part of the orgartisation. The various factors analysed above contribute to the limitations of strategic planing, either making planing ineffective or making lesser degree of planned work.

CONFLICTS BETWEEN STRATEGIC PLANNING AND OPERATIONAL PLANNING

There are certain conflicts between strategic and operational planning. These conflicts may be generated because of the different nature of two types of planning or because of the different groups of people involved in them. Most of the common conflicts between strategic and operational planning are as follows:

(1) First source of conflict between strategic and operational planning may be period of futurity. Strategic planners think in terms of long term future of the organisation, sometimes even at the cost of immediate gains. On the other hand, operational planners may concentrate more on near future. Strategic planners may think in terms of long term profitability as new projects may affect short term profitability adversely because of their long gestation period.

(2) Strategic planning is likely to proceed at a more leisurely pace than operational planning. Operational planners focus on their present resources, have major day-to-day operating responsibilities and are under pressure to immediately accomplish a higher level of activity at lower cost. They have to meet the more specific targets in the organisation on which their survival in organization is determined. Under such circumstances, each group may exaggerate its importance in the organisation and combining the two types of planning may become even necessary.

(3) Strategic planners are more prone to change while operational planners may not relish changes. For example, the growth prospects of an organisation can best be served by broadening or shifting the base into areas with more potential for development. Such shifts, however, are likely to decrease efficiency as new products with which the organisation has had little or no experience are scheduled to be developed and manufactured. The *status quo* therefore, as far as product lines are concerned, may be more attractive organisational policy for functional managers.

The above factors may lead to conflicts between strategic and operational planning. However, since operational planning contributes to strategic planning, it is essential that both are properly integrated. Corporate planning makes an attempt for this integration.

REASONS FOR INADEQUATE PLANNING IN INDIA

There are many factors which affect the corporate planning and are not quite conducive to Indian organisations. The need for an extent of corporate planning within any economy is governed basically by the following factors:

(a) Scarcity of resources

(b) Government policy and control

(c) Competition facing the firm

(d) Size of the firm.

There is substantial interdependence among these factors and the intensity of impact of each one of these factors may vary from country to country from firm to firm within the same country, or from time to time within the same organisation. A study related to the cross-cultural management philosophy, practices and effectiveness with particular reference to India have suggested the following propositions:

All other factors being the same, the higher a firm's score on the management philosophy (*i.e.*, attitudes toward various components of society internal and external to the firm) index, the greater will be its concern for long-range planning.

The greater the degree of competition, the greater will be the need for long-range planning by the individual company.

The greater the degree of economic and political instability, the lesser the likelihood that private industrial enterprises will undertake systematic long-range planning.

The greater the degree of government control over prices and the availability of raw materials, the lesser the likelihood that the firm will undertake systematic long range planning.

The greater the degree of governemental hostility toward the business community, the lesser the likelihood that a firm will undertake systematic long-range planning.

The implication of the above propositions is given usually low score on management philosophy among Indian organisations: these constraints are likely to be stronger enough to subdue the passion for long-range planning, apart from management philosophy. Following characteristics of Indian environment work against formulation of the plans by Indian organisations:

(1) As regards the size of the organisation, the Monopolies and Restrictive Trade Practices Act, 1969, sets constraints on expansion and diversification strategy through the limits on assets size (Rs. 20 crores) and market share (33.3 per cent). Thus area of expansion and diversification-most important area of LRP for larger organisations is defined by Government regulations. Further constraints are out on organisations, with foreign-majority equity holding and public sector organisations, though there is a basic difference. The former organisations area of business is determined by Government, thus narrowing the scope of discretionary planning. In the case of the latter, business goals in terms of areas of activity are pretty clear and stable.

(2) There is not enough degree of competition among sellers because of sellers market conditions. Though in some consumer goods, the conditions of the market have changed, there is high rate of returns. Thus for most organisations, a fair amount of rate of return is assured. The market is further accentuated by growing population and market size, fairly stable consumer tastes, progressive deeming of areas of business by Government in which organisations can go. As such many organisations do not see any need for systematic planning. This is supported by non-existence of separate planning division in most of the organisations.

(3) Lack of resources, in general also creates barriers in formulation and implementation of plans. There is a competition for claims for resources—specially materials, infrastructural facilities, such as, power transport finance, managerial manpower. Since many of these resources are canalised and controlled through Government agencies, there is no competition in the supply resources. It verges more on monopoly-rationing supplies to a large number of competing organisations. Many of the organisations view that constraining forces in effective plan implementation are the Government policy, licensing policy, delay in procurement of

machinery and equipment, erratic supply of raw materials, shortcomings in transport and communication facilities, and delay in implementation of projects in other sectors.

Thus either because of lack of appreciation of need for planning or because of prevailing conditions working against effective formulation and implementation of plans, some organisations do not make attempts to look beyond a year and others accept the conditions as constraints in their attempt at planning. The factors—degree of competence, ownership professional training of management, and perception of Government attitude towards the companies—may account to some extent for the difference in attitudes.

FACTORS OF MAKING STRATEGIC PLANNING EFFECTIVE

It is not sufficient to say that managers must take actions to make strategic planning effective, but they must be clear as to what actions can be taken in this direction. Following factors are important for making planning effective:

(1) **An Open Systems Approach.** The problems of planning should be dealt through open systems approach. It suggests that managers must take into account interactions with their total environment in every respect of planning. Open systems approach makes it necessary on the part of the managers that they take into account the environmental variable such as, technological, social, cultural, legal, political, and economic. Further, they must also take into account the internal interaction pattern that is, how their planning process is affecting others and is affected by others. When managers take all these factors into account is affected by others. When managers take all these factors into account, they are in better positions to plan and execute their actions.

(2) **Participation in Planning.** As discussed above, planning progress should be a joint one. The best planning is likely to be done when managers are given an opportunity to

contribute to plans affecting the area over which they have authority. Participation in planning affecting managers areas of authority at any level through their being informed contributing suggestions and being consulted, leads to good planning commitment, loyalty, and managerial effectiveness.

The various methods of participation in planning process may be followed in the organisations depending upon their requirements and understanding of the people.

(3) Integration of Long-term and Short-term Plans. Managers often focus their attention only on very short - term plans, even if they plan. As discussed earlier, a good planning process involves integration of long-term and short-term plans. A short-term plan contributes towards the achievement of the long-term plan. Thus, if a manager is planning for very short period, he must take into account his long-term plans also. He must constantly watch and review that his short-term plans contribute to his long-term plans. If this is not the situation, he must modify his course of action which may include modification in both long-term and short-term plans.

(4) Communication of Planning. Many planning efforts fail because managers do not adequately emphasise the role of communicating various planning elements, such as, goals, strategies, policies, and planning premises. If these are communicated clearly, adequately, and timely, the managers are motivated and initiated to take planning process. Which may be necessary for them. When a manager understands the various aspects of planning he is in a better position to foresee his future course of action and may develop a habit of planning every course of future action.

(5) Initiative. Planning to be effective must have the initiative and support of top level management. It is the top level which is responsible for success or failure of any organisational process, and planning is no exception. The basic objectives which are set at the top level must be two-way process which involves people at other levels also. Further, when top management rigorously reviews subordinates programmes, it naturally stimulates planning interest throughout the organisation. The planning action by top management does not suggest in everything will come from the top and subordinates will do nothing, rather the planning process should be a joint one.

(6) **Establishing a Climate.** The managers should try to establish a climate where every person in the organisation takes planning action. Every superior managers should remove obstacles to planning and present facilities for planning of his can be done by setting clear goals, establishing and publishing applicable significant planning premises, involving all managers in planning process, reviewing subordinate plans and their performance, and assuring appropriate staff assistance and information at all levies of management.

ORGANISATIONAL OBJECTIVES

Organisational objectives seek to direct the efforts of all members of a team while personal goals are motives of people working in the team. Efficiency is high when the two types of objectives are mutually supportive or compatible. Organisational objectives are the goals established to guide the efforts of the company and each of its components. Objectives are variously referred to as purposes, goals, missions, or targets. The establishment of objectives is a very important step in planning. Planning can be effective only if objectives are carefully selected. A clear statement of purpose understood by one and all is the best guarantee of effective management. Objectives must be actionable, that is, meaningful to the manager who is to achieve them. Objectives or goals must be specific and capable of accomplishment. They must be identified in such a way that ultimate success or failure can be determined.

The above description reveals the following characteristics of organisational objectives:

1. Every organisation has number of economic, social and human objectives rather than a single aim. As stated earlier, objectives are required in every area of business where the success and survival of the business is important. Every department or division has its own objectives in addition to the overall objectives of the organisation. Different objectives should be balanced with one another. A business firm has both general and specific objectives are narrow in scope *e.g.*, to reduce absenteeism. Organisational goals are sometimes divided into *(a)* maintenance goals, and *(b)* productivity goals. Maintenance goals are the expression of the desire to ensure the existence of the enterprise, while productivity goals aim at improvements in performance.

2. Objectives are the ultimate ends or results towards which an organisation and its members strive at all times. All activities and, resources of an enterprise are directed towards the achievement of common and specified objectives.

3. Objectives are the standing plans which recurringly guide action. They are the basis of other plans such as policies; procedure programmes, etc. Objectives are the concrete expressions of the purposes of an enterprises. Primary or major objectives provide the principal reasons for the establishment of the enterprise while collateral objectives supplement and contribute to the primary objectives. Organisational objectives are the basis of long range planning whereas departmental objectives provide the basis for short range planning. Different organisations have different objectives and there is no universal set of objectives. Objectives must, however, be practicable, consistent and clear cut. There must be proper coordination between major and derivative goals and between long range and short range objectives. Objectives should be specific,

verifiable and well planned. There must be active participation of all concerned in the determination of objectives.

4. Objectives are arranged in a hierarchy which is known as the 'Ends and Means Chain.' Objectives of a lower order act as the means for the achievement of higher level objectives. For instance, the organisational objectives are more basic than the departmental objectives.
5. Objectives may be long-term or short-term. Long-term objectives refer to the objectives to be achieved over a long period of time while short-term objectives are to be achieved within a period of one to two years. Short-run objectives are steps towards long-term objectives.

Impact on Strategic Planning Programme

(a) Clear and specific objectives avoid conflicts and misunderstanding. They facilitate unified action and integration of efforts on the part of members of the organisation. When objectives are clearly defined and there is agreement on them, every individual tries to adjust his actions and this leads to voluntary coordination. Thus objectives serve as the important tool of management. They define excellence in organisational performance. Without objectives, the manager possesses no tools for deciding whether performance is satisfactory or disappointing. By delimiting the course of the operations, objectives help to avoid misdirecting of the resources and to ensure maximum utilisation of the assets of the firm.

(b) Well-defined objectives help in effective delegation and decentralisation of authority. By providing clear-cut guidelines for action, they avoid the need for detailed and specific guidance on the part of management. Knowledge of objectives helps to transform random behaviour into systematic efforts. Goals are vital links in planning process.

(c) As there exists an ends and means relationship between objectives, objectives make for consistent and unified planning. Objectives provide the common denominator for different types of plans. The entire process of management concerns itself with means to achieve objectives.

(d) Objectives serve as the standards with which actual performance can be evaluated. They are also helpful in fixing responsibility. In this way, objectives provide the basis for control. Performance can continually be evaluated in terms of how well the organisation is moving in the direction of its objectives.

(e) Objectives provide a sense of purpose. They improve the motivation and morale of members of the organisation by making the job meaningful and worthwhile. They serve as guide-posts to action and efforts. Objectives are key to effective planning as plans have no meaning unless they are designed to achieve certain well defined objectives. By defining objectives, management establishes the image or character of the firm.

In the words of Ordway Tead, "it is difficult to overstress the notion of the purpose, aim, objective or goal of the organisation as fundamental to every view of or element in administration."

Planning can be a useful managerial function only if objectives are properly spelled out. Therefore, every enterprise should state its of objectives precisely and clearly.

❒

5

Corporate Planning and Environment

Corporate planning consists of both strategic planning and operational planning which have been described earlier. It may be viewed as an input-output system. Its input is the information used to formulate, execute and review strategies. These inputs are transformed through the process of environmental scanning, corporate appraisal, strategy making and strategic management. Various types of plans are its outputs.

Planning is an integral part of every manager's job. It involves determination of a desired future state and the choice of actions to attain the desired future.

According to Hussey, "the formal process of developing objectives for the corporation and its component parts, evolving alternative strategies to achieve these objectives and doing this against the background of systematic appraisal of internal strengths and weaknesses and external environmental changes; the process of translating strategy into detailed operational plans and seeing that these plans are carried out."

According to Drucker, corporate planning is the continuous process of making present entrepreneurial (risk taking) decisions systematically and with the best possible knowledge of their futurity, organising systematically the efforts needed to carry out these decisions and measuring the results of these decisions against the expectations through organised systematic feedback.

On the basis of foregoing description the following characteristics of corporate planning can be identified:

(i) Corporate planning is a formal and systematic process. It is an organised or structured process consisting of a particular sequence of steps. It involves analysis of internal and external environment, setting corporate objectives, formulating and executing strategy and review of progress as well as strategy.

(ii) Corporate planning is basically concerned with the future impact of present decisions. It is based on the belief that while future is uncertain and the environment is complex, it is possible and necessary to cope with them through active intervention.

(iii) Corporate planning is an ongoing or continuous process. It is a dynamic exercise that goes on throughout the corporate life. Continuous review of the whole planning process is a fundamental feature of corporate planning.

(iv) Corporate planning provides an integrated framework within which each of the functional and departmental plans are tied together.

(v) Corporate planning is a rational process. It requires imagination, foresight, reflective, thinking, judgement and other mental faculties.

Objectives of Corporate Planning

Peter Lorange has identified four specific objectives of corporate planning.

(i) Allocation of scarce resources like funds, managerial talent and technological know-how. Such allocation among product/market alternatives (*e.g.,* expansion, acquisition, diversification etc.) decides the strategic direction of the firm.)

(ii) Coordinating strategic activities so as to reflect the firm's own internal strengths and weaknesses in order to achieve efficient operations. Such integration provides a direction for building on the firm's strengths and avoid its weaknesses. Integration can take several forms, *e.g.*, development of strategic programmes to achieve particular objectives. Adaptation and integration purposes are complementary to each other.

(iii) Assisting the firm to adapt to environmental opportunities and threats. Such adaptation helps to improve company's success by providing an effective strategic fit with the environment. This outward looking search helps to identify strategies options and to employ resources in such a way that they yield the best return.

(iv) Instilling systematic approach of management development through learning from the outcomes of its past strategic decisions. Planning is a vehicle for more effective managerial learning so that the executive team of a company can systematically increase its strategic decision-making capabilities over time. A properly designed and executed planning system contributes to management development in two ways. *First,* the process of developing, discussing and executing plans serves as a valuable learning experience. *Secondly,* planning serves as a self-improvement system by setting down a basis for monitoring progress towards goals. The learning and self-improvement aspects of planning underscore the important roles of performance monitoring and management motivation within the context of corporate planning.

Approaches to Corporate Planning

Ackoff suggests three approaches to planning:

1. Satisficing. Under this approach, planning is designed to attain a satisfactory level of performance. Objectives are set at a level that is practicable or feasible. The aim is to do well enough. The planner searches for ways to achieve the aims that are acceptable but not necessarily the best. This approach shies, away from organisational changes as it is concerned more with survival than with growth.

2. Optimizing. This approach to planning aims at the highest possible level of achievement. A search is made for the best way as opposed to a merely satisfactory way of achieving results. Efforts are made to maximise (sales or profits) or minimise (cost of operation) something.

3. Complexity of Business. In a complex business, it is very difficult to make correct estimates of future possibilities. Complex operations require detailed analysis. In order to deal with such complexities, the corporate planner may require models of understanding and explaining the interactions among complex variables. Continuous interaction and feedback from operating managers may be necessary on current operations and problems.

4. Adaptivising. In neither of the above two approaches, there is an explicit attempt to improve the planning process itself. Adaptivising approach places as much emphasis on searching for better ways of planning and control as on finding better solutions to problems. It is designed to manage the planning system in such a way as to minimise the future need for retrospective planning. It is directed towards removing deficiencies produced by past decision.

5. Planning Skills. In most of the firms which are regularly engaged in corporate planning, a planning department or cell is created to coordinate the planning efforts of divisional or functional groups. The planning cell is assigned the responsibility of making forecasts, collecting and analysing data, reviewing the plans prepared by lower levels and advising the chief executive on the viability and adequacy of such plans. Where the planning cell is possessed of required skills, it is likely to play a more active role in plan formulation. In the absence of such skills, plannaing becomes essentially a process of negotiations between departmental/divisional heads and the chief executive.

6. Ownership Patterns. In general, corporate planning is a more formalised process is professionally managed companies than in closely-held or family-owned companies. Surveys on corporate planning practices reveal reasons for such difference. Family-owned companies depend largely on intuition, common sense, experience and entrepreneurial skills. Therefore, corporate planning is such companies tends to be more informal, more centralised and less interactive. On the other hand professionally managed companies depend more on analytical method, participation and a formal setup.

7. Management Attitudes. The philosophy or attitude of management exercises a significant influence on plan formulation. Autocratic or paternalistic management formulates corporate goals without consulting subordinates. In such a case, the plan formulation becomes a one-step process wherein goals are handed down to subordinates who are expected to accept them and work for their accomplishment. Under participative or democratic management, on the other hand, plan formulation is an interative process wherein subordinates are actively involved in goal setting and strategy formulation.

8. Nature of Demand. In a company which manufactures and sells consumer goods, demand is direct. In case of direct demand, sales forecasting is comparatively easy. For example, a steel utensil manufacturer can forecast future demand for his products on the basis of consumer price index, analysis of income groups, festivals, etc. In such cases, demand forecasting is simply one-stage process.

On the other hand, a firm supplying producers or intermediate goods enjoys derived demand. For instance, steel is used by other industries to produce products used by the consumer. Demand forecasting in such cases is a multi-stage exercise. First, the demand for the ultimate product would have to be forecasted. From such demand, the firm will have to go back and forecast the demand for steel by the intermediate industry.

9. Time Lag. Plan formulation is a simple process when the time lag between a decision and its implementation is nominal. As the decision takes effect immediately or soon after, it is taken, there is little chance of any change in the variables affecting the outcome of the decision. In such cases there is little need to plan to take a decision. Similarly, it is not necessary to evaluate different alternatives and their possibilities. In such a situation, corporate planning becomes deterministic. If the lag between a decision and its effect is long, plan formulation becomes complicated. Since the possibility of change in the underlying variables is high, it becomes essential to evaluate various alternatives. The decision once taken may have to be reviewed and revised before it is fully carried out.

10. Market Dynamics. When the market for the company's products and services is stable, demand can be forecasted with reasonable accuracy and plan formulation becomes comparatively a simple process. On the other hand, if the market is uncertain and less predictable, corporate planning becomes a difficult and complex exercise. Accurate prediction of demand in such a case requires much effort and analysis. Thus, the formulation of corporate plan is conditioned to a great extent by the predictability of demand or dynamics of the market.

Steps in Corporate Planning Process

The main steps in the process of corporate planning may be described as follows:

1. Environmental Scanning. Every organisation functions within an environment and environmental forces exercise a significant influence on its functioning. Therefore, it is essential to analyse and understand the environment before formulating any plan. Environment refers to the aggregate of all conditions, events and forces that surround and affect an organisation. Business environment is complex as it consists of numerous elements. It is dynamic or keeps on changing. A thorough scanning of the external environment will reveal the opportunities and threats which the organisation is likely to face in future.

OPPORTUNITIES AND THREATS PROFILE

Opportunities in the Environment

1. Favourable economic climate with a clearer thinking in the key policy areas.

2. Increasing demand potential abroad for exportabe products.
3. Higher plan outlay and liberalisation of import policy.
4. Short gestation periods.
5. Long term fiscal policy.

Threats in the Environment

1. Tendency towards economic nationalism. Hostile propaganda from indigenous competitors.
2. Price controls that inhibit profits.
3. Restriction into the entry of large concern and foreign firms into certain areas without minimum export commitments.
4. Growing public sector shutting out openings for the private sector.
5. Expansion and diversification requires dilution of foreign shareholdings.
6. Heavy tax doses prticularly on company's tobacco products.
7. Borrowings from public financial institutions entail government control on ownership and management structure.

Corporate Appraisal. Corporate appraisal or self appraisal refers to analysis of internal environment of the enterprise. Such appraisal helps to identify the strength and weakness of the enterprise in terms of resources, products, profit ability, market share etc. It indicates what the enterprise can do and where does it stand.

COMPANY'S STRENGTHS AND WEAKNESSES

1. Strengths

1. Management

(a) Very strong top management with administrative expertise

(b) Open-minded management, no infighting

(c) Very little internal politicking

(d) Solid management in subsidiaries

(e) Lean management

(f) Management integrity

(g) Flexible organisation structure

2. ***Marketing***

(a) Strong image among consumers particularly for quality, performance and aftersale service.

(b) Sound relations with industry, government and reputation for fair play.

(c) Five established brand names.

(d) Effective low cost distribution network.

3. ***Finance***

(a) Rs. 50 lakhs internal resources available for expansion, progressive dividends and retentions record.

(b) A capacity to raise a debt of Rs. 10 crores.

(c) Good credit standing with banks and other institutions.

(d) Ability to adjust debt-equity ratio for increasing profitability.

(e) High current ratio.

4. ***Production***

(a) A strong R&D base with research oriented bias in activities.

(b) New plant and equipment.

(c) Dispersed production units to take care of regional contingencies.

(d) Access to technology and know-how at home and abroad.

(e) Assured supply of raw materials.

(f) Optimum size units with capacity to meet extra demand.

5. Personnel

(a) A high level of technical expertise.

(b) Rising labour productivity.

(c) Progressive collective bargaining.

(d) Strong grievance handling machinery.

(e) Attractive wages and fringe benefits.

(f) Healthy industrial relations with no strike in the last 10 years.

2. Weaknesses

1. Management

(a) Chief executive aged 65, no obvious successor.

(b) Weak middle management cadre.

(c) Coordination between Departments lacking.

(d) Lack of depth of management.

(e) Lack of innovation and result orientation.

(f) Marketing manager incapable of handling any expansion.

2. Marketing

(a) About 80 per cent of profits accrue from product A whose market is declining by 5 per cent per annum.

(b) Lack of consumer orientation.

(c) 5 products contribute no profit and have no potential.

3. Personnel

(a) Low morale due to nepotism in promotion.

(b) Constant line staff bickerings.

(c) High turnover of skilled labour.

(d) Too many status seekers and waste makers.

(e) Poor labour management relations.

(f) Manpower planning imbalances; too many unskilled and too few skilled workers.

4. Production

(a) Frequent production and transportation bottlenecks.

(b) Lack of scientific inventory control and quality control.

(c) Inadequate capacity utilisation.

(d) Irregular supply of materials and spares.

(e) Poor quality of materials and spares.

(f) Obsolete machinery.

5. Finances

(1) Substantial capital tied up in stocks.

(2) Over-dependence on imports.

(3) Overtrading on stocks with inadequate cash at various points of time.

(4) High rate of royalties and repairiations due to foreign collaboration.

(5) Poor public relations.

(6) Inappropriate capital gearing with heavy fixed interest obligations.

3. Strategy Making. The next step in corporate planning is to identify and evaluate strategic options and to choose the most suitable option. This is the heart of the corporate planning process. Strategy indicates the basic thrust of the company and serves as a bridge between objectives and actions. Like a magnifying glass it focuses attention on the key result areas. Strategy should match the strengths with opportunities.

4. Defining Mission and Objectives. After identifying opportunities, threats, strengths and weaknesses, the next step is to define the mission and objectives of the organisation. Mission and objectives reflect the desired future position of the enterprise. Since

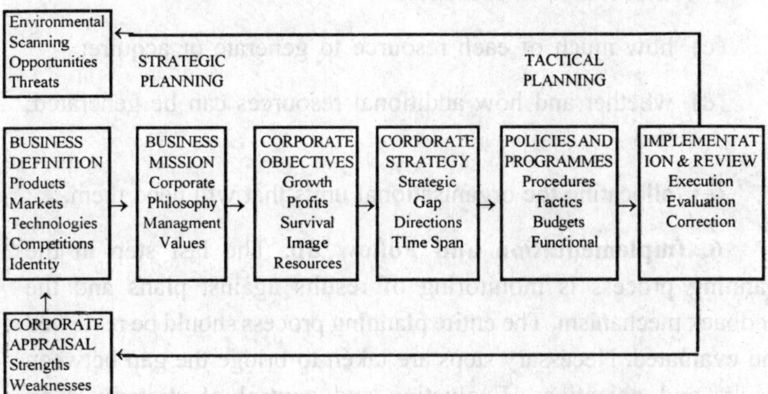

Fig. 5.1 Model of Corporate Planning Process

the aim of planning is to provide a rational direction of activities towards desired results, a corporate plan cannot be drawn up without clarifying objectives. Comparison of the present position with the desired position will reveal the strategic gap to be filled by the corporate plan.

5. Action Planning. Policies, programmes, budgets, etc. are required for effective implementation of chosen strategy. This step is the tactical or operation planning phase of corporate planning. Action programmes are set-up for all functional areas.

An action programme consists of:

(i) The main job and other jobs to be accomplished.

(ii) A work schedule specifying the critical time elements.

(iii) Sequence of jobs and activities.

(iv) Assignment of work responsibilities.

Action programming also involves resource planning which consists of:

(a) determining amount and type of each resource that will be required for each year in the planning period;

(b) estimating how much of each type of resource canbe expected to be available:

(c) how much of each resource to generate or acquire;

(d) whether and how additional resources can be generated; and

(e) allocating the organisational units that will need them.

6. Implementation and Follow up. The last step in the planning process is monitoring of results against plans and the feedback mechanism, The entire planning process should be reviewed and evaluated. Necessary steps are taken to bridge the gap between results and objectives. Evaluation and control of strategy is an important element of corporate planning. Continuous monitoring is required to judge performance and the functioning of the strategy. Remedial steps in performance and strategy must be taken at the right time. Modifications in strategy may become necessary due to unexpected changes in environment. Implementation of strategy also involves developing an appropriate organisational/structural framework, formulating and integrating functional plans and managing the behaviour of individuals and groups through proper leadership. Necessary adjustments, therefore, must be made in the plans and the planning process.

Environmental Analysis and Diagnosis

As stated earlier a business enterprise operates within an environmental framework. It has to constantly interact with the environmental forces and adapt or adjust its objectives and strategies to changes in the environment. Otherwise it cannot survive and grow. The environment in which an organisation exists could broadly be divided into two parts—external and internal environment.

External Environment. External environment consists of all the forces, institutions and events that are relevant to an organisations operations but beyond its control. It includes all the outside factors that provide opportunities and pose threats to the organisation. The main components of the external environmental of business are as follows:

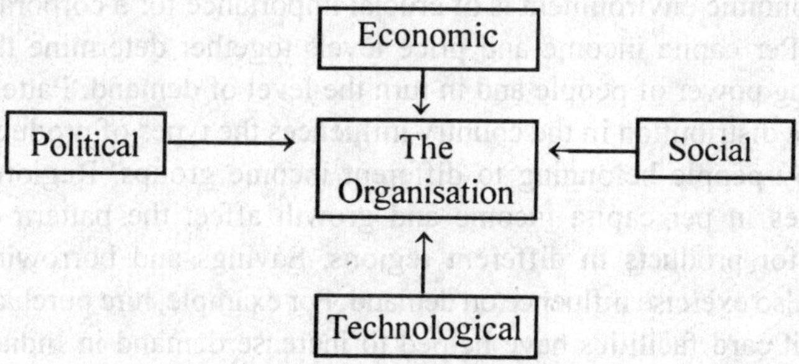

Fig. 5.2 Environmental Components

Economic Environment. Economic environment exercises the most significant and pervasive influence on a business enterprise. It consists of macrolevel factors related to the means of production and distribution of wealth. It includes all such forces of economic development which affect the product market scope of the enterprise. Some of the important factors operating in the economic environment are as follows:

(i) The stage of economic growth existing in the country.

(ii) The country's economic structure *e.g.* capitalistic, socialistic or mixed economy.

(iii) Economic policies *e.g.* industrial, monetary and fiscal policies.

(iv) Economic planning *e.g.* five year plans, annual budgets, etc.

(v) Economic indices *e.g.* gross national product (GNP), National Income, distribution of income, per capita income, disposable personal income, rate of savings and investments, price level changes, balance of payments, exports and imports, etc.

(vi) Industrial infrastructure such as transportation and communication facilities, banks and financial institutions, sources of energy, etc.

Economic environment is of crucial importance for a corporate planner. Per capita income and price levels together determine the purchasing power of people and in turn the level of demand. Pattern of income distribution in the country influences the types of products needed by people belonging to different income groups. Regional differences in per capita income and growth affect the pattern of demand for products in different regions. Savings and borrowing patterns also exercise influence on demand. For example, hire purchase and credit card facilities have helped to increase demand in India.

In comparison to general economic conditions,conditions in the particular industry exercise a more direct and immediate influence on a business enterprise. Long term growth or decline of the industry, stability of demand for products and stage in product life cycle are important elements of the industry's condition. The nature and needs of customers should be analysed by the corporate planner. Supply of necessary inputs, *e.g.*, raw materials, labour, managers, power and capital directly influence the operation and success of an enterprise.

Some examples of the influence of economic environment in India on business are as follows:

(a) Liberalisation of the economy in recent years has given the necessary freedom to companies to alter their product mix and capacities.

(b) Bad conditions of roads, high taxes on vehicles and spare parts, and delays at checkposts have a negative impact on the cost and timely delivery of raw materials to industry.

(c) Shortage and high costs of power have affected production in energy intensive industries, such as aluminium, cement, fertilisers, steel manufacturing, refineries, etc.

(d) Acute shortage and high costs of raw material (bamboo) forced Grasim Industries to close its pulp factory at Mavoor in Kerala temporarily in 1985.

(e) Liberalisation of imports and entry of multinationals has led to increased competition and some companies are unable to survive competition from multinationals.

Market Environment. Market or competitive environment is closely related to economic environment. In recent years competition in most of the industries has increased due to growing industrialisation, expanding size of operations, rapid advancements in technology and liberalisation. Therefore, managers have to be fully aware of the market environment and formulate strategies to cope with competition. The important components of market environment are as follows:

(i) Customer factors — needs, preferences, attitudes, values, bargaining power, buying behaviour and satisfaction of customers, etc.

(ii) Competition factors — number and types of competitors, market shares of the competitors, growth rate of the industry, general level of profits, cost of entry and exit from the industry, etc.

(iii) Middlemen factors — level and quality of customer service, distribution channels, costs, logistics, delivery systems, etc.

(iv) Product factors — demand, image, utility, design, life cycle, differentiation and substitutability of the product.

Competitor related factors are particularly significant to the corporate planner. Analysis of market share gives an idea of the firm's competitive strength. A high growth rate of industry and high level of profits result in less aggressive behaviour on the part of competitors. High costs of entry and lack of economies of scale also lead to less aggressive competition. With increase in competition, market research, advertising sales promotion, research and development, total quality management and aftersale service phase become more significant.

Technological Environment. The technological environment consists of Jorces concerning knowledge applied and the materials and machines used in the production and distribution of goods. Technology affects the size and efficiency of operations, cost and quality of products, "market structure, organisation structure, etc. New technology imay result in the creation of entirely new products or new.uses for existing products. Technological changes canillter customer groups and functions and competitive pattern of the firm :rechnology can create new markets and new business segments. 'For example, rising petrol prices have increased the demand for fuel efficiency cars and two wheelers in India. A corporate planner must be on the look out for changes in the 'technological environment which offer opportunity or entail risk to the organisation. Some of the important factors in the technological environment are as follows:

(i) Sources of technology-company's research and development, foreign and other external sources, cost and transfer of technology.

(ii) Technological development-stages of development, rate of change in technology, research and development.

(iii) Impact of technology on the manmachine system, on human beings and on the environment.

Social Environment. The social environment consists of factors concerning human relationships. The main factors in the social environment are given below.

(i) Demographic characteristics, size and distribution of population, changes in population, age composition, inter State migration, rural-urban mobility and income distribution.

(ii) Education levels, awareness and consciousness of rights, works ethics, etc.

(iii) Social attitudes, customs, rituals, values, changing life styles, etc.

(iv) Social concerns such as the role of business in society, environmental pollution, corruption, use of mass media, consumerism, status of women and minorities, etc.

(v) Family life and structure, attitudes towards and within the family, family values.

Socio-cultural environment exercises a significant influence on business operations, Growth and age composition of population affect demand pattern. Mobility of population and education levels result in greater demand for consumer durables, books and magazines. Emergence of the middle class as a powerful socio-economic group in India has been a major social change affecting business.

Political Environment. The political environment consists of the forces concerning management of public affairs and their impact on business. Some important components of the political environment are as follows:

(i) The political system—its nature, ideologies, political parties and power centres.

(ii) The political structure—Centre State relations, stability of government, its goals, etc.

(iii) Political philosophy and role of the government.

(iv) Political processes—party system, elections and their funding.

(v) Regulatory framework—constitutional framework, policies, procedures and rules concerning promotion, operation, expansion, etc. of business enterprises.

India is a democratic country wherein the government plays an active role as planner, promoter and regulator of business activities. Political changes exercise a very significant influence on the investment decisions of business firms. For example, Coca Cola and IBM were forced to move out of India due to strict policy of the Janata Pprty Government during 1977-1980. These multinationals have again come to India because of the liberal policy of the Congress Government during 1991-1996. Enron in Maharashtra is another such example.

Environmental Analysis. It is the process of monitoring the economic and non-economic environment to determine the opportunities for and threats to a business enterprise. Such an analysis involves data collection, information processing and forecasting to provide a rational basis for developing objectives and strategies of business. No organisation can afford to ignore changes in the environment. A business firm can set its future directions and performance targets only when it has visualised and perceived the opportunities and constraints that lie ahead. Environmental analysis enables the management to predict future developments and take timely actions to make a constructive use of these developments.

Environmental Diagnosis. Environmental analysis or scanning results in a mass data relating to different segments of the environment. A technique is required to comprehened this data. This technique is called environmental diagnosis. Under it the more important environmental factors are identified and the impact of each such factor on the business is assessed together with the probability of such an impact.

Environmental analysis leads to the identification of various issues that affect the enterprise. Environmental diagnosis, on the other hand, judges these issues on the basis of intensity and relative probability of their impact on the enterprise. Fig. 5.3 provides a matrix for identifying the high priority environmental issues or factors.

In Fig. 5.3 environmental issues are distributed among the nine cells of the matrix. The issues which are most likely to have a high level of impact on the organisation are the critical issues and require immediate attention. High priority issues are those which have a medium to high probability to impact. The issues having a high level of impact but a low probability of occurrence need to be watched. All other issues couid be considered low priority items. However, their continuous monitoring is necessary because conditions might change.

Probability of Impact ↑ / Impact on Business ←	High	Medium	Low
High	Critical	High priority	Low priority
Medium	High priority	Highpriority	Low priority
Low	To be watched	Low priority	Low priority

Source: William R. Boulton — Business Policy — The Art of Strategic Management. 1984. p. 120.

Fig. 5.3. Diagnosing Environmental Factors

With the help of environmental diagnosis, the corporate planner can know the range of environmental factors on which attention should be focused.

Factors Influencing Environmental Analysis and Diagnosis

(i) Nature of Business. The pattern of environmental analysis and information needs depends on the present and intended type of business activity of the firm. A firm currently engaged in manufacturing glass containers and intending to do the same in future requires a limited scanning of the environment. On the other hand, a diversified or conglomerate company will require a very broad scanning to collect the wide variety of information required for strategic decisions.

(ii) Size of Business. Large organisations more frequently take on new ventures and are exposed to greater risks. Therefore, they interact more frequently with various environmental forces and require a more intensive environmental scanning. These are also required to respond to various laws applicable to large organisations. Small enterprises are not influenced by these laws *e.g.* MRTP Act, FERA, etc.

(iii) Age of the Enterprise. An old enterprise with experienced managers is selective in environmental appraisal. Its managers know what and how much information to collect and how to reckon the environment. But a hew enterprise has no such experience and therefore it has a wider scope of environmental search.

(iv) Influence of the Enterprise. The more powerful an enterprise is in relation to its environment the lower is its need for appraisal of the environmental forces. For example, monopolistic organisations such as Indian Oil Corporation and BHEL need not analyse competitive environment.

(v) Volatility of Environment. When the environment is highly turbulent and heterogenous a more intensive search is required. But if the environment is homogenous and relatively stable a limited search adequate.

(vi) Geographical Dimension. The area of operations of an enterprise also influences its environmental scanning. Multinational corporations, for example have to appraise the national as well as international environment. But a local firm with operations confined to one region need not analyse national and international environment.

(vii) Calibre of Management. Professionally qualified managers show a greater concern for environmental scanning than less qualified managers. One of the reasons why multinationals carry out a systematic and comprehensive study of the environment is their rich technical knowledge and managerial expertise.

(viii) Managerial Attitudes. Attitudes styles and beliefs of top management determine the importance given to environmental appraisal. Dynamic and enterprising chief executives with an open mind and global perspective are always on the lookout for environmental opportunities. Similarly, forward looking managers attempt to anticipate changes in the "environment and act before threats occur. Aggressive managers make strategic change a way of life and periodically review its strategy irrespective of performance.

Techniques of Environmental Scanning

The main techniques of environmental analysis and diagnosis are given below:

1. SWOT Analysis. It is a systematic approach to understand the environment. SWOT is the acronym for strengths, weaknesses, opportunities and threats. It is also known as WOTS-UP analysis. An opportunity is a favourable condition in the environment. It enables the enterprise to consolidate its position. Growing demand is an example of an opportunity. A threat is an unfavourable condition in the environment. It creates a risk *e.g.* threat of growing competition. A strength is an inherent capacity which an organisation can use to gain strategic advantage over its competitors. Superior research and development facilities, for example, enable a firm to develop new products and thereby gain competitive advantage. A weakness is an inherent limitation or constraint which creates a strategic disadvantage. For example, overdependence on a single product is potentially risky.

SWOT analysis helps an enterprise in matching its strengths and weaknesses with opportunities and threats operating in the environment. An effective strategy is one that capitalises on the opportunities through the use of strengths and neutralises the threats by minimising the impact of weaknesses.

A profile of strengths, weaknesses, opportunities and threats is as follows:

Instant foods industry is one of the sunrise industries that has come up well in India in the recent past. Essentially meant for middle and upper-middle class urban consumers, instant foods are a product line that offers considerable potential for growth.

The business environplent in which the instant foods industry exists at present could be explained in terms of the opportunities and threats operating currently. Opportunities are supported by factors like:

(a) High demand potential, estimated at around Rs. 20,000 crore. At present the total industry output is just Rs. 300 crore.

(b) Availability of packaging material to keep instant foods fresh and unadulterated.

(c) Rising personal incomes, emergence of nuclear families and rise in the number of working women.

(d) Spread of television as a media for advertising.

Threats arise due to factors like:

(a) Problem of acceptability, as Indians are typically used to eating fresh vegetables and foods.

(b) High taxes, as instant foods are considered a luxury item; direct and indirect taxes constitute 70 to 80 per cent of the price of processed foods.

(c) High raw material costs.

(d) High overhead expenses.

2. Forecasting. Forecasting is the technique of estimating the future events that are likely to have a significant influence on the enterprise. It involves anticipating probable occurrences so as to reduce uncertainty surrounding the future. It is based on past experience and present assumptions about the future to predict what will occur.

3. ETOP. It is the acronym for environmental threat and opportunity profile. It involves dividing the environment into different sectors and then analysing the impact of each sector on the enterprise.

❐

6
Ethical Leadership in Business

Leadership represents an abstract quality in a man. A leader mayor may not be a business executive but a business executive must be a leader. The executive must have that quality so that he may be able to inspire confidence in those who are working for the organisation of which he is the incharge. He has no alternative but to provide an inspiring leadership. Leadership, according to Koontz and O'Donnell, "is the abiility of a manager to induce subordinates (followers) to work with confidence and zeal"

According to Koontz and O'Donnell, "Leadership is generally defined simply as influence, the art or process of influencing people so, that they will strive willingly toward the achievement of group goals."

According to Encyclopaedia of Social Sciences, "Leadership refers to the relation between an individual and group around some common interest and behaving in a manner directed or determined him (the leader).

According to Peter Drucker, "Leadership is the lifting of man's visions to higher sights, the raising of man's performance to higher standard the building of man's personality beyond its normal limitations."

According to Alford and Beatty, "Leadership is the ability to secure desirable actions from a group of followers voluntarily without the. use of coercion."

According to Chester 1. Barnard, "Leadership refers to the quality of the behaviour of individuals whereby they guide people on their activities in organised efforts."

"The essence of leadership is followership," Koontz and O'Donnell assert. It is the followers who make a person leader. An executive has to earn followers. He may get subordinates because he is in authority but he may not get a follower unless he makes the people willing to follow him. Only willing followers can and will make him a leader.

The concept of leadership, therefore, lies in the creation of followers. Surely because of this concept thinkers have asserted that "leaders are born not made." Another group of thinkers assert that "leadership can be acquired." This assertion of some of the thinkers have given rise to the concept that "leaders are both born and made." It is this school of thinking which has led to a thought that if one has a leadership quality he can use it undoubtedly to his best of abilities and can succeed in his mission. But those who don't have can develop the qualities to a greater extent by shear indulgence and hard work and use the same to better advantage through experience if they are given a chance to lead.

CHARACTERISTICS OF LEADERSHIP

From the above definitions the following characteristics of leadership may be deduced:

1. Leadership helps others in choosing and attaining specified goals to the maximum satisfaction of both the leader and the follower.

2. Leadership is a personal quality of character and behaviour in man which enables him to exert personal influence.

3. The leader leads his groups with authority and confidence.

4. The leader unifies his group and motivates the group to work for the attainment of a goal.

5. The leader establishes relationship between an individual and a group around some common interest.

6. The leadership is the process of *(i)* directing, *(ii)* guiding, and (iii) influencing the people to do their best for the attainment of a specified goal.

7. Leadership must have the following.

Importance of Leadership

Importance of leadership may be studied conviently under the following heads:

1. Motive Power to Group Efforts. Management provides leadership to the organisation. The management while providing such a leadership is interested in:

(a) getting the work done.

(b) realising the objectives.

(c) inspiring group efforts and team work.

(d) getting cooperation and wholesale attitude for the accomplishment of assigned task.

Leadership is a quality and has the requisite power to pull group efforts upon the highest degree of efficiency in which sincerity of the purpose is omnipresent throughout the entire functioning. The leader by his personal conduct and behaviour infuse confidence in others and incite them for hard, sincere, purposeful and honest work. It is in this context that LP. Urwick has said that "It is not what a leader says still less what he writes, that influences subordinates (and the followers). It is what he is. And they judge what he is by what he does and how he behaves. George R. Terry confirms when he says that "A leader shows the way by his example. He is not a pusher, he pulls rather than pushes."

2. Aid to Authority. Managing people is rendered difficult if a manager does not possess managerial qualities. A manager for all practical purposes is a leader. He must, therefore, possess the leadership quality if he and his organisation aim at success. A leadership quality in managers help them in exercising their authority to get the work done successfully. Initiative and resourcefulness cannot be of much help to the manager unless he has the leadership quality. A manager lacking leadership quality may not be able to inspire his working force. Inspiration is the greatest force for tangible results. Leadership in the words of S.S. Chatterjee, contains all the essential ingredients of direction for inspiring people and providing the will to do for successful work accomplishment. And in this respect leadership is in aid to authority.

3. Basis for Co-operation. Good two way communication, man to man personel relationship, creation of opportunity, better participation and satisfaction and instrument for eliciting co-operation from the working force which a good management aims at. An effective leadership is able to attain this aim of management and thus forms the very basis of co-operation needed from the working force.

4. Motivation and Leadership. To motivate the rank and file of the organisation so that their efforts may be effectively channelised in a manner in which maximum utilisation of their skill, knowledge, training and experiences is possible, is the first task of any management. This is the biggest problem which a management faces in the "modern business and industrial world. This however could be easily done by effective leadership. A leadership inffuses a will in the man to do his best. It secures best contribution. It mobilises and then channelises the human energy. A group works on a direction and this direction has to come from the leader of the group. The group which is meaningfully "led can perform miracles. But the same group disintegrates in the absence of purposeful, dynamic and effective leadership. In such a case team spirit is destroyed, human energy is wasted and desire to accomplish falters.

A leadership is responsible for creating cordial relation in the organisation at all levels and between all the personnel working in and for the organisation. Fostering the human relation and toning up the efforts are the functions of management which it attains with the help of motivation activity. It is the leadership that guides, inspires and directs group members for achieving a unity of purpose and efforts, asserts Satya Saran Chatterjee.

THEORIES OF LEADERSHIP

The theories of leadership are broadly categorised into the following four heads:

1. Traitist Theory. This is a classical theory which owes its base to different traits in a human being. This theory believes that leadership behaviour is sum total of the traits (the qualities) the leader possesses. A leader cannot behave other than what his personnel traits are. He may either inherently posses these traits or may have acquired through learning, training and experiences. But he himself is what his traits are and he therefore behaves within the limits of his traits. A leader is expected to possess the following traits:

(i) Good personality

(ii) Tirelessness

(iii) Courage

(iv) Enthusiasm

(v) Ability of quick decision

(vi) Alertness

(vii) Intelligence

(viii) Imagination

(ix) Physically fit

(x) Persuasive voice

(xi) Reliability

(xii) Intellectually sound etc.

The above traits have been grouped by psychologists into the following four categories:

(i) Physical

(ii) Psychological

(iii) Intellectual and

(iv) Qualities pertaining to character.

It has been maintained by the traitists that these traits can either be inherited or can be developed with the help of training and experience or can both be inherited and acquired. Some of the traits have come to a conclusion that these traits cannot be wholly acquired through training and experience. Inheritance is also a must. It has therefore, been widely accepted that the leadership traits can both be inherited. This is why it has been maintained that a leader is not only born but hoe is made also.

The Weakness of Traitist Theory

The traitist theory is widely accepted. But it suffers from certain weaknesses which are enumerated as given below:

(i) Traitists have not supplied an exhaustive list of leadership qualities. Various thinkers have supplied different list of qualities of leadership. Neither of the thinkers have listed them in order of their importance. The list sometimes confuses the students and practitioners alike.

But this weakness does not take away the merits of the theory. Agreed the traitists have not agreed on a common list of leadership qualities. But he should not forget the management is a behavioural science and it changes with the dictate of time, situation and human behaviour. Traits may be added and deleted as and when found necessary.

(ii) Leadership traits are neither common in nature nor are universal.

(iii) Traitists have earlier assumed that leaders are born. The traits hence cannot be acquired and developed. This approach really weakness the theory. But latter pronouncements amply reveal that the traitists too have accepted that leaders are not only born but they are made also. Hence, they accept the theory that leadership qualities can be acquired and developed.

(iv) Traitists do not consider situational factors which influence the leader more than their own traits. In fact traits are helpful in facing the situation but traits cannot wipe off the situation which may arise from time to time and which a leader is required to face time and again. Situation forces a decision. A leader possessing requisite traits of leadership may come out from all the situations with flying colours.

2. Situation Theory. This theory believes in situational behaviour of the leader and hold that leadership is strongly affected by the situation in which he works. The theory believes that it is the situation which develops a leadership and from which a leader emerges. A leader is made as per the thinking of this theory. Traits are only helpful. A leader is he who succeeds. But situationalists believe that a leader may succeed in a given situation but he may not succeed in some different situation. This thinking amply proves that it is the situation which produces a leader. This theory further believes that there exists an interaction between a group and its leader. The people are prepared to follow only the leader who is capable of fulfilling their aspirations. For acquiring such a capacity the leader is required to recognise the needs, to study the situation and to visualise the aspirations of his followers.

The Weakness of Situation Theory

The situationalist theory too suffers from its own weaknesses which are enumerated as under:

(i) Over-emphasis on Situation. The leadership is the product of situation and a leader emerges as per the dictate of the situation. This thinking over-emphasizes the situation aspect. True situation effects, the decision and influences the thinking of the leader but it is not everything.

(ii) Completely Overlooks the Traits. By over-emphasising the situation aspect this theory completely overlooks the traits which obviously play a significant role in the emergence of a particular leader. The head and heart of a leader plays a definite role in every situation. But this theory completely ignores this fact.

3. Follower's Theory. This theory may also be known as acceptance theory. The followers must accept their leader and his leadership. A leader or his leadership cannot exist without followers asserts this theory. According to this theory followers may form groups and the followers groups naturally have their own characteristics and needs. According to the characteristics and nature of followers groups needs are ascertained. The needs require fulfilment. Every group will naturally want its needs satisfied. The person leading them has to satisfy at least the basic needs of the groups. Unless he does not he can neither be called as good leader nor he will be allowed to function as such. Here the need of the followers groups is most important and guiding factor in deciding the leader and his leadership.

The followers theory suffers from a major weakness that it ignores the trait side of the leader or his leadership. But modern business managers are of the opinion that it is the followers theory which is now playing a significant role in managing the people today. The traitist and the situationalist theories have taken a back seat. In India since 1967 it is the followers theory which is dominating the Indian political science and certainly it had an impact on the business and industrial leadership.

4. System Theory. System theory of leadership is based on all the variables of leadership *viz.* the leader, his leadership traits, situation in which he acts, goals which he has to attain the environment in which he works, the followers groups which have been formed its contents, nature, characteristics and needs, role behaviour of the leader and his co-ordinating efforts. The theory believes that it is the act of the leader which influences his followrs most instead of his leadership traits. His act, the role he plays and the role-behaviour stimulates his followers to act and try to attain the objectives.

The system theory is also known as modern theory of leadership. The modern business world feels that we are in era where the system theory is rather more acceptable to those who are being led as compared to other theories of leadership.

QUALITIES: OUTCOME OF TRAITIST THEORY

Many theories of leadership have been advanced. Various theories indicate diverse qualities of leadership on the basis of which these theories have been propounded. Traitist relating to qualities theory is based on the quality of a leader which he inherits and acquires and develops.

Distinguished thinkers differ in their views so far as the essential qualities of a leader is concerned. F.M. Viscount Shim has given six basic qualities of a leader. His list is as given below:

1. Courage
2. Will power
3. Judgement
4. Flexibility
5. Knowledge
6. Integrity

Ordway Tead had not agreed with the above qualities. While enumerating the qualities which a leader should possess. Tead has given the list of ten qualities. His list is as given below:

1. Physical and nervous energy
2. Sense of purpose and direction
3. Enthusiasm
4. Friendliness and affection
5. Integrity
6. Technical mastery
7. Decisiveness
8. Intelligence

9. Technical skill
10. Faith

Supporting Ordway Tend Marshall E. Dimock writes that "the executive is he who commands the best balance of physique, mentality, personality, technical equipment, philosophical insight, judgement, ability to understand and a sense of social purpose and direction."

Ordway Tead and Marshall Dimock have combined physical, mental and philosophical traits and they are thus of the opinion that a manager is a aim of all these traits. But the best combination of these traits has been given by C.W. Briggs. He summarised the requirements for a good manager in six categories in the following words:

A manager (business leader) should be:

1. An organiser
2. A controller
3. A diplomat
4. A Father confessor
5. A Friend
6. A student of human psychology

Chaster I. Bamard has not quoted the lines of the above thinkers. He depends less on physical traits. Instead he bases his leadership qualities more on mental and philosophical traits. The following is his list of traits (qualities);

1. Vitality and Endurance
2. Decisiveness
3. Persuassiveness
4. Stability of behaviour

5. Intellectual capacity
6. Knowledge

Henri Fayol has taken both physical as well as mental traits into consideration. However, he has not touched the philosophical side of the trait. He has summarised the leader's, qualities in the following five broad categories:

1. Health and physical fitness
2. Intelligence and Mutual Vigour
3. Moral qualities
4. Knowledge
5. Managerial ability

Mrityunjoy Banerjee, the Indian thinker, has given the following six groups of leadership qualities obviously basing his classification on traitist theory but taking into mental and psychological side of the picture into consideration:

1. Intelligence and technical competence
2. Initiative
3. Power of judgement and ability to deal
4. Sense of responsibility
5. Ability to deal with people
6. Ability to inspire and integrate

Psychologists Enumeration

From the above six lists it is clear that there is an absence of agreement between various thinkers so far as the essential qualities of a leader is concerned. Here the psychologists have stepped into and have first broadly divided the qualities of a leader into the following four broad categories:

1. Physical qualities
2. Psychological qualities
3. Intellectual traits
4. Qualities of character

Thereafter the psychologists have sub-divided each of the traits of .a leader into different subdivisions. The full list of psychologists appear as enumerated below:

Under first physical qualities:

(i) Sound health to fulfil his obligations

(ii) Vitality and endurance to face all hardships

Under second the psychological qualities:

(i) Personnel magnetism

(ii) Enthusiasm

(iii) Co-operation

(iv) Ability to inspire and integrate

(v) Resourcefulness

(vi) Exerting

(vii) Fact and skillful handling

Under third the intellectual traits:

(i) A high degree of intelligence

(ii) A capacity to deal in every situation courageously

(iii) A sound judgement

(iv) A scientific approach to the problem with open mind

(v) As astute displomat. A best teacher

Under fourth the qualities of character:

(i) Integrity

(ii) Self-discipline

(iii) Ethical Leadership in Business

(iv) Good natured

(v) Willingness to work hard

(vi) Willingness to accept and share responsibilities

(vi) Good mannered and courteous

(vii) Courageous. Initiative

(viii) Zealous

(ix) Humanist

(x) Ethical

Leadership

Ethical leadership is akin to that of captaincy of a team. In both classes the goal is to bring out the best out of every team member. This cannot be done simply by committing a foul, but by bringing out the best possibilities from the players. This is the kind of leadership that is best suited to the contemporary needs of entrepreneurship and business management. This style of leadership is quite unlike the tycoon variety, when a single person, by sheer will power, magnetism and extra ordinary drive, overpowers all opposition and extracts work from cowering subordinates.

An important reason why ethical ledership is the order of the day is because technology has become so developed that it really needs the combined offer of all to make a single task succeed, much like a team playing a match. For maximum efficiency of contemporary technology, knowledge, needs to be widely disseminated at all levels.

Under these circumstances one needs a team captain and not a frightening tycoon. To be a successful captain of a team it is essential to know the strengths and weaknesses of your side. It is important therefore to Know Your Company. This is how a captain is best able to marshal the talent in the team. The captain, too, is as much a participant as a member.

Taking Responsibility

Leadership with integrity requires extra commitment such that the spirit of the rules is put into practice. Sometimes integrity is linked ina straight forward way in terms of loyalty to the company; others could argue that integrity is doing one's job by the book of rules. Leadership is all this and more. Ethical leadership creates partisans in excellence in pushing the limits of capabilities much further than passive adherence to routine.

In addition, taking responsibility alters, and sometime adds to, each of the other meanings of integrity in subtle, and yet significant, ways. Loyalty to the company can also imply that it is alright to do whatever it takes as long as the companys' bottom line looks healthy. In this case, it is easy to condone unethical and sharp practices for it can be argued that all this is for the greater good of the whole. While this sounds reasonable at first blush, a situation could easily arise when the company has to pay a high price for allowing unfair and illegal practices in its functioning. An ethical leader would find that unsatisfactory.

Going strictly by the book could also mean blind adherence to rules. In which case nothing is ventured nor is anything gained. There are scores of officials and managers who are honest but not enterprising because they do want to take responsibility. To be able to combine the two is the true test of an ethical and enterprising manager.

Transparency is not just a question of keeping one's books in good order. Here again, once transparency is linked with the notion of taking responsibility, its horizons are significantly extended. Transparency would now include a much greater openness to criticisms from all quarters as well as a willingness to learn from them.

Taking responsibility is to be able to stand up and be counted. The test is when things do not go right. It is very easy for all to take credit. But to take responsibility is to be able to walk tall, take the blows, and learn from them. Organisations that encourage their executives and employees in this direction are ultimately the most ethical enterprises. Remember, its difficult to lead from the front if you're always looking over your shoulder instead of boldly leaving your imprint you are constantly trying to cover up your tracks.

Leadership Moments

All professional organisations have a set of rules and norms for conducting everyday business. While most of these stated regulations are, by and large, unproblematic, there are many occasions when a seemingly straightforward policy is neither satisfactorily established nor practiced. This is a perennial source of executive despair.

At times like these it is tempting to get cynical. One frequently hears the refrain that certain things look good only on paper, and cannot be implemented on the ground. But look at it another way, and you will find that these are precisely the opportunities for exercising leadership; these are leadership moments.

Here are some examples:

1. Take a simple matter like the misuse of office stationery. If senior executives believe that this is an issue within the organisation then it certainly needs to be addressed. Probably the amount lost in monetary terms is not much, but it is symptomatic of a serious flaw in office morale. It would have a great demonstration effect on the staff if, for example, senior executives would go across from their offices, walk past other employees, and do a significant chunk of their photocopying themselves.

2. Office punctuality is often quite a nettlesome affair. Senior executives can once again set an example by adhering to office timings. On occasions, they could come in a little earlier and seen to be fully set for the day by the time the

office hours commence. This again would be a very demonstrative manoeuvre designed to send a message to everybody—from the telephone receptionist upwards. Office attendance and punctuality are bound to improve as a consequence.

3. The injunction against making personal calls on the company paid mobile phone is also quite often a niggling problem. Senior executives can set the tone by highlighting all personal calls (both local and outstation) and reimburse the company for such calls. Such a practice again is very demonstrative in nature. Everybody will know about it.

Even when certain matters appear trivial, a demonstrative exercise in leadership has quite an impact down the line.

It is up to the senior executives to devise how exactly they would like to take advantage of these leadership moments. They should be crafted to suit the natural inclinations of the executives so that they do not become one off affairs. But most importantly, make sure that these leadership moments are demonstrative and easily visible to the naked eye.

Good Manners

An ethical leader through practice gives evidence of what good manners are all about. The business community has often been portrayed as boorish and lacking in civility. It has been commended on the economic front but as far as refinement goes they have received really bad press.

This is very unfair!

Let it be clear that it was not the aristocratic circle that created good manners. Good manners also came with the rise of entrepreneurs and business people. In princely courts, hierarchy and arbitrariness ruled. Court societies did whatever the monarch did, and underlinings down the line followed this example. If the king picked his teeth in full view with a knife, it was just fine. If he threw bones under the table or at his servants, other did the same. The term courtesy originally signified deference to superiors. Nothing should ever be done to offend those on top even if it hurts all the way.

All of this changed once those engaged in business and industry gained social ascendance. They introduced good manners by standardising rules such that they applied equally to all. This is what brought about refinement. If rules were different for different people then one could hardly call the society civilised in the true sense of the term.

Social refinement expressed itself in a variety of ways. On the economic front it was manifested in industrial laws, structures on child labour, statutes on minimum wages, financial transparency and so on. The latest in the long line of corporate refinement is the advocacy of business ethics. More than anything else business ethics is principally about extending good manners.

❐

7

Market Economy in Business

It can be argued that ethics or corporate social responsibility (CSR) begins where the law ends (Friedman, 1970). Organisations are expected to observe the law but of course there will always be the issue of interpretation of that law. Legal departments found in many organisations are evidence that understanding and interpretating the law consume resources and time. Organisations also can and do quite legitimately become involved in the formation and farming of law either directly or through their industry associations. Lobbying of governments is a sophisticated activity in many parts of the world, the object being to restrain moves to tighten legislation perceived to be against business interests or to attempt to gain relaxation of laws which are perceived to be inhibiting.

In a market economy business organizations are allowed a significant degree of discretion. They are ostensibly free to choose what goods and services they produce, the markets they aim to serve and the processes by which they produce. The state will play a greater or lesser part in these processes depending on the social and political complexion of society at large. The legislative framework of any country will include a raft of laws, statutes and precedents which will affect how organizations are able to go about their business. In the European Union much of this legislation is being harmonised but throughout the world there is likely to be found laws relating to employment practices, restrictive practices, consumer protection, financial reporting and conduct and many other areas of business life.

Whatever the legislative framework many organisations can and will choose to use their discretion to go beyond the legal baseline and this can be conceived as exercising ethical judgement (Carroll, 1979, p. 497). The reasons why business organisations may choose to do this are many and complex. It can be that there is a particular culture which was imprinted on the organisation in earlier times. For example some organisations had Quaker origins and these values have been carried forward into the present time resulting in organisations almost unconsciously accepting an ethical role in all their dealings. Alternatively it may be that adverse publicity in some area may have prompted a firm to embark on a process to restore a battered image. One view is that business not only reflects the values of society but also plays a part in creating those values.

Issues in a Command Economy

Business and State. In large parts of the world, until recently, the relationship between the state and business was highly integrated. Central planning was the instrument by which many countries ran their business. Enterprises were state owned and highly prescribed in terms of their activities. The state decided what was to be made and how. It also decided how the output was to be distributed and to whom. It prescribed how much labour would be used and how much they were to be paid.

Business Discretion. Overall managers in these enterprises had very little discretion and were frequently subject to political pressure to sustain the state ideology. In these circumstances responsibility for most activities of a strategic nature were not in the hands of the management and ethical judgements were probably only articulated in meeting the demands put on the enterprise by the state and reflecting the values of the government.

The objectives of the state in terms such as production or hard-currency earnings were dominant and one outcome of such policies is reflected in the high levels of environmental pollution and the dangerous state of plant and machinery frequently found in many of the former communist countries.

Issues in the Public Sector

Since public sector organisations are essentially there to serve the public it might be assumed that these organizations do not face the dilemmas of the profit-seeking private sector between commercial pursuit of profit and notions of ethical behaviour.

Recent experience both in Britain and elsewhere indicates that public sector strategies are changing dramatically and in some instances throwing into sharp focus ethical and social responsibility issues. Many public utilities have been privatized and this has fundamentally changed their operating paradigm and strategies to pursuit of profit rather than purely service delivery. Of the organisations remaining in public ownership attempts are being made to create a business ethoc within them. Examples of this are the trust status of hospitals and the internal market created, the creation of agencies from civil service activities and the opting out of schools to grant-maintained status.

It could be argued that these moves have been made to bring a more economic or commercial perspective to strategy in the public sector. The stated aim of the present government is to achieve higher efficiency and better-quality services. Whether this conflicts with the wider social responsibilities of the public sector is a matter of great debate. The government argues that it is not a matter of economic versus social imperatives but that social goals are achieved through a tighter economic framework. Opponents argue that the government is simply attempting to cut public expenditure of budgetary and dogmatic reasons and are imperilling the ability of many public service organizations to carry out their basic task.

The Role of Charters

One continuing criticism of some public sector organizations is that they are inflexible, remote, bureaucratic and unresponsive to the public they are designed to serve. Machine bureaucracy is perhaps endemic in large mature organizations in relatively stable environments. In addition, many public sector organisations were and are professionally driven, for example education and health where the 'customer' is given what is good for them by the professionals.

Notions of social responsibility here can revolve around what is best from a professional point of view rather than what the customer may require.

To cope with this and also the fear that in many of the privatized utilities a monopoly situation still exists leading to charges of exploitation of the customer, the British government has introduced a series of charters (examples are those related to railway travel and the Inland Revenue) which specify individuals' rights when they deal with public sector organisations. Other organizations have followed suit—for example the banks have a collective charter for customers and British Telecom specify minimum service levels in theirs.

Issues in International World

Organizations with activities crossing international boundaries can be faced with a particular dilemma with regard to their ethical stance. Firstly, it is quite possible that the organisation can be larger in terms of the resources at its disposal than a small overseas country in which it locates part of its activity. To that extent the organisation is extremely powerful and could exercise its power for its own interest where this conflicts with the interest of the host country.

This may result in the organisation imposing its own style and culture either consciously or unconsciously. Few of the larger multinationals have escaped the charge of cultural imperialism. The issue here could be whether organisations are pursuing local or global strategies.

Organisations that aim for an integrated production policy on a global basis may make the manufacturing strategy dominant with local variations at a minimum. Hence, adaptations to local custom and practice may be secondary. McDonald's aim to present an identical service wherever a McDonald's found in the world. The strategy will be perceived by some as cultural imperialism but McDonald's would probably argue that people have the discretion to buy a Big Mac or not and franchisees in many countries are willing to accept the franchise as it adds to rather than replaces existing eating places. However, if an organization is serving a local market as part of its world-wide strategy it is likely that some recognition will be made for local custom and practice. The degree to which an organisation brings its 'back home' values into another society should be one aspect of its global strategy. This area like many other ethical issues is fraught with dilemmas. One example could be an organisation setting up in a country where wage rates were very low. If the company pays the prevailing low wages it could stand accused of exploitation. On the other hand if it paid somewhat better wages to get better quality employees it could stand accused of being irresponsible by disturbing local wage patterns. A recurring dilemma was posed for many years for many companies in relation to South Africa. International companies who did not pull out of South Africa believed they were being responsible to their black employees and improving their lot.

ORGANISATIONAL PHILOSOPHY FOR CORPORAE SOCIAL RESPONSIBILITY (CSR)

In market economies where organizations and managers do have a considerable degree of autonomy, the way organisations incorporate notions of CSR into their policies and strategies becomes in itself a matter of discretion and one where an organization's needs to develop a clear philosophy or stance:

(a) It is possible to conceive of organizations who are leaders in the field-setting the pace. They are the ones who go way beyond what the law requires and set an agenda of best practice.

(b) There are many organizations who are followers. They observe the pace-setters and make a decision as to how and where they might reasonably act.

(c) A third category could be described as the minimalists. They do what the law requires and no more unless there is some pressing reason.

Another view of the varying stances of CSR suggests that three broad approaches are often found:

(a) ***Special Obligation.*** Companies who do what is only absolutely necessary or required by law are acting according to social obligation.

(b) ***Social Responsibility.*** Those who recognize a wider circle of relationships and are willing to make charitable donations as well as interact with stakeholder groups who have an interest in what the company does, are acting according to the principle of social responsibility.

(c) ***Social Responsiveness.*** Other companies are far more open to social influence and communication with external groups. They give attention to broad ethical principles of right and wrong behaviour. Frederick *et al.* say these companies are acting according to the principle of social responsiveness.

The stance any organization takes in terms of CSR is likely to arise from both custom and practice and/or, more recently, a carefully worked out position. However, any position taken is likely to be subject to change as social expectations change. The progressive companies are likely to bell the fore-front of developments in their position and the more conservative organizations will be likely only to change their position along with changes in legislation. But as society becomes more complex and turbulent it is likely that many organizations will feel it necessary to review their stance on social responsibility.

ARGUMENTS IN FAVOUR OF CSR

Organizations which take a progressive stance may argue that there are several good reasons for them to do so.

(a) ***Balances Power with Responsibility.*** Modern corporations have considerable power and alongwith this should go responsibility. If not the company will ultimately attract hostility from many quarters.

(b) ***Promotes Long-run Profit.*** A well-rehearsed argument. The belief is that a positive policy builds trust and respect and consequently the company enjoys a good reputation.

(c) ***Good Company Image.*** This is clearly related to the previous point. Surveys appear to suggest that business has not enjoyed a good public image. Events such as insider dealing and other financial scandals only serve to confirm some of the fears held. The effect could be reluctance to deal with low image companies or sectors and public support for repressive legislation.

(d) ***Discourages Government Legislation.*** This is attractive to many groups, not least executives themselves. Self-regulation is perceived to be preferable since legislation can prove draconian, costly and restrictive. In addition if legislation is called for by other interest groups goodwill is likely to have already been lost.

Overall the proponents of social responsibility sum up the case in terms of good business. There is no real alternative and a positive policy actually promotes enlightened self-interest. To that extent, corporate strategy and a strategy for CSR are interwined. Even in emergent and bottom-up strategy making scenarios where formal strategy making processes are not dominant, a defined and accepted policy on CSR will be a factor in conditioning the decision making of all those involved in the process.

ARGUMENTS AGAINST CSR

Very few firms would say they oppose social responsibility but they would take up the minimalist position of doing no more than the law prescribes. The reasons against going beyond the legal minimum might be:

(a) ***Lower Economic Efficiency and Profits.*** Incurring unnecessary costs could jeopardize the whole operation to the detriment of all stakeholders.

(b) ***Compromises and Confuses Objectives.*** A former chairman of British Steel Corporation was reputed to have once asked the government if British Steel existed to make steel or to act as an arm for the Department of Employment. At

this time the economic objective of making steel profitably was in sharp conflict with the responsibility (perceived to have been thrust on British Steel by the government) to maintain jobs. Confusion about objectives may be dysfunctional to the executives of the organization. Taken together the critics of corporate social responsibility would argue that pursuing active social responsibility policies adds burdens on both business and society without producing the intended effect of social improvement.

(c) ***Firms penalize Themselves Against Competition.*** In being responsible a company might put itself at a competitive disadvantage if others do not follow suit. A case in point here is the issue of training in the U.K. Some companies might feel severe foreign competition from firms in countries (particularly developing countries) where the legal minimum is much lower. The belief of the British government in opting out of the Social Chapter of the Maastricht Treaty was that the obligations to employees that it would impose would prejudice the competitive position of British industry.

A STAKEHOLDER APPROACH TO CSR

To whom are Organisations Responsible? Possibly the most difficult question for corporate executives is to whom the organization believes it has a responsibility. At one level it is clear that in the private sector the responsibility is to the shareholders; the owners, whilst in the public sector the responsibility is to the politicians as elected representatives of the people.

At a broader level the stakeholder concept is useful to give a wider view of relationships the organisation has. With these relationships come responsibilities.

What is a Stakeholder? Those who depend on the organization for the realization of some of their goals and in turn the organisation depends on them for the realisation of its goals.

Any organisation relates to a wide range of stakeholders and each one will have an interest or expectations of the organisation. This interest, when examined will indicate the perceived relationship between the organization and each stakeholder or stakeholder group.

Some stakeholders will have a vital interest for the achievement of their own objectives in the decisions the organization makes and the way it performs and behaves. For others the interest may be more marginal. In considering relationships with stakeholders from a strategic perspective writers such as Mitroff and Edward Freeman (Freeman, 1984) refer not only to interest but power. It is asserted that the stakeholders who need most carefully monitoring and managing are those with both a high interest in the focal organisation and high power as well. Other stakeholders will have low interest and low power and from a strategic point of view demand less time and effort from management. In dealing with stakeholders from the management strategy point of view, it is usually difficult to fully take into account all the perceived expectations of the wide number of stakeholders. The result is that the focus of strategy is likely to be directed on the key stakeholders, *i.e.* those with high interest aim high power as they provide most direct threats or opportunities.

When examining stakeholders from the point of view of social responsibility it may be questioned whether responding to stakeholders on the basis of power and interest is adequate. It could be argued that organisations should not determine their responsibilities on the basis of power and interest as this in itself would be socially irresponsible. Weaker stakeholders may not be taken into account where a strategic move is deemed necessary but it may be argued that longer from responsibilities to the wider constituency demand action. The dilemma is whether an organisation in formulating its strategy accepts responsibility to each stakeholder or to stakeholders collectively.

The relationship between strategy and social responsibility can be very close. Key strategic moves by organisations such as acquisitions, rationalisation, relocation, product diversification and so on, inevitably result in an increase in satisfaction for some stakeholders but dissatisfaction for others. Modern organisations facing an increasingly turbulent environment often need to make significant strategic moves for defensive or offensive reasons. It is at this stage that firms may find themselves facing serious dilemmas. Closing a plant will pose a threat to employees but may help the organisation to remain viable. The firm is faced from a social responsibility point of view with conflicting obligations to one stakeholder (some employees) and the wider constituency of stakeholders.

MAKING CSR WORK IN PRACTICE

Devising a Process for Managing CSR. The formulation of most strategies tends to be incremental and evolutionary. For most organizations the movement towards a strategy of social responsibility proves to be the same. In addition early efforts may be fragmented and piecemeal—almost being made up as issues arise. Dominant values and precedents will prove to be important at this stage alongwith considerations of economic implications.

For many of the larger companies this becomes intolerable because reacting to stimuli as they arise is likely to lead to contradiction and inconsistency and also some degree of puzzlement on behalf of affected stakeholders. Consequently, many large organisations have developed and published position statements on a corporate view of social responsibility. These are sometimes issued as codes of conduct or codes of practice.

Some of these may be quite general - attempting to encapsulate the company's philosophy or they may be directed at particular stakeholder groups. The banking code of practice alongwith the charters produced by some of the privatized industries, such as British Telecom, and some government agencies such as the Inland Revenue, are primarily aimed at one stakeholder group - the customer. The process is still incremental, however, despite the published positions since organizations will find that as developments occur in society and new expectations arise they will be frequently revising and updating their stance.

Most social responsibility policies emanate from senior management/the board. It is difficult to imagine any policy which could be so far reaching in terms of the conduct, style and nature of the company having any credibility either inside or outside the company unless it had the active support of the people at the top.

Implementing CSR. If companies are to avoid the situation of 'good intentions unfulfilled' then positions on social responsibility need to be turned into action programmes. Successful implementation requires several elements.

First and foremost it needs the commitment of senior management and other high profile champions. It needs a place in the formal or informal structures implying stffing and other resources. Resources may also be necessary for research, development and dissemination of the policy. There may also be a need for a training programme and possibly some type of change management initiative.

The method of implementation is likely to be dependent on the existing style and culture of the organization as well as how well developed is the sense of social responsibility within the organization. In addition, implementation may be affected by how management wish to see it working.

Some organisations may conceive such an initiative as a cultural change. They may wish it to be enshrined in the core values of the organisation so that it is a factor in almost every decision taken by all managers. On the other hand a bureaucratic organisation which is governed by rules and procedures may draft new rules and set up systems to ensure that these rules are adhered to. Both approaches are valid but the rule-driven approach, facing the wide ranging and complex issue of social responsibility, runs the risk of running out of rules as new situations arise.

One other aspect which can be of great value in any policy change is symbolic action at the top. Symbols playa very significant part in the management of any organization and often indicate the closeness or otherwise between what is espoused and what is the reality. Tom Farmer, chairman of Kwik-Fit used to give his telephone number and invite dissatisfied customers to ring him personally. Not too many chairmen are known to do that. Symbolic action on the part of top management may also help reduce the cynicism which often surrounds any change in organizations. If the senior management are seen to act out the policy then others inside and outside the organizations are more likely to take it more seriously.

One fundamental question about implementation is how to judge when it is complete. With a complex and developing issue like social responsibility it is probably true to say it is never complete but as it develops new aspects of policy will have to be implemented. Perhaps implementation may be judged to have happened when everyone has the new rulebook or it may be when one perceives fairly consistent behaviour throughout the organization. Clearly monitoring is only possible if there is some clear and general understanding of what outcomes are expected and these, as already indicated, are likely to be very different between organizations and within a specific organisation at different stages of its development.

Evaluating Outcomes. Evaluating CSR is problematic and likely to remain so. In some areas it is possible to look for a measurable return. For example, attempting to act more responsibly towards customers should have the effect of gaining new customers and nct losing existing ones. If this were not happening then it should be closely scrutinized to see if policy or implementation are failing. Similarly it might be anticipated that good employee policies should reduce turnover, attract better quality staff, and encourage higher commitment. Some measurable return is possible here. Responsible behaviour to suppliers is hoped to bring better and closer relationships. Improvements in quality, delivery performance and cooperation are measurable on a variety of parameters. Community programmes are perhaps less easy to evaluate but many large organisations attempt to assess the impact of their community programmes on their corporate image. This sort of assessment has led some organizations to focus their community activities on areas where they have an accepted competence.

❐

8

Corporate Code of Ethics

Ethical codes are statements of the norms and beliefs of an organisation. These norms and beliefs are generally proposed, discussed and defined by senior executives in the firm and then published and distributed to all the members. A code of ethics specifies the ethical rules of operation. Most important thing is developing and continuing dialogue around codes and values. Occassionally, employees react to codes with suspicion, believing code and values are window dressing. But Carter McNamara points out "that when managing a complex issue, especially in a crisis, having code is critical" He further highlights that "continued dialogue and reflection around ethical values produces ethical sensitivity and consensus."

CONDITIONS FOR MAKING CODES EFFECTIVE

In a recent Dutch Study Kaptein and Klamer (1991) list six conditions for effective codes of ethics:

(i) **A Valid Motivation for its Introduction.** It should insist on important benefit for adopting and complying with the code.

(ii) **Broad Acceptance within the Company.** Involve representatives from all departments in the process of elaborating the code. The code should be discussed, checked and redefined before it is finally laid down.

(iii) **Integration into a Broad Company.** The set of ruels should be part of a wider ethical mission statement. This may involve staff training programmes, a company ethical committee or discussions with external stakeholders.

(iv) **Continuous Feedback.** Difficulties occur during the implementation of the code, and also norms on how to act in specific situations change. This calls for feedback. Living up to a code is not simply a matter of blindly applying rules it is part of a process.

(v) **Sanctions and Control.** Compliance with codes needs enforcement—both positive and negative. In order to become effective, some system of sanctions must exist. Free—wheeling permissiveness would only lead to lip service. Many companies do now have severe sanctions against, for example, bribery.

(vi) **Verification and Control.** Any inconsistencies between rules and practice should be disclosed. One method of achieving this is peer discussions. New guidelines should be drawn up if the rules prove inadequate in any way.

However, the basic difficulty with codes of ethics is that they do not establish priority between norms and beliefs. The priorities are true values of a firm and they are not included. As an example, one division in a firm is faced with declining sales and profits; the question is whether to reduce employment and cut over head costs (the classic downsizing decision).

Norms are, of course, are standards of behaviour; they are the ways the senior people in the organisation want the others to act when confronted with a given situation. An example would be, "employees of this company will not accept personal gifts with a monetary value over Rs. 400 in total, from any business friend, and they are expected to pay their full share of the costs for meals or other entertainment (theatre, sporting events etc.) that have a value above Rs. 400 per person." The norms in an ethical code are generally expressed as a series of negative statements (list of thing a person should not do).

The beliefs in an ethical code are standards of thought. They are the ways that senior people want others to think. It is to encourage ways of thinking and patterns of attitudes that will lead towards wanted behaviour. Beliefs in ethical code are generally expressed in a positive form. Examples:

(i) "Our first responsibility is to our customers."

(ii) "We wish to be good citizens of every community in which we operate."

DIFFICULTIES TO IMPLEMENT CODES OF ETHICS

However, the basic difficulty with codes of ethics is that they do not establish priority between norms and beliefs. The priorities are true values of a firm, and they are not included:

(a) As an example, one division in a firm is faced with declining sales and profits; the question is whether to reduce employment and cut overhead costs (the classic downsizing decision), but code of ethics says in one section that we respect our employees and in another section that we expect "fair" profits. How do we decide? The code of ethics does not tell us.

(b)Another example, whether direct distribution from factory "to retailer would be economical" when our code of ethics says "we will work closely with distributors, for they too deserve a profit." But we can reduce our prices to our customers and gain a competitive advantage for ourselves, if we eliminate the wholesalers and ship directly. The code does not tell us to choose.

(c) Are ethical codes-effective at ensuring that the moral standards of senior executives are known and followed throughout the organisation. If yes, then some events can be just anomalies such as for years, GE has been regarded in USA as one of the examplarly companies, a breed ground for managerial excellence, a good corporate citizen. But unfortunately GE was convicted 3 times of crimes, *i.e.* price fixing, bribery and fraud, GE pleaded guilty of charges of defrauding the government on missile-warhead contracts.

In such a case we have to examine causes of unethical actions in individual cases. In this connection an example of code of ethics of Johnson & Johnson, Inc. helped managers in time of crisis.

Johnson & Johnson spent over $ 100 million removing Tylenol from shelves of every store after non-prescription drug was found to have been deliberately poisoned in Chicago area during 1982, causing death of 4 individuals. James Burke, Chairman of Johnson & Johnson, credits that code with guiding the actions of his company. This document of code of ethics spells out our responsibilities to all our constituencies: consumers, employees, community, stockholders. It served to guide all of us during the crisis, when hard decision had to be made. All our employees world-wide were able to watch the process of Tylenol, withdrawal and subsequent reintroduction in temper-resistant packaging. There was a great sense of shared pride in the knowledge that the credo was being tested and it worked. I think we can agree that the employees of J & J should be proud of the response of the firm which put consumer safety ahead of company profits."

ETHICAL RESPONSIBILITIES OF SENIOR MANAGEMENT

How can the conflict between economic and social performance be resolved by senior executives. This has to be done as part of the strategic planning process (SPP).

(i) Ethical issues have to be made a part of SPP, and no longer ignored or pushed down onto operating levels. Hard ethical questions have to be asked by the managers in the units, and specific answers to be supplied by corporate executives, *e.g.* We can substantially increase our bank revenues by charging Rs. 10 per month for all accounts below a minimum balance, but this will place burden on many older, retired customers, should we make a charge?"

We can reduce our costs by replacing the wholesale distributors who helped us in building the market, should we start direct sales?

(ii) Managers in units also ask themselves hard questions, *e.g.*, "What are the residues of this chemical process and how are those waste materials being handled?

What is the failure rate of this product, and are these failures being satisfactorily repaired?

Now how these ethical questions to be answered? With character and courage. This is the character to face issues that have adverse social impacts. Associated with each of the alternatives and the courage to evaluate each of these alternatives following economic, legal and moral forms of reasoning and then arrive at a decision.

This is the character to recognise that personal costs may be associated with the choice, due to the biased nature of the planning, control and motivation systems, and the courage to bear those costs.

Those who differ with this approach is due to their differences in their perspectives or in their beliefs in the importance of economic outcomes, under moral values of justice and liberty. We make ethical decisions based on our sense of responsibility to others; it is a test of our character and a measure of our courage.

CATEGORIES OF CORPORATE CODES OF ETHICS

Category I

"Be a dependable organisation citizen":

1. Demonstrate honesty and fairness in relationships with customers, suppliers and employees.
2. Dress in business like attire.
3. Comply with safety, health and security regulations.
4. Be reliable in attendance and punctuality.

Category II

"Don't do anything unlawful or improper that will harm the organisation":

1. Maintain confidentiality of customer, employee and corporate records and information.
2. Make decisions objectively without regard to friendship or personal gain.
3. Avoid outside activities which conflict with or impair the performance of duties.

4. Do not provide false or misleading information to corporation or government agency.

5. Acceptance of any form of bribes is prohibited.

6. Do not use company property or resource for personal benefit.

7. Conduct personal and business dealings in compliance with relevant laws, regulations.

Category III

"Be good to our customers":

1. Strive to provide 'products and services of highest quality.

2. Convey true claims for products.

Category IV (Undustered)

1. Exhibit standards of personal integrity and professional conduct.

2. Racial, religious or sexual harassment is prohibited.

3. Protect quality of environment.

FOR PROFESSIONAL GROUPS

Professional Associations lay down code of ethics for their members—behaviour required or expected of its members, Doctors, Personnel Managers, etc.

These codes give clue to what type of response is expected in given situation. It comprises of norms and standards of discipline, honestly and integrity and professional ethics to be followed and enforced by association.

As an illustration extracts from some codes of conduct of professional bodies are mentioned.

(A) Codes of the Medical Council of India

The codes cover 33 principles:

(i) General principles.

(ii) Doctor to doctor relationship.

(iii) Duties to profession.

(iv) Duties to patients.

Example. They should educate public on correct and ethical use of drugs.

List of misconduct as well given, *e.g.* refusing to perform a sterilisation operation on religious grounds.

(B) Ethics for Chartered Accountants in Chartered Accountant's Act

Some misconducts are:

(i) if he allows any person to practise as CA. if he is not one.

(ii) If he advertises or solicits work.

(iii) He certifies a statement without adequate scrutiny.

(iv) If he accepts a position held by another CA. without communiating with him.

(v) If he discloses confidential information about his dinet.

(C) The Engineers' Code

The National Society of Professional Engineers had a code, which requires professionals to:

1. Dissociate themselves from organisations that are of a questionable character.
2. Further the cause of public good.
3. Advise clarity, the consequences, if a technical opinion is overruled by a non-technical person.
4. Maintain confidentiality.
5. Avoid engineeringly unsafe good.

(D) Code for Marketing Managers

A code of ethics for marketing managers is issued by the American Marketing Association. It includes:

1. **Basic Guidelines.** Not doing harm knowingly, accurate representation of their education and training, following the laws in letter and spirit.
2. **Follow the well Understood Principles of Rights and Duties in the Process of Exchange.** Products should be safe, communications not deceptive in good faith adequate processes for redressal of grievances.
3. **Honesty and Fairness.** Serving customers, clients, employees, distributors and public, avoid conflict of interest, employ equitable fee schedules of payments or receipt.
4. **Promotion.** Avoid false, misleading, high pressure and manipulative tactics.
5. **Distribution.** No coercion, ensuring free channels, etc.
6. **Product Development.** Safety standards, any component substitution to be advised to the customer, extra cost and added features.
7. **Organisational.** Avoid adverse organisational behaviour.
8. **Pricing.** Neither predatory nor rigged.
9. **Market Research.** Prohibit selling under the guise of market research, research integrity, confidentiality and privacy of respondents.

(E) Code of Ethics of Public Relations Practitioners

1. The core philosophy of the code is to uphold the Universal Declaration of Human Rights of the UNO.
2. It requires behaviour, in a manner, as to develop the confidence of those, with whom they come in contact, whether clients or employers.

3. It upholds the free flow of information.

4. The practitioners must avoid ambiguous language and maintain loyalty to the clients and employers.

5. They must never manipulate to create sub-conscious motivations.

6. They must protect the interests of the organisation they serve and the general public.

7. They must never impair human dignity and integrity.

8. They must never compromise on the truth due to other requirements.

(F) Code of Ethics of the Association for Computer Machinery (ACM)

The ACM has five canons. An ACM member should:

1. Act with integrity at all times.

2. Strive to increase his own competence and the competence and prestige of the profession.

3. Use his knowledge and skills for the advancement of human welfare.

4. Act with professional responsibility.

5. Accept responsibility for his work.

(G) Code of Advertisers issued by the Advertisement Council of India

1. Moral and religious sentiment should not be offended.

2. Advertisements should not directly and adversely compare products with those of the competitors.

3. Rhetoric like offering to refund money, if the product is not good should be avoided.

❐

9

Strategy Implementation in Business Ethos

The strategy formulation and the relationship between strategy formulation and strategic implementation should be studied. This is because the formulation and implementation process are intertwined in real life. The two linkages existing between strategy formulation and strategy implementation are: *(i)* forward linkage, and *(ii)* backward linkage. The forward linkage deals with preparing the organisational activities including organisational structure, leadership, culture etc, necessary for the strategic implementation.

The backward linkage deals with the influence of implementation on strategy formulation. In other words, once the strategy is selected and implemented, it is found in the reality that there are certain deviations due to the different ground realities. These deviations force the strategist to reformulate the strategy based on the ground realities. Therefore, the past strategic actions and experiences should be taken into consideration in formulating strategies.

ISSUES AND STRATEGY IMPLEMENTATION

A number of issues are normally involved in strategy implementation. The important issues are project, procedural, organisational, structural, behaviour considerations, production/ operations, human resources, financial and marketing.

1. Project Implementation. Project is defined by the Project Management Institute of the US as, "a one-shot, time limited, goal-oriented, major undertaking, requiring the commitment of varied skills and resources." Thus, a project is a highly specific programme for which the time schedule and specific costs are determined in advance. Projects create all necessary conditions and facilities for the strategy implementation, the discipline of project management. The goals for a project are devised/derived from the plans and programmes which are based on the strategies adopted. A project passes through various phases before a set of task can be accomplished:

(i) Detailed planning related to different aspects of the projects such as infrastruture engineering designs, schedules and budgets, finance etc. has to be completed.

(ii) The phase is an extension of strategic formulation phase of the strategic management. Ideas generated during the process of strategic alternatives and choice consideration from the core of the future projects that may be undertaken by the organisation.

(iii) After a set of projects have identified and arranged according to the priority they have to be subjected to a preliminary project analysis which examines the marketing, technical, financial and economic aspects. This analysis is done to find out whether it would stand the scrutiny of the financial institutions, banks and investors. After this screening the viable projects are taken up and feasibility studies conducted.

(iv) The detailed engineering, material, awarding contracts, civil and other types of construction, etc., have to be undertaken during the implementation phase leading to the testing, trail and commissioning of the plant.

(v) The final phase deals with disbanding the project.

2. Procedural Implementation. Strategy implementation also requires executing the strategy, based on the rules, regulations and procedures formulated by the government. Though, many procedures are simplified with the liberalisation, privatisation and globalisation of Indian economy, certain procedures are still applicable in the process of strategy implementation. Therefore, the strategists should study the following procedural aspects before implementing the strategy. They are: licensing procedures, foreign collaboration procedures, Foreign Exchange and Regulation Act requirements, environmental requirements Monopolies and Restrictive Trade Practices requirements, import and export requirements, incentives and benefits, requirements of labour laws and other legislations.

3. Organisational Structures and Strategies. Companies build structures for their organisations based on their strategies. There are a number of methods/ways that the organisations can be structured. The simple strategies require simple structure whereas the growth strategies require flexible structure and complex strategies necessarily influence to build matrix structures. In fact, the stable strategies require a mechanistic organisation and a growth strategy require an organic structure.

4. Organisational Growth. Organisational structure is a means to an end of achieving organisational mission and objectives. Thus, it is an important means for strategic implementation. Organisational structure refers to the methods of allocating duties and responsibilities to individuals, and the ways what individuals are grouped together into units, departments and divisions. The formal organisational structure represents the relationships between people and functions as designated by management and conveyed in the organisation chart. It also defines the number of levles in the organisational hierarchy. The informal organisational structure represents the web of social relationships among various members of a company.

5. Entrepreneurial Structure. Generally, the small businesses and the businesses when they are started consist of an owner-manager and few employees. These types of organisations do not require an organisational chart and formal assignment of responsibilities. Organisation structure is fluid with each employee often knowing how to perform more than one task and with owner-manager involved in all aspects/areas of business.

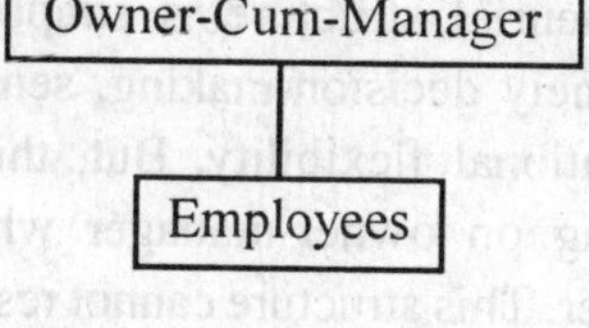

Fig. Entrepreneurial Organisational Structure (Start-up)

The small firms, if,they are successful during the first years of crucial period, it would be due to the increased demand for products or services. The entrepreneurs develop the business and increase the size of the firm to meet the increased demand. The business begins to evolve from fluidity to a status of more permanent division of labour due to the growth. The owner-manager, who was performing all functions in the initial stage now finds that he has to perform more managerial activities than operational activities. The growth demands the owner to employ new candidates and this results in assignment of specialised functions to these employees.

The business growth results in expansion of organisational structure both vertically and horizontally. The entrepreneurial organisational structure with growth is depicted in Fig. given below. As can be seen from this figure, the operative functions of manufacturing are assigned to manufacturing manager and the operative functions of marketing are assigned to the marketing manager. These two managers perform the activities with the help of employees. The owner-manager performs managerial and strategic functions.

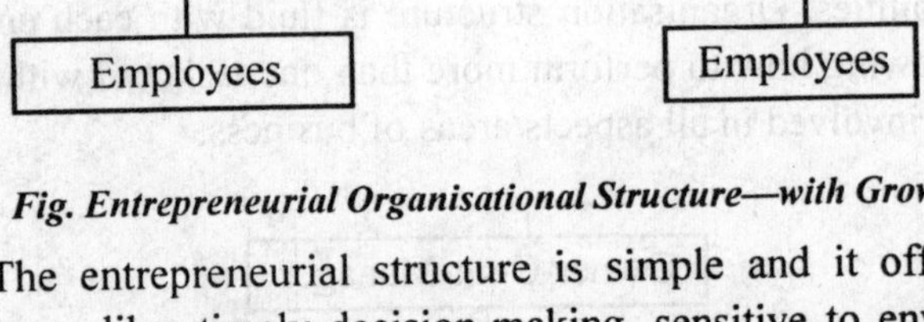

Fig. Entrepreneurial Organisational Structure—with Growth

The entrepreneurial structure is simple and it offers some advantages like: timely decision-making, sensitive to environment demands and operational flexibility. But, this structure results in excessive depending on owner-manager who is normally not a professional manager. This structure cannot respond to the increasing demand beyond a point. Thus, this structure is mostly suitable to the strategy catering to the needs of a local market by being small.

6. Vertical/Tall Organisations. Vertical/Tall organisations refer to increase in the length of the organisation's hierarchy chain of command. The hierarchical chain of command represents the company's authority— accountability relationship between superiors and subordinates. Authority and responsibility flows from the top to the bottom through all the levels of the hierarchy, accountability from the lowest level to the highest level. Fig. given below shows the vertical/tall organisation. Employees at each level should report to their superior, who in turn should report to his boss. Thus, the activities are reported to the top. Authority is more centralised in tall organisation.

Fig. Tall/Vertical Organisational Structure

The advantage of tall organisation include: effective analysis of factors and efficient decision making are possible as a number of managers at different levels supervised and check the activities. The organisation can formulate effective policies, programmes and control mechanisms. Further, it provides promotional avenues to the employees.

But, too many hierarchical levels results in bureaucratic characteristics rather than commercial characteristics to the business firm. Tight operational control delays the decision making process. This process makes the organisation incompetent. Too many controls may reduce the cost of operation.

Tall and centralised organisations allow for better communication of company's mission, goals and objectives to all employees. It also enhances coordination of functional areas to ensure that each area will work closely witht the other functions. Since, all employees are centrally directed, coordination become possible.

Tall organisational structure is appropriate for the firms having bleak growth opportunities, problem children and dogs. Further, firms with cost minimisation strategy and firms in maturity stage can adopt tall organisations. Thus, this type of structures are well suited for environments that area relatively stable and predictable.

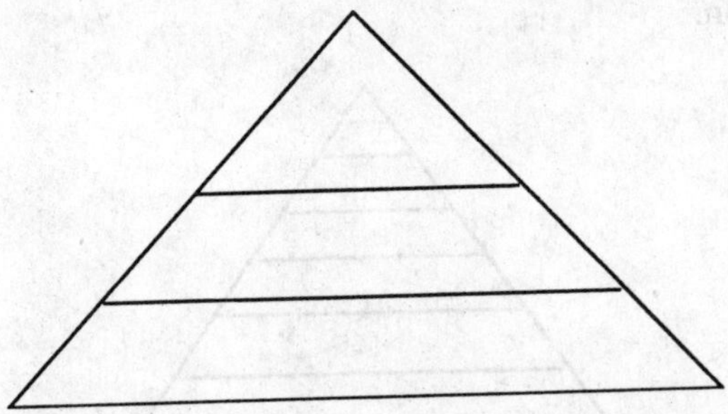

Fig. Flat/Horizontal Organisational Structure

7. Horizontal/Flat Organisations. Horizontal/flat organisations refer to an increase in breadth of an organisation's structure. Fig. given above presents the model of horizontal/flat organisation. The number of levels in the organisational hierarchy are a few. The span of control is relatively large.

The increasing bio-professionalisation and multi-professionalisation and wide acceptance for empowerment allowed even the large business firms to reduce the number of hierarchical levels of their organisations. Consequently, large sized firm also started adopting horizontal/flat organisation by delayering. In fact, this structure is well suited for the small size business firms.

Authority is more decentralised in relatively flat structures. Managers with broad span of the control must grant more authority to his subordinates. Decisions are more likely to be made by the employees who are at the helm of affairs and more familiar with the situations and ground realities. Organisational activities are mostly performed informally. Professional managers are treated as real profession lists.

The major advantage of flat structure is quick decision-making. Thus, it enables the management to take decisions in right time. Other advantages of this structure include: low adminsitrative costs, freedom and autonomy to the managers to operate, decision making by the managers who are at helm of affairs and empowerment of managers. These benefits motivate the managers to accept responsibility and commit themselves towards organisational objectives. Further, these characteristics enable the organisation to be duly sensitive to the environmental demands. The employees also become innovative and creative.

The horizontal/flat organisational structure are appropriate for the organisations with horizontal and vertical growth strategies, stars and cash cows. Thus, these structures are useful for competitive and dynamic business firms.

8. Resources Allocation. Resource allocation is the process of allocating organisational resources to various divisions, department and strategic business units (SBUs). Resource allocation deals with the procurement and commitment of financial, physical and human resources to strategic tasks for the achievement of organisational objectives. Resource allocation is a powerful means of communicating the strategy of the organisation as it gives the desired signals to all concerned. It will demonstrate what strategy really is in operation. If the resource shift is not in line with the official strategy, the latter will remain only as a paper strategy.

Resource allocation decisions are linked to the objectives. Several questions have to be dealt within resource allocation. What sources can be tapped for resources? What fact affect resource allocation? What different approaches could be adopted?

How does resource allocation take place? Decision about dividend is important in relation to objectives and long-term ability of the company to attract capital. How to distribute the expected profits among investors, employees and the company's own needs is an important resource allocation decision from the viewpoint of long-term implementation of the strategy.

Methods for resource allocation are *(i)* B.C. G. Matrix, *(ii)* Budgeting systems.

9. Functional Policies. Functional policies provide guidelines to operating managers, so that *(a)* coordination across functional units take place. Once the strategy of the company is decided, modificational functional policies may become necessary to meet the demands of the new business. *(b)* similar situations are handled consistently *(c)* strategies are implemented and *(d)* executive time in decision making is reduced.

10. Communication of Strategy. Communication of strategy covering the mission objectives market scope, technology and all the issues relating to implementation, to different level in organisation is very important for its success. This is so because strategy is implemented through people who ought to be clear about the roles they have to play in relation to each other.

11. Leadership. Developing appropriate leaderships is one of the most important elements in the implementation of a strategy. Appropriate leadership is necessary, though not a sufficient condition for developing effective structure and systems for the success of strategy. Leadership is the key factor for developing and maintaining right culture and climate. There are several aspects of leadership styles and skills, some of them appropriate to the context, content of strategy, while others are desirable attributes in general for the success of an organisation. The challenges of leaderships is in implementation are the gravest as leadership in most scare resources.

12. Challenge of Change. The strategy implementation process generally invovles a change. The change can be minor or major. If it affected a large number of people, cuts into deeper issues like beliefs, values etc., it is major change. The process of change has three stages namely infreezing, moving and refreezing.

13. Pre-Implementation Evaluation of Strategy. Before the implementation of strategy it is advisable to go for a final scrutiny so as to avoid failure due to weaknesses in the analysis, if any and to ensure that strategy decided for the organisation is optimal. It is something like checking all the electrical connections before switching on the circuit. There are several check-points that may be used for evaluation.

The process of strategy formulation is referred to in current literature as 'Strategic planning' and is distinguishable from Management Planning and Control for strategy implementation. Strategic planning is defined as "the process of deciding on the objectives of the organisation, on the changes in the objectives, on the resources used to attain these objectives, and on the policies that are to govern the acquisition, use and disposition of these resources. It involves matching of the external economic, political and social environments to corporate capabilities and setting the long-term objectives and goals of the organisation as well as the policies and strategies to achieve the objectives. As Anthony has put it. "Strategic planning is a process having to do with the formulation of long-range strategic plans and policies that determine or change the character or direction of the organisation. In an industrial company, this process includes planning that effects the objectives of the company; the acquisition and disposition of major facilities, divisions, or subsidiaries; policies of all types, including policies as to management control and other processes, the markets they serve and distribution channels for serving them, the organisation structure, research and development of new product lines, sources of new permanent capital, and dividend policy; and so on."

As distinguished from strategic planning, the system of 'management planning and control' is associated with the ongoing administration of an enterprise. It is the process by which managers assure that resources are obtained and used effectively and efficiently in the accomplishment of the organisation's objectives. It accepts the corporate objectives evolved by strategic planning as 'givens' and attempts to relate the organisational resources to the objectives in order to arrive at a time-phased statement of the corporate goals and objectives and operational plans. Thus, the management planning and control system may be regarded as the medium through which the strategic objective, policies and plans are translated into more specific, measurable, attainable and meaningful goals and plans. Conceptually, it is a part of the total concept of strategy—a segment of the strategy implementation phase.

The management planning system involves the preparation of annual plans formalising the overall corporate goals and objectives in terms of sales, costs, margins, profits and return on capital, broken up, as necessary, in relation to products, operations, and geographic location of the activities. It may also involve the development of longer term (say, five-yearly) 'action' plans defining the possible ranges of sales and market share, cost, profits, capital expenditure, expected return on investment, and the operational plans in terms of money, men and materials which would be required over the time span in order to achieve the pre-determined corporate objectives. The formal planning system should ensure that the executives, with participation from managers at lower levels, break down the institutional objectives into functional and divisional objectives, thus translating strategic considerations into management considerations for specific time periods. The planning and control system to be effective requires the organisation structure to be such that it defines authority and responsibility in terms of jobs to be accomplished.

For effective implementation of strategy, the essential elements of the planning and control system should consist of:

(a) an appropriate organisation structure that defines authority and responsibility in terms of the job to be accomplished;

(b) a reporting system that can quickly diagnose deviations from the desired results, particularly in those areas which represent key variables in operations;

(c) goals and targets of organisational units based on the input-output relationship in the relevant operations;

(d) participation and support of all levels of management and supervisory personnel;

(e) a follow-up mechanism to ensure prompt remedial action by proper analysis, review and coordinated action.

The planning device commonly used to implement strategy is the budget. As an instrument for putting plans and policies into effect. The budget enables management to formalise goals and targets in quantitative/financial terms. Moreover, budgeting requires the participation of managers at different levels in the development of plans and policies. A motivational force is thus built into the process of planning and control, which is a vital necessity for successful implementation of the strategy. Its usefulness, notwithstanding budgeting has also its inherent limitations. But on balance many of the limitations may be found to lie not in the budget or the process of budgeting but in the lack of management awareness of the limitations, or the improper use of budgets.

RELATIONSHIP BETWEEN STRATEGY FORMULATION AND IMPLEMENTATION

The relationship between strategy formulation and implementation can best be described by their interdependence. These have been divided primarily from the point of view of orderly study as well as the skill requirements for these two aspects of strategic management. The requirement of strategy formulation is primarily conceptual and analytical skills while that of implementation is administrative skills. But in real life, the processes of formulation and implementation are interwined. Both can be thought of reiterative in the sense that both are affected by each other. For example, the strategy is formulated in a particular environment which is dynamic. The feedback from the operations, a result of strategy implementations, gives notices of the changing environmental factors to which strategy should be adjusted. Thus this is on-going process which should be seen in continuity rather than in discrete form. The formulation of strategy does not end where its implementation begins; both should be taken as a continuous process.

The interdependence of formulation and implementation of strategy does not, however, mean that managers should not distinguish between the two. While interdependence helps management to take corrective action in the light of the feedback given by the implementation, the distinction between the two helps in putting right perspective on organisational resources, both human and physical. Strategy formulation should not be assigned to management below certain level because of its dependence on contingent factors; implementation can be assigned to this level of management. This is possible because once the overall strategic decisions are made, detailed implementation plans can be developed for the various functional areas of operations. Thus various levels of management come into the picture of strategic management. As will be seen later, when the strategy is put into action through the process of development of internal plans, the feedback mechanism emphasises the need to continually assess implementation of strategy and organisational performance in order to determine any change required in the strategy. Thus those who are responsible for strategy formulation can not be relieved from the task of its implementation.

TECHNIQUE FOR STRATEGY FORMULATION

I. Scenarios. Scenario generation is one of the methods which strategic planners have found useful for the interpretation of a fluid, rapidly changing business environment with an uncertain future. Scenarios constitute an effective device for sensing, interpreting, organising and bringing to bear diverse information about the future in planning and strategic decision-making. Simply stated, scenarios may be regarded as stories about the future. But more precisely speaking, these are descriptions of plausible alternative futures of the macro-environment. The primary purpose of scenario generation is to delimit the range of uncertainties in the most critical factors in an environment. Typical scenarios include qualitative and quantitative descriptions of uncertainties in the most critical factors in an environment. Typical scenarios include qualitative and quantitative descriptions of the more important social, political, economic, demographic, technological and other conditions. They often describe the basic trends, assumptions, conditions and dynamics of the factors relating to the future period that the scenario covers. As such scenarios are not forecasts or predictions. Probability estimates are hardly associated with the elements of the scenario. Hence scenarios are said to be fuzzy, too imprecise and hard to apply. Also scenario generation is an expensive process. There is no doubt that scenarios represent a significant departure from the traditional methods of forecasting like the single or multiple variable extrapolation and regression methods. However, most of the environmental factors are not amenable to easy prediction on account of their complexities and the rapidity of changes. Under the circumstances scenarios are found to be an ideal complement to the various other methods of forecasting and planning.

II. Gap Analysis. The basic question that strategic planners have to face with regard to environmental forecasting is how far ahead will they look, that is about the time horizon for forecasting. For, to respond strategically to a perceived environmental change in future, the strategic decisions have to be taken well in advance. It may be a matter of technology of production envisaged by the planners. Thus, for instance, it will take a considerably longer period to create production facilities for computer hardware than for production (say) a newly designed software. A technique which has been found useful in determining the time horizon for environmental forecasting is that of 'Gap Analysis'. Application of this technique will be clear from the following diagram which depicts a typical situation.

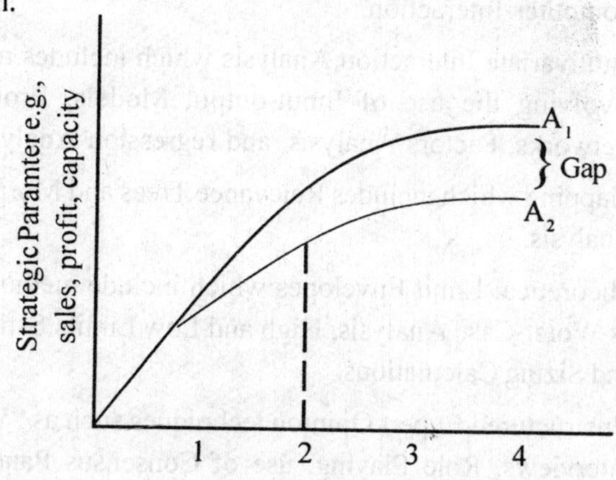

Gap Analysis

It will be seen in the diagram that between line A_1, and line A_2, which show the desired change in a strategic parameter like sale, profit, etc. and what will happen if there is no change in strategy, respectively, a gap has emerged by the second year. The gap widens with the passing of time. The planners should know how long it will take for current decisions to begin to fill the gap. If it is a question of creating capacity for computer hardware, two years will be too short a period for the purpose unless it is decided to acquire an existing plant.

Once the time horizon for forecasting is determined it is necessary that objective data should be processed and then analysed for making forecasts, taking into account the probabilities of occurrence and the risks involved. One or more of the following forecasting techniques may be adopted in this context:

(1) Unstructured Inexpert Opinion techniques such as person-in-the-street interviews, brainstorming, etc.

(2) Structured Inexpert Opinion techniques include use of questionnaire, interviews and surveys.

(3) Structured Expert Opinion techniques which include 'delphi' technique, highly structured interviews, and on-line Computer Interaction.

(4) Multivariate Interaction Analysis which includes mehtods involving the use of Input-output Models, Probability Networks, Factors Analysis, and regression Analysis.

(5) Mapping which includes Relevance Trees and Morphology Analysis.

(6) Theoretical Limit Envelopes which include methods such as Worst-Case Analysis, High and Low Limits Estimation, and Sizing Calculations.

(7) Unstructured Expert Opinion techniques such as "What if" Interviews, Role Playing, use of Consensus Panels, and Scenario Generation Forecasting technology change in particulary rendered easier by scenario generation.

(8) Dynamic Models which include Historical Analogues, Time-lags, and Stochastic Modelling.

(9) Single variable extrapolation. Variants of this techniques include linear extrapolation, life-cycle curves, power-series expansion, exponential smoothing, and others, Single varibale extrapolation is found useful if it is possible for the firm to identify a key environmental variable, on the assumption that the past is a guide to the future. However, a single environmental variable is generally insufficient. Thus, multiple regression techniques may have to be used.

RESOURCE ALLOCATION

A strategic plan is the representation of hopes and aspirations of strategists. Project implementation is for the creation of infrastructure to enable them to put such a plan into action. Procedural implementation provides the 'go-ahead' signal. But nothing really happens until resources are procured and allocated to tasks for accomplishment of objectives. Resources allocation deals with the procurement and commitment of financial, physical, and human resources to strategic tasks for the achievement of organisational objectives. Resource allocation is both a one-time and a continuous process. When a new project is implemented, it would require resources. An on-going concern would also require periodic allocation of resources. Strategy implementation should deal with both these types of resources allocation. Several questions have to be dealt with in resources allocation; what sources can be tapped for resources? What factors affect resource allocation? What different approaches could be adopted? How does resource allocation take place? and, finally, what difficulties are encountered? We deal with these questions in the following sub-sections.

Factors Influencing Resource Allocation

Resource allocation deals with the commitment and distribution of resources. Since resources are almost always scare, the process of resource allocation is quite complex. The basic question before the strategists is how to allocate scarce resources to competitive strategic tasks that lead to the accomplishment of organisational objectives. It would be easier for strategists to allocate resources to the strategic priorities are clear. But setting clear priorities practically is often a daunting task. This is so because a variety of factors affect the process of resource allocation. These factors would be the objectives of the organisation preference of dominant strategists, internal politics, and external influences.

There are a number of objectives. Some are official while others are operative (or implicit). Employees of any organisation tends to judge the importance given by strategists to tasks on the basis of the amount of resources allocated to them. If the chairperson of a company, while presenting the annual report, waxes eloquently on the virtues of human resources but the actual resource allocation does not reflect the importance given to these resources, then human resources development is certainly not a priority strategic task. Operative objectives tend to affect the pattern of resource allocation to the maximum extent.

The dominant strategists-most often the chief executive, tend to affect the process of resource allocation. Their preference are reflected in the way how resources get allocated. Except SBU, divisional and departmental heads know that such preferences matter and try to present their demands in line with them or attempt creating interest in the dominant strategists for their demands so that resources can be attracted easily.

Resources are often misconstrued as power. Those department units which are able to attract more resources are considered more powerful. Executives who are in a position to affect the process of resources allocation in their favour are perceived to be more effective. These perceptions make resource allocation a rational-political process. Internal policies within the organisation, therefore, affects the process of resource allocation.

Apart from internal politics, external influences also affect resource allocation. These influences arise due to government policy and stipulations, the demands of external shareholders, financial institutions, community and others. For instance, conditions imposed in the letter of intent issued to a company may require additional investments in pollution control and safety equipments before its conversion to an industrial licence. The shareholders may expect a higher dividend or bonus shares and resources may be to be diverted to them. Financial institutions may impose restrictions or require companies to invest in technology upgradation. The discharging of social responsibilities such as contribution to community services may require allocation of funds. Thus, external influences affect the process of resources allocation considerably.

Procurement of Resources

The different types of resources-financial, physical, and human-are derived from different sources. But finance is generally considered to be the primary source; it is used for creation and maintenance of other resources. We deal with sources of finance here. Basically, there are two types of finances-long term and short-term. Long-term finance is required for creation of capital assets. Short-term finance is for working capital. Both types of finances can be procured form internal and external sources.

Internal sources include retained earnings, depreciation provisions, taxation provisions, and other types of reserves like development rebate and investment allowance reserves. External sources consist of equity and loans (generally for long-term finance) and bank credit, hire-purchase debt, trade credit and fixed deposits (generally for short-term finances). While both internal and external sources carry benefits as well as disadvantages, given a choice, a business firm would prefer the internal sources. But much depends on management policy related to financing. The cost of capital from different sources has to be considered.

When modernisation, expansion, and diversification strategies lend to the creation of a new company or require additional investments, and when external sources of financing are tapped, certain important issues have to be considered. There are the requirements for the Controller of Capital Issues and financial institutions, and the stipulations, stock exchanges. The Controller of Capital Issues would consider the total capital most outlays and the scheme of finance for project, debt-equity ratio, and equity-preference ratio. The financial institutions have their own norms and specific areas and types of financing. The primary support for working capital is provided by commercial banks.

Having procured financial resources, the strategists set out to implement the strategies in right earnest. The first task is to distribute the resource within the organisation to different SBUs, divisions, departments, functions, tasks and individuals.

MEANS OF RESOURCE ALLOCATION

1. BCG-based Budgeting. The BCG matrix can also be used for resources allocation. In a BCG matrix, SBUs or products are identified as 'stars', 'question marks', 'cash cows' and 'dogs'. Investment and cash flow decisions can be made on the basis of the type of SBU. For instance, resources can be diverted from a 'cash cow' to a 'questions mark' or a 'star'. The BCG matrix, can, therefore, play a useful role in a multi-SBU-division or department company where resources have to be allocated.

2. Strategic Budgeting. Budgeting is a common technique used as a planning coordination, and control device in management. Its use is widespread in organisations. The topic of budgeting is covered exhaustively in texts in the area of financial management. But apart from traditional budgeting where stress is on accounting, a budget increasingly being used as a dynamic management tool. The difference lies in the way budgeting exercise is carried out in an iterative manner between different managerial levels and the assumptions made before the formulation of budgets. Position papers on different aspects such as environment, distinctive competence, marketing, past performance, etc are prepared and presented to the top management which uses them in formulating corporate policy guidelines and stating long-and short-term goals. The operating management meanwhile prepares operational plans and sets targets which are coordinated with the corporate objectives through the executive management. Based on resources availability and corporation guidelines the strategies budget is prepared by the executive-level committee and presented to the top management for approval and sanctions. The strategic budget then communicated down the line and the tasks of implementation taken up.

As can be seen from the above description, strategic budgeting is an iterative process involving a multi-level, organisation-wide effort and, therefore, needs to carry the approval of all concerned. More importantly, it takes into account strategic factors such as environmental changes and their likely impact on the implementation of strategies, and the corporate distinctive competencies and their probable effect on the objective achieving capability of the organisation. This is the reasons why it is termed as a strategic budget. Besides, this type of budgeting, there are also other means of resource allocation.

3. Zero-Based Budgeting. Zero-based budgeting is an operation planning and budgeting process that requires each strategist to justify resource allocation demand not on the basis of previous years' budget but on "ground zero", which is based on a fresh calculation of costs each time a plan is to be implemented. The strategic plan is divided into operational plans, goals and activities, and resource requirements are calculated everytime a budget is prepared. ZBB can be used for effective resource allocation among competing units on the basis of strategic priorities since costs are related to benefits for each strategic task undertaken.

4. PLC-Based Budgeting. Resources allocation could be linked to the different stages in a product's (or SBU's) lie cycle. A product in the introduction and growth stages may attract more resources and these resources may be diverted from the high-profit yielding products that have reached the maturity stage of their life cycle.

5. Capital Budgeting. Resources allocation for new projects or products could be done on the basis of capital budgeting. Existing projects, in cases of restructuring and modernisation, could also use capital budgeting for resources allocation.

6. Parta System. The parta sysem is an indigenous form of control device used for exercising management control. Though essentially, parta is a control tool used for the daily assessment of net cash inflow from operations before tax and dividends, the budgeted parta is a pre-determined amount agreed upon between the chairperson of the company and the business unit in charge. The total parta sysem is a daily budgeting and reporting system.

Difficulties in Resources Allocation

The previous sub-section described the factors that affect the process of resource allocation. These factors, combined with the fact that the resource allocation process is highly complex, create several difficulties for the strategists.

The first difficulty arises due to a scarcity of resources. Financial physical, and human resources are hard to find. Firms will usually face difficulties in procuring finance. Even if finance is available, the cost of capital is a constraint. Those firms which enjoy investor confidence and high credit-worthiness process a distinctive competence as it increases their resource-generation capability. Physical resources would consist of assets such as land, machinery and equipment. In a developing country like India many capital goods have to be imported. The government can provide a limited amount of foreign exchange and this places a restriction on firms wishing to procure physical resources. Human resources are seemingly in abundance but the problem arises due to the non-availability of skills that are specially required. Computer professionals, advertising personnel, and chemical engineers are currently scarce in India. This places severe restrictions on firms wishing to attract and retain personnel. In sum the availability of scarce resources is a very real problem faced in resource allocation. Within organisations, there are several difficulties encountered in resource allocation. The usual budgeting for existing SBUs, divisions, and departments places restrictions on generating resources for newer units and those with a greater potential for growth. Overstatement of needs is another frequent problem in a bottom-up appraoch to resource allocation. The budgeting and corporate planning departments may have to face the irks of those executives who do not get resources according to their expectations. Such negative reactions may hamper the process of strategic planning itself. When strategic budgeting is used for resource allocation, powerful units may be divested of resources for reallocation to potential units. "Budget battles" may ensue if resource allocation affects vested interests. It must be pointed out, however, that the chief executive has a major role to play in managing the process of resource allocation. Strategic management, based on participative mode, and communication of stratgic plan to all executives creates a congenial environment where the resource allocation decisions may be taken amicably.

APPROACHES TO RESOURCE ALLOCATION

1. First alternative approach is the product life cycle system of budgeting resources which suggests that resource allocation should be in tune with the stages in the product life cycle. The basic proposition in this approach is that resources needs vary at different stages in the life-cycle of a product and the strategic choice is also influenced by changes in the state of its life cycle. Thus, for instance, with retrenchment strategy assigned to a product division, one may suggest that it would be useful to adopt zero-base budgeting which implies that resource allocation should depend on the budget requests being justified in detail from scratch and not being considered in the light of allocations of the previous period. Even as a general approach to resource allocation, zero-base budgeting may help management to evaluate expenditure proposed and make trade-offs among current operations, development needs, and profits.
2. The second approach is the analytical conceptual models used for strategic choice (the Growth-Share matrix, 'Stop-light', and Directional Policy matrix models) are considered to be useful for resource allocation in multi-divisional firms. The Growth-Share Matrix suggests that business segments with low growth/high market share position should be allocated resources so as to maintain the present market share and the cash flow generated to be shifted to segments with high-growth/low market share. Thus, resources allocation may be governed by considerations of competitive capabilities/market share/business strengths of

the one hand, and growth prospects/industry attractiveness of business segments on the other.

3. A third approach to management decisions on resources allocation is provided by the budgeting system carefully geared to the chosen strategy.

   As the first step in the process, the corporate objectives and strategy are stated along with the environmental and competitive conditions to be communicated to the SBUs (organisational units), which in turn draw up preliminary budgets after defining the unit-wise objectives and strategies. The preliminary budgets are reviewed by top management and approved if found consistent with the strategy. Summary budgets are then prepared and subsidiary budgets developed including the operating budget, financial and expenses budget. The process involves a series of negotiations among managers at the SBU and corporate levels. For instance unit managers having defined the objectives and strategy of the unit prepare premises and forecasts which are sent for approval by top management. Tentative allocation of resources take place at the corporate level and budget proposals are called for on that basis. The preliminary budgets indicate changes in the resources requirements as compared with the previous period. Only on approval of the preliminary budgets the units draw up their plans and programmes. In large organisations the budget department at the headquarters provide all information to the SBUs and advises them in connection with preparation of budget proposals.

UNSUCCESSFUL IMPLEMENTATION OF STRATEGY

Before going into the details of how a chosen strategy is implemented, it is desirable to identify the factors which cause unsuccessful implementation of strategy so that managers can take adequate safeguard against these factors. There are several such factors:

1. First factor that can lead to unsuccessful implementation of a strategy is the defect in the strategy formulation itself. For example, if a strategy is beyond the capability of the organisation, it can not be successfully implemented. In such a case, the implementers may face serious problems and the organisation may lead to bankruptcy. Therefore, the strategic choice should always be correlated with the organisation's ability to implement it. While formulating and implementing a strategy, adeuqate precuations should be taken against these factors. In the light of these factors, various tools of strategy implementation should be adopted.
2. Unsatisfactory coupling of the strategy to the actions necessary to implement it both within the organisation and in the external decision situations with which it is concerned may cause unsuccessful implementation of the strategy. This type of difficulty can result from a number of causes and conditions. For example, unsatisfactory coupling of the new strategy may be due to the lack of explicit decoupling from previous strategy and commitment with the organisation itself. This decoupling may be caused, in turn, by the existence of a sizeable group of people within the organisation who are convinced that the new strategy is not practical and that the previous ways and activities are best. Another factors responsible for this unsatisfactory coupling may be misperceptions by the strategists of the impact of the newly proposed initiatives on the organisation and its people. It is sometimes assumed that the new initiatives will be accepted by the organisation with a minimum of time and effort from all those who are involved. In actual practice, however, much more work is necessary to ensure that the strategy is accepted and implemented than to prepare it in the first instance. Another reasons for unsuccessful coupling may be cause of different perspectives of strategists and implementers. In most cases, majority of people are concerned with the current operations. Their primary task is to ensure that these operations are

conducted smoothly and efficiently. Their perspective is involved with the avoidance of change and of the factors that could interfere with the operations in their area of responsibility. Strategies, in other hand, seek out changes and determine whether it can be used to the advantage of the organisation. These different perspectives can result in the two groups becoming alienated from each other. For successful implementation of the strategy, a link between these two groups is necessary.

3. Another major factors causing unsuccessful implementation of the strategy is insufficient attention to the negotiation of outcomes in the external decision situations. It is a tendency to assume, once the strategy is formulated, that all that is necessary for the success of the organisation is the aggressive pursuit of the strategy. However, this assumption holds good only so long as there is no change in the decision situations. If these situations change, there should be correpsonding change in the strategy also. For this is essential that the structure of the strategic decision situations in which the organisation is involved should be kept clearly in view throughout the implementation. If this is done, changes in the conditions surrounding those decision situations can be taken in stride. Contingency strategy made during the strategy formulation process can be brought ino operation when appropriate.

❐

10
Value of Management Ethics

Ethics can be defined as the systematic attempt to make sense of individual, group, organisational, professional, social, market, and global moral experience in such a way as to determine the desirable, prioritised ends that are worth pursuing, the right rules and obligations that ought to govern human conduct, the virtuous intentions and character traits that deserve development in life, and to act accordingly.

Sometimes the term morality is used interchangeably with ethics in everyday conversation, but at other times it can be conceptually distinguished from ethics. The morality of a society is related to its mores the customs accepted by a society or group as being right and wrong as well as to those laws of a society that add legal prohibitions and sanctions to many activities considered to be immoral. Morality, therefore can be defined as the customary, socio-legal practices and activities that are considered importantly right and wrong; the rules that govern those activities; and the values that are embedded, fostered, or pursued by those conventional, socio-legal activities and practices. In some instances, management morality and management ethics are diametrically opposed to each other. For example, in the South before the Civil War, the fugitive slave, if recaptured, was often maimed by his or her managers/owners, frequently by chopping off one foot. Although this act of maiming was condoned by customary morality and socio-legal practices at the time, some ethically sensitive, progressive managers objected to it. They argued that this cruel and vindictive act may have been morally acceptable but was ethical repulsive. Whereas management morality may allow one to succeed temporarily by conforming to current social norms or organisational mazes, management ethics calls for a sensitive, reflective, and systematic endorsement of those norms only after they have withstood critical challenge. A classic business example of a transition from stakeholder morality to stakeholder ethics is represented in the Ford v. Dodge lawsuit from the turn of the century. Henry Ford wanted to share profits from his automobile company with his employees to improve the quality of their lives, but the Supreme Court sided with the position of Dodge that the fiduciary moral relationship with investors precluded the ethical sharing of profits with employees. Subsequent to that case, however, profit sharing the gain sharing with designated stakeholders has been ethically justified in terms of prioritized ends and obligations that overcame the conventional morality of earlier forms of capitalism. Many times moral managers and ethical managers engage in the same behaviour patterns but the latter must critically challenge accepted norms before endorsing them.

In addition, moral values are part of a person's philosophy of life. A philosophy of life consists of ongoing, critical reflection about logically fundamental beliefs regarding what is real, true, and of value and acting in accord with those reasoned commitments, as graphically illustrated in Figure 10.1. Moral values alongwith economic, aesthetic, political and other values, indicate what people regard as important in life and worth acting on. Reflection on beliefs about what is real, called metaphysics, and reflection on beliefs about what is true, called epistemology, can result in either religious or secular conclusions and both can provide conceptual foundations for moral values. For example, a person who believes that a real God created the world and humanity, that these truths are known by faith in divine revelation disclosed through sacred writings, and that his or her highest ethical value is spiritual salvation after death has adopted a religious foundation for ethics. Another person who believes that nature is the only reality that always existed, that, humans created gods out of fear, that these truths are known through science and reason, and that the highest moral value is ethical integrity in this life has adopted a secular foundation for ethics.

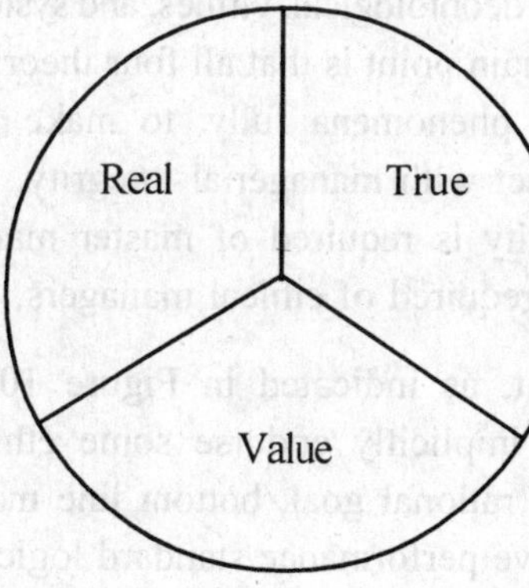

Figure 10.1 Fundamental beliefs in a personal philosophy of life

In addition to reducing tangible and intangible costs, management ethics adds value to individual, group and organizational performance. Management ethics can be defined as the descriptive and normative study of moral awareness, judgement, character and conduct as they relate to all levels of managerial practice. Individual business judgement and performance can be enhanced through management ethics in the following ways:

(a) Stimulation of the moral imagination

(b) Moral identification and ordering moral evaluation

(c) Tolerating moral disagreement and ambiguity

(d) Integrating managerial competence and moral competence

For a manager, exhibiting ethical integrity involves achieving good consequences or ends (outcome-oriented theories emphasized in telelogical ethics), by adhering to standards of right conduct (duty-oriented theories emphasized in deontological ethics), while habitually being motivated by proper intentions and developing virtuous character traits (character-oriented theories emphasized in virtue ethics), in an ethically supportive, holistic context (system-oriented theories emphasized in system development ethics). Although all four theories of ethics (teleological, deontological, virtues, and system development) can be isolated, the main point is that all four theories are necessary to understand moral phenomena fully, to make balanced ethical judgements, and to act with managerial integrity. Just as handling behavioural complexity is required of master managers, handling moral complexity is required of ethical managers.

More important, as indicated in Figure 10.2, management theory and practice implicitly endorse some ethical values over others. For example, rational goal, bottom line managers who use results as the exclusive performance standard logically endorse and tacitly choose to accord outcome oriented ethical values pre-eminence over other ethical values. Rational goal managers, who have strong role competencies in directing and producing, implicitly subscribe to outcome-oriented ethical values in their daily practice. Internal process managers, who exhibit strong role competencies in monitoring and coordinating implicitly subscribe to duty-oriented ethical values in their daily practice. These "by the book" managers who use compliance with internal policies as the exclusive performance standards are tacitly endorsing and logically choosing to accord duty-oriented ethical values priority over other ethical values. Human relations managers who have strong role competencies in facilitating and mentoring, implicitly subscribe to a virtue oriented ethical value in daily practice. These "true grit" managers who focus on the right stuff in persons and use virtuous character as the exclusive performance standard are tacitly endorsing and logically choosing to accord character oriented ethical values preeminence over other ethical values. Finally, open systems managers, who excel in innovating and brokering for resources implicitly subscribe to systems oriented ethical values in daily practices. These change agent managers who use continuous system improvement as the exclusive performance standard, are tacitly endorsing and logically choosing to accord systems oriented ethical values priority over other ethical values.

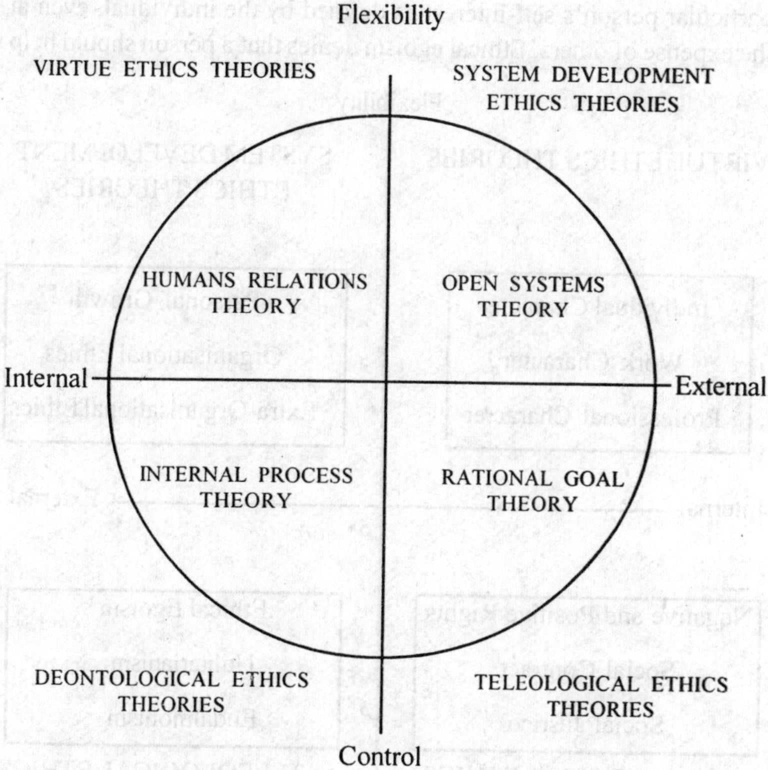

Figure 10.2 Management theories and ethics theories

Teleological Ethics Theories

Teleological ethics theories maintain that good ends and/or results determine the ethical value of actions. If on balance, more benefits than costs are obtained by the relevant stakeholder(s) than by any other alternative, teleological ethics endorses the goodness of that choice. Three major types of teleological ethics are egoism, utilitarianism, and eudaimonism. They and other major types of the key ethics theories are depicted in Figure 10.3.

Ethical Egoism. In the lower right quadrant of Figure 10.3 Ethical egoism, is a teleological theory that holds that an action is good if it produces or tends to produce results that maximize a particular person's self-interest as defined by the individual, even at the expense of others. Ethical egoism denies that a person should help others when the person will get nothing out of it. Psychological egoism is different from ethical egoism in that the former theory claims that people always and only want something out of it for themselves when they act, thereby denying the reality of genuine altruism. While genuine altruism, as the international sacrificing of one's self-interest or welfare for the sake of others, has been used to refute psychological egoism, it has provided a rationale for enlightened egoism. Englightened egoism emphasizes long range self interest while allowing for altruistic concern for the wellbeing of

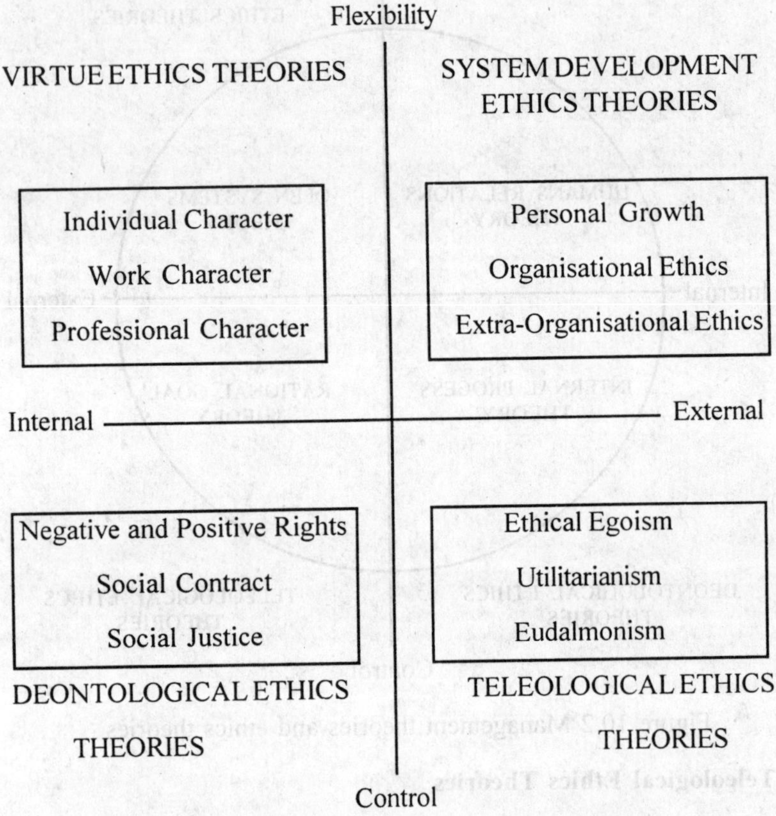

Figure 10.3. Major types of key ethics theories

others (Gauthier, 1986; Holmes, 1993; Olson, 1965). An enlightened egoist, for example, may well avoid cheating and support community projects, not so much because these actions benefit others but because they help achieve some ultimate goal for the egoist, such as social image enhancement that could lead to career advancement within an organisation.

Utilitarianism. Utilitrarianism is a teleological theory that holds that an action is good if it produces or tends to produce the greatest amount of satisfaction for the greatest number of stakeholders affected by the action; for example, if I as a manager create an annual employee vacation schedule only after soliciting vacation time preferences from all employees and honoring those preferences, then I would be acting in a way that would maximize the pleasure of all employees.

Most business students routinely adopt either an egoist or a utilitarian perspective (whether act or rule based) because of their conceptual roots in classic economic theory and emphasis on maximizing investor wealth (self-interest and utility). Growing businesses to increase profits, market share and sales has led to high consumption societies and widespread material satisfaction in the economically developed world.

Eudaimonism. Eudaimonism is a telelogical theory that holds that an action is good if it promotes or tends to promote the fulfillment of goals constitutive of human nature and its hapiness; for example, if I as a manager enforce employee health and safety standards at work, I am ensuring fundamental, natural components of human happiness (Aquinas, 1250/1959; Aristotle, 350 B.C./1985; Finnis, 1980; Pegis, 1945). Aristotle maintained that happiness was the quality of a whole human lifetime characterised by the degree to which the following "goods" were achieved and sustained: health, wealth, friendship, knowledge, good luck, and virtue. He argued that there was a difference between having a good time (maximizing pleasurable utility) and leading a good life (maximizing happiness) and that the latter outcome was to be preferred to the former. Impulsive and understrained acquisitiveness and consumption, though pleasurable, are vices of immoderation for Aristotle that ultimately lead to unhappiness.

The rational goal theory of management, therefore, stresses productivity and profits as the criteria of effectiveness and managers who excel in or endorse this approach demonstrate concious or subliminal support for telelogical ethics. In concrete terms for managers, this approach emphasizes the bottom line and the timely achievement of organisational objectives. Managers who adopt this perspective implicity accept the dictum. "All's well that ends well," regardless of the means used to produce the results.

DEONTOLOGICAL ETHICS THEORIES

Deontological ethics theories maintain that responsibility fulfilling obligations, following proper procedure, doing the right thing, and adhering to moral standards determine the ethical value of actions. Deontological ethics maintains that actions are morally right independent of their consequences; for example for the secularist, it is right to keep promises and for the religious, it is right to obey the Ten Commandments regardless of personal costs or benefits. Among the major types of deontological ethics are negative and positive rights theories, social contract theories, and social justice theories.

Negative and Positive Rights Theories. In the lower left quadrant of Figure 10.3 Negative rights theories, hold that an action is right if it protects an individual from unwarranted interference from government and/or other people in the exercise of that right; for example, if I have a right to privately use, sell, or dispose of my personal property as I choose, this means that every other person has the correlative duty not to prevent me from privately using, selling, or disposing of my property as I freely choose (Locke, 1690; Nozick, 1974). Positive rights theories hold that an action is right if it provides any individual with what ever he or she needs to exist; for example, if I have a right to adequate health care to survive, this means that other agents (perhaps the government) have the correlative duty to provide me with my entitled adequate health care, not merely to avoid interfering with its competitive acquisition (Dworkin, 1978; Kant, 1785/1938). Much of domestic and global public policy conflict over moral rights can be interpreted as differences over the kind and degree of dignity that is to be accorded to persons and whether negative or positive rights should be accorded priority. Political conservatives for example, argue that government activities should be restricted to protecting people's negative rights rather than also providing for people's positive rights (*e.g.*, right to health care, welfare benefits, housing, and jobs), as political liberals maintain.

Social contract theories hold that an action is right if it conforms to the terms agreed upon, conditions, or rules for social wellbeing negotiated by competent parties; for example, the U.S. Uniform Commercial Code and the United Nations Code of Conduct of Transnational Corporations both specify normative guidelines arrived at by consensus (Donaldson, 1994; Donaldson & Dunfee, 1994; Mayer, 1994; Rousseau, 1762/1959-1969).

Social Justice Theories. Social justice theories hold that an action is right if it promotes the duty of fairness in the distributive, retributive, and compensatory dimensions of social benefits and burdens; for example, if secondhand smoke injures non-smokers at work, the fair distribution of that health risk burden, the imposition of reasonable punishments on responsible parties and the compensation due injured parties would all be factors in social justice determinations (Plato, 367 B.C/1968; Rawls, 1971; Velasquez, 1994).

The internal process model of management, therefore, stresses dutiful compliance with stable standards as the criterion of efficiency, and managers who exceed in or endorse this approach often exhibit conscious or subliminal support for deontological ethics. In concrete terms for managers, this approach stress monitoring adherence to standard operating procedures and rewarding persons for adhering to contractual agreements in a coordinated manner. Managers who adopt this perspective tend to "run a tight ship" and to make decisions "by the book," regardless of the consequences.

VIRTUE ETHICS THEORIES

Virtue ethics theories maintain that habitual development of sound character traits determines the ethical value of persons. For the virtue ethicist, building character is what life is all about? Character is the pattern of intentions, inclinations, and virtues that dispose a person or organisation to be ready to act ethically. Persons with strong character have soundly cultivated intellectual, moral, emotional, and social virtues to achieve the self-discipline to do the right thing or want what is truly good for them (Himmelfarb, 1994). Persons with week character find themselves doing the wrong thing or wanting what is truly harmful to them and making excuses for their irresponsible life choices. Character is to be distinguished from personality in that the former provides the substantive moral foundation for one's actions, whereas the latter projects the psychosocial image that creates surface impressions; for example, a manager may be fair but not look fair and vice versa (Giacalone & Rosenfeld, 1991; Greenberg, 1990; Paine, 1991). The alignment of strong character and hardy personality is one indication of individual integrity L. Josephson, 1992; Slote, 1992; Srivastava & Associates 1988).

Virtue ethics maintains that the sound, balanced character, motivation, and intention of an individual is more important than the person's actual conduct and its consequences (Pincoffs, 1985; Slote, 1992). The difference between merely desirable and truly admirable lives is captured in virtue ethics; the wholesome readiness to act out of good intentions constitutes the character of the good person for a virtue ethicist. Three major types of virtue ethics theories focus on individual, work and professional character.

Individual Character Ethics. In the upper left quadrant of Figure 10.3 individual character ethics, maintains that the identification and responsible development of the human traits of nobility such as courage moderation, justice prudence, gratitude, sense of humor, self-discipline, reliability, benevolence, authenticity, caring, sincerity, understanding and wisdom determine both the instrumental intrinsic value of all human ethical interactions for example, if as I age I lose my health, my wealth, and my loved ones through no fault of my own, I retain my dignity and prospects for happiness by living a virtuous life (Aristotle, 350 B.C./1985; Gilligan, Ward & Taylor, 1989; McAllister, 1995; Nussbaum, 1986; Sheaffer 1988; Solomon, 1990; Taylor, 1987; Wilson, 1993).

Work Character Ethics. Work character ethics maintains that the identification and responsible development of noble, reflective, practitioner traits at work such as competence, creativity, honesty, fairness, trustworthiness, coworker appreciation, task completion, honor, loyalty, shared work pride, diligence, resourcefulness, level-headedness, tolerance, dependability, civility, empathy, conscientiousness, discretion, patient urgency, cooperativeness, and supportiveness determine both the instrumental and intrinsic ethical quality of work life; for example, as a manager facing global competition, heightened productivity expectations and the need for effective teamwork, it is essential that the character of my work performance serve as a role model for task accomplishment and considerate relations at work (Cavanagh, 1984; Hosmer, 1994, 1996; Kruschwitz & Roberts, 1987; Schon, 1983; Solomon, 1992). As more and more occupations including management, undergo the process of professionalisation, standards for work character ethics increase (Bayles, Fukuyama, 1995; Larson, 1977; Trevino & Youngblood, 1990). As managers and information specialists, for example, are required to have extensive training with a significant intellectual component in order to provide services vital to the organised functioning of society, they are acquiring more technical autonomy, developing more organisational networks for members, and expecting to be treated in a more "professional" manner. In turn, as more employees become empowered in their work units, they expect a high degree of cognitive moral development, appropriate positive affect, and behaviour consistent with "professional" moral norms at work from their managers.

System development ethics theories maintain that the nature and extent of the supportive framework for continuous improvement of ethical conduct determines the ethical value of actions. Managers who are sensitive to the need to assess and develop work cultures supportive of ethical conduct implement ethics development systems that will sustain integrity-building environments. Managers who rely exclusively on the character of employees to sustain sound business practices, while neglecting to implement morally supportive intra-organisational systems and stable (variation reducing) processes, are unintentionally exposing their organisations to future ethical risk. Managers who do not implement recognition processes for exemplary moral conduct by employees or refrain from implementing processes for swift, fair enforcement of sanctions on wrongdoers at work are guilty of both moral and managerial malfeasance. Three major types of system development ethics theories are personal improvement, organisational and extraorganisational ethics.

Personal Improvement Ethics. In the upper right quadrant of Figure 10.3 Personal improvement ethics, holds that an action is good if it promotes or tends to promote personal responsibility for continuous learning, system holistic development improvement, and moral excellence; for example, a manager who generates new ideas out of a commitment to personal improvement directed toward company goals uses her company's educational benefits package to improve herself and her organisation. Both in the western and non-western traditions, family and friends who support personal improvement and moral progress provide the resources to energize on going personal development.

Organisational ethics holds that an action is good if it promotes or tends to promote the formal and informal organisational processes that enhance procedural, outcome, and systemic justice, respectful caring, and innovation in ethical work cultures; for example, if the organisation in which I as a manager work has neither a fair reward system nor an employee voice system for feedback, part of my responsibility is to improve those systems so that there are contextual forces that support individual and organisational moral development and override inertia or intense resistance to moral development.

Extraorganisational Ethics. Extraorganisational ethics holds that an action is good if it promotes or tends to promote the improvement of collaborative partanerships and collective and global justice creativity in the human and natural environments; for example, as a manager, I have a social responsibility to consider and respect global and domestic constituencies that represent diverse economic, political, legal, social, philanthropic and ecological concerns that affect the firm.

The open systems theory of management, therefore, stresses innovative adaptability and acquisition of external resources as the criteria of effectiveness and managers who excel in or support this approach exhibit conscious or subliminal endorsement of system development ethics. In concrete terms for managers, this approach emphasizes creative change management, entrepreneurial resourcefulness, respectful and sophisticated global negotiation, and collaborative networking with diverse global interests. Managers who adopt this perspective implicitly encourge organisational flexibility to adapt to reality better and to accept the system dictum that, to make organisational moral progress, it is necessary to concurrently manage both people and processes ethically.

❐

11

Ethical Marketing in Business

ETHICAL MARKETING AND ORGANISATIONAL FACTORS

Marketing ethics is the moral evaluation of marketing activities and decision as right or wrong. This behaviour is judged as ethical or unethical on the basis of principles of behaviour established by society, interest groups, organisation management, competitors and individuals. It is a function of mutual trust among individuals and organisations. An ethical violation makes contninuous trust in marketing exchanges difficult if not possible. There we can see the costs resulting from unethical behaviour in the form of reduced sales or loss of goodwill. Ethical considerations continue to capture the spotlight because of well-publicised cases of unthical practices in politics, sports, businesss and religion. Ethical behaviour often goes unnoticed while unthical conduct receives a great deal of media attention. Reporting on the thousands of ethical decisions individuals make daily is difficult if not possible.

The businesses do not understand how people make decisions when faced with ethical dilemmas. How people form thier ethical standards and what causes them to encourage in unethical behaviour may help business reduce the unethical activities. The following factors influence a person's ethical behaviour:

(1) **Moral Philosophies.** It is a set of principles which directs the right and moral way to behave. Normally the masses term all these principles their families, society and education imparted to them. Moral pholosphies can be divided into utilitarian and humanistic categories.

Utilitarian philosophy seeks the maximum satisfaction to the target number of individuals. A particular activity achieves the greatest good for the greatest number can be determined by a social cost benefit analysis in which the sum of all costs of a particular action is substracted from the sum of all the profits. If the result is positive, the action under consideratin is considered ethical and if the result finds negative form then this action is unethical.

On other side people and organisation follow the humanistic philosophy which is focused on individuals rights and values. If the potential of product poses harmful to any worker or customer then it is taken off the market.

(2) Organisational Factors. In the competitive world of business it is believed to get the secrets of competitors at any cost and rate. It is in fact unhealthy and therefore unethical profit. Many successful business houses loses tenders, contracts, offers done the leakage of inside information.

In order to get the work done, gifts and tips to the key executives be given. In this way the finance officer has to pass the payments to parties. Here the power might be misused by delay tactics to get the payment in time the business parties give annual gifts/festival valuable gifts.

To make favours is another unethical tactics which is rapidly increasing in the society. Favouring goes on the basis of cost, colour, creed, sex, blood relations, son/ daughter of social consideration. Such practice leads to break the norms set by the laws and in this way the high position officers use their powers and achieving result is not good.

(3) Marketing Environment. The comman ethical problem faced by the marketers is of conflict interest. Such conflict arises when an individual acts to further his/her own selfish concerns rather than the long term interest of the organisation. For example, when bribe is taken in the form of gifts, payments etc. obtain the new customers or to satisfy the customers; a conflict of interest occures. Communications in the form of advertising may pose ethical problems in the marketing environment. False advertising and personal selling tactics are unthical and create consumer dissatisfaction.

In the world of business corruption is practiced with invisible art of cunning. It is unfortunate that a business house supports and justifies such corrupt practices that it is a worldwide phenomenon. The practices of corruption make the environment of business unfit for society, it directly put impact on the mind of consumers and due to such practices the reputation of business is hurt when it is exposed among the masses. For a good marketing environment the interest of organisation should be kept in mind for the betterment. If the marketing environment is not fit than the whole show will be spoiled.

LEGAL ASPECT OF MARKETING

Marketing decision cannot be taken without taking into account the developments in political and legal field. The viability of business depends upon the ability with which it can meet the challenges out of political and legal enviornment of a country is influenced by political stability, organisation, government's intervention and constitutional provisions affecting business, foreign policy etc.

Following are the legal enactments of marketing environment:

* The Prevention of Food Adulteration Act of 1954.
* The Agricultural Produces (Grading and Marketing) Act of 1937.
* The Drugs Act of 1940 and the Drugs Control Act of 1954.
* The Standard Weights and Measures Act of 1956.
* The Monopoly and Restrictive Trade Practices (MRTP) Act of 1969.
* The Company's Act.
* The Essential Commodities Act of 1955.

* The Trade Marks and Merchandise Marks Act of 1958.
* The Display of Prices Order of 1963.
* The Packaged Commodities (Regulation) Order, 1975.
* The Consumer Protection Act of 1986.
* I.D.R. Act.
* Import and Export Trade Control Act.

Some of the important acts are disscussed in brief to highlight the Acts regarding marketing:

1. MRTP Act. The MRTP Commission, under this Act, is empowered to enquire into: *(i)* any restrictive trade practice upon receiving a complaint of facts from any trade of consumer's association or Central and State Governments or upon its own knowledge and information and *(ii)* any monopolistic trade practice upon a reference by the Central Government or upon its own information.

Twin objects of the Act are "*(1)* To ensure that the operation of the economic system does not result in the concentration and economic powers to the common detriment and *(2)* to prohibit such monopolistic and restrictive trade practices as are prejudicial to public interest."

After investigation the report of the MRTP Commission, the Central Government may make order for any of the following measures: *(a)* regulating the product, supply distribution or control of any goods or service and also fixing of price *(b)* prohibiting monopoly undertaking to continue any such act any more; *(c)* fixing the standards of the products; and *(d)* declaring unlawful any agreement which may lead to monopolistic practice, etc.

According to the Act, monopolistic trade practice means a trade practice which has, or is likely to have, the effect of:

- Maintaining prices at an unreasonable level by limiting, reducing or otherwise controlling the production, supply or distribution of goods of any description or supply of any services or in any other manner.
- Limiting technical development or capital investment to the common detriment or allowing the quality of any goods

produced, supplied or distributed, or any service rendered, in India to deteriorate.

- Unreasonably preventing or lessening competition in the production supply or distribution of any goods or in the supply of any services.
- Increasing unreasonably the cost relating to the production, supply or distribution of goods or performance of any service or increasing unreasonably the prices or the profits also treated as monopolistic trade practices.

2. Import and Exports Trade Control Act. This Act states about India's imports and exports policies. The import policy seeks to *(i)* maintain prices in the local markets by importing the necessary supplies; *(ii)* protect the domestic capital goods industries by charging higher taxes on imported capital goods; and *(iii)* ban imports of non-essential consumer goods, similarly, the export policy of India seeks to : *(i)* raise the export marketing of value-added items, *i.e.*, finished goods rather than raw materials of semi-finished products; *(ii)* fix a floor price for certain goods in which inter-se competition is severe among Indian manufacturer-exporters; and *(iii)* impose restriction on export trade when the supply in the domestic market is insufficient to meet the demand.

3. I.D.R. Act. The Central Government under this Act may secure equitable distribution and availability at fair prices of any article relatable to any scheduled industry and may provide for; *(i)* controlling the prices; *(ii)* regulating by licences, permits, or otherwise the distribution, transport, disposal, acquisition, possession, use or consumption of any such article; *(iii)* prohibiting the withholding from sale of goods ordinarily kept for sale; *(iv)* fixing by agreement a controlled price; *(v)* regulating or prohibiting any class of commercial or financial transactions which are likely to be detrimental to public; and *(vi)* requiring persons engaged in the distribution and trade and commerce to mark the goods with sale prices, etc.

The Development Councils constituted under this Act may suggest, among others, measures for: *(i)* better marketing, *(ii)* better distribution and sale of goods and *(iii)* standardisation of products which would be satisfactory to the consumer.

4. Essential Commodities Act. Under this Act, the Central Government may exercise the powers same as those stated under the I.D.R. Act above with respect to the control, production, supply and distribution of commodities and of trade and commerce, in certain specified essential commodities including coal, textiles, drugs, sugar and foodstuffs, etc., in the interests of the general public.

Legal environment is determined by the help of laws and court decisions which put pressure on the business and marketing managers.

MARKETING SERVICES

A service is any act or performance that one party can offer to another that is essentially intangible and does not result in the ownership of anything. Its production may or may not be tied up to a physical product. A service is an intangible product that provides benefits to consumers and often involves human or mechanical effort.

The term of service is rather general in concept, and it includes a wide variety of services. Services vary as to whether they are equipment based (automated car whases) or people based (windows washing). Some services require the client's presence. Service differ as to whether they meet a personal need (personal services) or a business need (business services).

There are the business and professional services such as advertising, marketing research, banking insurance, computer-programming, legal & medical advice. There are services which are provided by professionals but consumed for reasons not of business, rather for leisure, recreation, entertainment and fulfilment of other psychological and emotional needs such as education, fine arts etc.

Characteristics of Services

Services have five characteristics which affect the design of marketing programme:

(1) Intangibility. The primary characteristic that distinguishes services from other products is intangibility. Unlike physical products, they cannot be seen tasted, felt, heard or smelled before they are bought when you buy sugar, you can feel it, see it, touch it, smell it and see it. Teaching is a most intangible service. But by travelling in aeroplane has both tangible and intangible aspect *i.e.*, the benefit which we are deriving is a service and in a particular plane in which we fly has some tangible aspect. The goods & service continuum highlights the fate that most of the services are in reality a combination of both tangible & intangible aspects. There are only a few truly pure tangible products or pure intangible services.

(2) **Inseparability.** In case of 'products' or 'physical products', the activities of the production and distribution are separated from the act of consumption. Thus, a computer, chocolate, shoes and the like are produced in anticipation of demand and are sold as and when they are demanded. While on the other hand, in case of services, the production, the distribution and the consumption are taking place simultaneously. In most cases, the service cannot be performed unless the customer is present or drectly involved in the production process. Therefore, service cannot be separate from the person of firm providing it. A plumber has to be physically present to provide a service and alike. The service encounter cannot be completed successfully unless customers have the skills needed to participate in the transaction.

(3) **Heterogeneity.** Most services are performed by people, and people are not always consistent in their performance. This inconsistency or variation in performance is referred to as the heterogeneity of services. Performance may vary from one individual or service to another within the same organisation, or in the service one individual provides from day to day and from customer to customer. The doctor who gave you his complete attention in your last visit may behave a little differently the next time. Many people take their automobiles to a favorite mechanic at a certain service station because of his better service. But even a favourite mechanic may provide inferior service in the next visit.

Thus services are much more difficult to standardize than tangible goods.

(4) **Perishability.** Services can not be stored and therefore perishable in nature. A company selling goods would deal the problem through inventory control. But service not fully utilized represent a total loss. For example, empty seats in movie's theatre in one show and due to heavy rush many people returned in another show, heavily booking in trains in peak seasons and empty seats in other days shows fluctuating demand pattern which aggravates the perishabiliy characteristics of services.

(5) **Ownership.** When you buy a product you become its owner—be it a pencil, book, shirt, refrigerator or car. In the case of a service, you may pay for its use but you never own it. By buying a ticket you can see the evening film show in the local cinema theatre; by paying wages you can hire the service of a chauffeur who will drive your car; by paying the required charges. You can have a marketing research firm survey into the reasons for your product's poor sales performance, etc. In case of a service, the payment is not for purchase, but only for the use or access to or for hire of items or facilities.

A service is purchased for the benefits it provides. If we closely examine the reasons why products are purchased, we find that they are bought because they provide certain intangible benefits and satisfactions.

Developing Marketing Strategies for Services

Like marketer of tangible goods, service marketer must strive to satisfy consumers by developing a marketing-mix for the target market.

Product Strategy. The marketing of services can be success only if there is a proper match between the service product from the customer's view point and the supplier's view point. To have a proper match, as a marketer, it is essential to analyse the following services.

- the customer benefit concept
- the service concept
- the service offer
- the service forms and
- the service delivery system.

Promoton Strategy. Because services are intangible-dominant products and therefore difficult to advertise. That's why, advertising of services should emphasize tangible cues, or symbols of the services that are more easily perceived and understood by the consumers.

Pricing Strategy. The intangible nature of services makes establishing prices difficult.

Hotels & airlines offering lower rates in off-season and lower telephone charges for outstation calls after peak hours are examples of how pricing strategy can be used to offset the perishable characteristics of services. Higher the intangibility, more difficult to calculate cost, such as doctors', lawyers' fee when fees settled sometimes through negotiation. On the other hand, services like drycleaning based on tangible component, easier to calculate the cost as a unit basis and have a uniform price policy. The above pricing based on market-oriented pricing while bank charges, electricity & water charges, rail or air fare etc. either controlled by Govt. or industry associations and are cost-based pricing.

Distribution Stategy. Due to special features of services namely 'intangibility' and 'inseparability', they cannot be stored, transported, stocked and hence poses a distribution constraint since they are able to serve only a limited localised market. The other characteristic of services which affects the distribution strategy is the fixed location of services such as universities, restaurants and hospitals which necessitates the customer to go to the service location.

Other service industries make use of different types of marketing intermediaries. Travel agencies for instance, help facilitate exchange between consumers and airlines, hotels etc. ATMs serve as electronic intermediaries for financial services. Master cards and VISA credit cards have enabled banks to extend their credit services to consumers in widely dispersed geographic area.

INTERNATIONAL MARKETING

International Marketing grows and prospers because of certain economic and political factors. The existence of global marketing over many centuries justify its existence. Some of the industrially advanced nations enjoy huge production capacity and surplus of goods. National market becomes inadequate to them. They must export so that their economies develop and expand. The need for international marketing is universally accepted because it is beneficial to all the countries. More than ever before international marketing has become important, now, because fastest means of transport and communiation has well-linked all the countries. The following factors necessitate international marketing:

(i) **Rapid Industrialisation.** Countries are economically dependent on one another. Every country has to import certain goods and also to export so as to pay for imports. The third world countries are dependent on the western countries for superior technology to achieve faster economic growth. International marketing has become prominent because of international interdependenec and growing industrialisation.

(ii) **Cost Benefits.** Due to certain favourable factors, some countries can produce certain commodities with low cost of production. International marketing is favoured by all in order to enjoy the comparative cost benefits. International marketing becomes the only option to exchange goods and export such goods where the countries enjoy cost benefit. A country will import such goods which either it cannot produce or will produce at a higher cost.

(iii) **Raised Standard of Living.** There is consciousness all over the world and people desire to raise the standard of living through the consumption of best quality goods procured from nook or corner of the world. International marketing also mobilises foreign investments, superior technology and international understanding. The standard of living of the people can be raised only by enabling them to consume quality products at reasonable prices, no matter from where they are procured. Even perishable goods are marketed within minimum possible time due to well-organised network of transport and communiation.

(iv) **Fulfils Economic Needs.** The increase in the rate of population growth has brought pressure on the Government to fulfil economic needs of growing number of its people. In order to provide basic amenities and luxuries to the increasing population imports and exports become obligatory. The growth of international trade is certainly because of increasing world population.

(v) **Cultural Exchanges.** Peaceful co-existence to a very great extent depends on economic, social and cultural exchanges. International relations can improve when people move to different countries on goodwill visits. Cultural differences separate the countries from one another. This gap can be well connected through international trade and exchange of culture.

(vi) **Maintaining International Prices.** It is not possible that varying prices will prevail in international marketing for long. Various countries market their goods at competitive rates. The comparative cost benefits enjoyed by one country in a particular item can be shared by other countries.

(vii) **Helps both Developed and Developing Countries.** International marketing is also required to narrow the gulf between advanced countries and less developed or developing countries. Even advanced nations must export their surplus so that under-developed countries can obtain their requirements. In turn, advanced countries must provide concessional terms so that developing countries have no option but to import superior technical known-how from developed countries. It is through international marketing that industrially advanced nations provide assistance to developing countries in their struggle towards economic growth. International marketing improves economic relations and reduces the chances of international conflicts.

Advantages and Benefits of International Marketing

International Marketing has number of advantages. Some of these briefly summarised below:

(i) Availability of goods which cannot be produced in the home country due to geographical factors and other natural limitations.

(ii) Proision of better standard of living to citizens by providing them with wide variety of goods and services.

(iii) Rational allocation of resources and the best use of the resources available at the international level.

(iv) Industrial development of the country, provision of massive employment opportunities to the people and full utilisation of natural resources available.

(v) Benefits of comparative cost difference as suggested in the theory of comparative costs. The benefits of division of labour and specialisation at the international level are also available through international marketing.

(vi) Interantional economic, political and cultural co-operation and world peace.

(vii) Social and cultral exchanges between different countries of the world.

(viii) Rapid expansion of tertiary sector which includes transport, insurance and shipping.

(ix) Special benefits during the period of emergency like famines and floods.

(x) Removal of deficit in the balance of trade and payments of participating countries through export promotion and import subsitution.

(xi) Effective utilisation of surpluse domestic production, introduction of new varieties of goods, improvement in the quality of production and promotion of mutual co-operation among countries.

(xii) Easy availability of foreign exchange for import of capital goods, modern technology and other essential requirements.

It may be noted that the above mentioned advantages or benefits are available only when international marketing is reasonably free from various restrictons and regulations. Unfortunately, almost all countries have imposed various restrictions on the free movement of goods. Such commercial restrictions are undesirable as they restrict the scope of free and fair international marketing.

PROBLEMS FACED BY INTERNATIONAL MARKETS

International marketing is a complex, difficult and intricate process in comparison to domestic marketing. There are differences due to different political entities, tariff, policies, restrictions, monetary system and other barriers.

The complexities caused by many factors, create following problems before the international marketing:

(i) **Trade Pattern Variations.** When one enters the international market, he has to deal with the existing trade patterns among the various countries of the world. The policies of the different countries, that govern their import and export should also be considered. These patterns, obviously impose restrictions on the international trade and the task of the international marketer becomes that of solving the problems through experience and expertise for attainment of the objectives in the best interest of the firm as well as its country.

(ii) **Different Regulatory Measures.** Now a days, every country wants that exports should be more than the import to maintain a favourable balance of payments. Furthermore, the trade patterns of a country are designed to serve the national purpose of achieving better trade position and in this it wants to export manufactured goods, surplus natural resources, agricultural commodities and avoids the import of such commodities it can be made available in the domestic market by the domestic manufacturers. This imposes certain restrictions on the trade with other countries. For this various barriers, as tariff (custom duties), quota restrictions. foreign exchange restrictions, technological regulation, state trading, preferential regulations, are brought into operation. All these present sever problems before the few and unrestricted flow of international trade.

(iii) **Unbalanced Development of Developing Countries.** There is a vast difference between the level of technological advancement and the developing economics. In contrast to the developing economies developed countries, have sophisticated technology capable of exploiting raw-materials and other resources and converting these into finished products. Whereas, the developing economies depend upon their old and outdated techniques of production, incapable of locating and exploiting all the economic resources available in the country. Such countries face problems due to their lopsided development and what actually happens is that, these countries export raw materials in the international market, which are converted into finished products by the developed economies and then again sold to the developing economies. The developed economies sell these commodities at the price which is always higher than their intrinsic value. A firm belonging to an under-developed economy suffers from this drawback of lopsided development.

(iv) **Economic Groupings of International Level.** There is a continuous and rising tendency among the nations to form unions at the international level, with the view of safeguarding their economic interests. Thus, the member countries of groups are in a better position than any other individual non-member economy. The union like ASEAN,

COMECON, EEC etc are some, which have in built growth and free flow of international trade in the contemporary world.

(v) **National Development Policy.** Every country aspires to attain self-sufficiency by exploiting its raw-material and other resources to the optimum. This aspiraton of self-sufficiency in industrial development, has resulted into the creation of many trade barriers on the free flow of international trade. Other countries must consider their trade barrier while framing their strategy. A country aspiring rapid development, implements strategy of importing capital goods and improves restrictions on the imports of less significant consumer goods to avoid, as much as it can, the deficits in trade.

(vi) **Procedural Complexities.** There is no common procedure relating to import and export, and every country has its own procedures, documents and practices relating to international trade. These are complex and difficult essentialities of international marketing these days, which pose, problems before the international marketing.

In addition to these problems, there are some more problems like, the fact that still, the business and industry have not fully recognised the value and importance of export trade. Again there are problems caused by inflation, high prices as well as black marketing. In the recent years the management of our national economy has been very bad to the extent that it has failed to supply for its own needs.

FACTORS AFFECT THE ENVIRONMENT OF INTERNATIONAL MARKETING

There is difference between various international markets as it differs from the domestic markets. The diversity in the environments of these factors are to be considered before planning any strategy of international marketing.

Follwing are the factors that act as determinants of the international marketing policies:

(I) Cultural Factors

Social values become the distinguishing factor between domestic and international marketing. Before stepping in the international market in any way, it is essential to understand the cultural dynamics of these foreign markets. The marketer must consider the cultural factors of the country in which it wants to enter in the international marketing. Culture has a broad meaning. According to M.J. Herks Kovits, "culture may be viewed as the sum total of man's knowledge, beliefs, arts, morals, loves, customes and any other capabilities and habits acquired by man as a member of society". To be more precise, culture is the, "distinct, way of life of a group of people, their complete design for living". Man has tried to solve the problems by borrowing from other cultures the various alternatives and by adopting it according to his environment and what is more appropriate for his society.

The borrowing by one society from another society is a process which is systematic and unending. It rather goes on inter-stingly. The adoption of a borrowed system or techniques is restricted to the environment of the society which is borrowing. This is why one product which is radically acceptable by one society is not liked by another society. In the like manner, a technique of selling workable in one society may not be successfull in another society. These differences occur because of differences in the way of living, customs, habits, beliefs, morals etc.

The existence of subculture *i.e.*, a culture within a nation's culture, is again a matter that attracts serious thought. Sub-culture arises due to differences existing within a culture. For instance in India, there is a distinction between the northern and the southern part of the country. Sub-cultures, may exist in the geo-political boundaries and sometimes they spread across all the political boundaries. For example, Bangladesh is very much like the West Bengal in India, as far as the cultural similarities are concerned. For the point of view of international marketing these differences between cultures and sub-customs, are very important because of their influence on the marketng plan as well as on the decisions about the selection of these markets. The demand for a product, influenced by cultural factors, must be ascertained to achieve success in the field of international marketing.

A marketer willing to enter an international market, must study following aspects of cultural background of a foreign market.

(a) **Material Culture.** This includes technology and economic aspects of that country.

(b) **Social Institutions.** This includes the consideration of social organisation, education system, and political system of the foreign country. The belief and family system and its kinds is also to be considered.

In additional to these, the Aesthetic part of culture including graphic and plastic art, folk lore, folkways and mores, music, drama, dance, etc. are also the aspect to be given consideration. And the last but not the least, is the language of the foriegn market.

Regarding culture, the changes that often take place in every society from time to time must also be considered as these caste effective impact on various aspects of peoples life. A firm desirous of entering international market must consider these factors and it should also evaluate the degree of influence and involvement of these factors, on the decision of international marketing policies.

There exists a feature of resistance of the cultural change. This reflects a certain degree of surprise on and apprehension about new products, ideas, and techniques. The degree and extent of this resistance differ from economy to economy. It has also been noticed that changes affecting the very basic structure of the culture face maximum resistence.

There is also a tendency, commonly present in all economies, to regard foreign goods as the things of social status. One more reason for the indication towards foreign products is the inferior nature of the domestic products, this feature is more common to the developing economies.

Thus for a successful international marketing, proper understanding of the culture is essential.

(II) Political Considerations

Political environment is another factor affecting the foreign market. It is necessary for an international marketer to assess the political environment since this affect has success as well as existence in such markets.

The study and assessment of the political environment include the following:

(a) **Political Systems.** The type of government *i.e.*, whether it is Socialistic, Capitalistic, Democratic etc must be analysed, since the philosophy of the government is reflected in its policies.

(b) **Philosophy of the Government.** It is essential to study government's philosophy in particular about, policy towards private sector and foreign business. Generally, the governments of the target foreign countries, specify their priority areas in which foreign business is encouraged. Many rules exist in the different countries. For example in india Foreign Exchange Regulation Act 1973, specifies guidelines for foreign private investment.

Infact, the government's philosophy towards foreign capital goes under change with the change of the party in power at a given period of time. From all this view points, it is essential for an international marketer, to assess the philosophy of the government in power, as well as the long run political prospectives.

(c) **Permanency and Stability of the Policy of the Government.** It is necessary to examine the extent of permanency and stability of government policy of the target foreign market. The marketer must always be careful about such changes in policy that lead to its destabilisation. It also involves the assessment of the long-run predicability of the governments policy.

The policy of a government in the field of trade may be rendered unstable, because of any one of the following factors:

(i) Change in Governments.

(ii) Growing aspirations of nationalism.

(iii) Shifting of political parties reaching the government at different levels. Due to certain causes, the products become politically vulnerable.

The attempt of the international marketer should be to minimise it.

(III) Economic Factors

An international markerter should assess the level of economic development of the concerned country. Since the level of development of the countries is not the same, so marketer must act according to making his best contribution to the economic development. It is also essential to assess the economic aspirations of the concerned countries. The factor of 'market potential' should always be kept in mind while studying the levels of economic development of a country.

A marketer should study following indications, in regard:

(a) Gross National Product.

(b) Per Capita Income.

(c) Purchasing power of the consumers.

(d) Rate of economic growth.

(e) Level and degree of industrialisation.

(f) The form of marketing channels and related infrastructure.

These factors play tremendous role in chalking out the marketing strategy of the firm deciding to enter the international marketing arena.

In addition to these factors, an interantional marketer should also study the policies, programmes and objectives of the international economic institutions like GATT, UNCTAD, UNIDO, IMF, World Bank, Asian Development Bank etc.

GREEN MARKETING

The firms which are accepting the societal marketing concept which do not harm the environment is called or considered Green Marketing. It involves the developing products and packages which are less harmful for the environment. It includes many areas which control the pollution for example. Procter and Gamble Company are producing the containers which are less harmful for our environment. In this way green marketing will provide benefit from better relations with consumers, suppliers, regulators and other firms in Industry. For successful green marketing programme a company must have the commitment of top management as well as in an internal environment that encourages employees to act as environmentalist. Many companies have established new positions such as vice president of environment, health and safety. Others reward employees for reducing waste or developing such kinds of products which are not much harmful for the environment. In this rapid growing industries era the pollution became a major challenge for us. Due to the mass production, the industries are demanded, one side we have benefits but other side we have to face the monster of pollution. The industries and top management are trying their best by acheiving new avenues in their field to put less harm by their industries. As individuals become more committed to the environment, green product will gain a competitive edge. But because environmental claims have to be used to mislead consumers, some firms find it difficult to successfully launch the green marketing programme. Successful green marketing requires being as precise as possible to enable consumers to understand the claims made in the message. As a result of all this same firms have retreated from making environmental claims about their products, even though they continue to develop products and packages that are good up to some extent for the environment. Pricing is also a big concern; since green products typically cost more than competing brands. Consumers prefer green products when they are readily available and their price and quality are similar to that of products.

Green Consumerism

The products demanding immediate eco-marketing are toilet soap, textiles, packages, paper, paints pesticides, drugs etc. These consumer goods with ecomark labels can spur the demand for Green Consumerism which is the prime aim of Ecomark Scheme. After that we can take other consumer goods like lubricating oil, petrol, wood substitutes, plastics, cosmatics, batteries, agricultural products etc. to get the ecomark stamp. The successful operation of the ecomark rests on the following assumptions:

(1) The consumers are environmentally conscious and are writing to buy them, and they are ready to exercise a choice if alternatives are available.

(2) Many products which can be demonstrated to be environment friendly and can be ecomarked.

(3) The manufacturers are also having environmental awarness and show their keen interest in the ecomark.

The Central Pollution Cotnrol Board of India is the final authority to implement ecomark scheme on voluntary basis. For example we do not have even soaps/detergents (not using phosphates) to be sold under ecomark stamp.

Implications for Marketers of Green Marketing

The various issues involved in green marketing may eventually imply a change in the prevailing quality of living standard and in the basics of consumer behaviour. Stocks, hosiery and clothing will for example be of higher quality, last longer and not need daring or mending too often ! But the customer will pay more for convenience, reflecting the value of the time that this convenience affords him or her. He or She may consume more quality but less quantity.

Forecasters suggest that consumers may return to demanding product attributes favouring quality, reliability, durability and safety. This change in behaviour reflects the beginning of a rejection of the "throw away society". The concept of the throwaway society is increasingly seen as untenable and unsustainable.

Sustainability is seen as a key issue within green marketing. A fundamental question is whether the marketing process is environmentally sustainable, or does it exploit that environment on an irrecoverable basis? For instance:

(a) Tropical deforestation, short term ranching, soil erosion, flooding and desertification; Or

(b) The planting of tropical or temperate hardwoods; the use of properly managed hardwood forests for furniture and construction materials (etc.); proper replanting to maintain eclogy and habitat.

The issue of sustainability can be placed within the context of consumption. Sustainability may become a key benefit required with the attribute set considered appropriate for any partiular usage requirement.

Some Key Principles for 1990's Green Consumer

Given the rapidly increasing awareness on the part of the general public of the importance and urgency of the green issues summarised above, Elkington and Hailes identify some key principles for the 1990's green consumer. These are that in general, the Green Consumer should avoid products (or services) which are likely to:

- endanger the health either of the consumer or of others;
- cause significant damage to the environment during manufacture, use or disposal;
- consume a disproportionate amount of energy during manufacture, use or disposal;
- cause unnecessary waste, whether because of over-packaging, an unduly short useful life or because they are not suitable to reuse or recycle;
- use materials derived from threatened species or from threatened environments;
- involve the unnecesary use of, or cruelty to animals, whether this be for toxicity testing or other purposes;
- adversely affect other countries, particularly in the Third World.
- The more widely these basic principles are promoted and understood by the general public as consumers, the greater will be the effect on consumer behaviour, and the greater

the resulting impact on the product-marketing strategies pursued by suppliers to consumers and industrial markets.

Environment consciousness, and green consumer behaviour are likely to diffuse through consumer, then industrial markets in the west at an increasing rate showing an increasingly potent "casade effect". This increasing public awareness and propensity to act in an environmentally conscious manner will simply reflect the wider socio-cultural and political climate as it develops in response to a (potentially) deteriorating environmental context, over-population (etc.).

CYBER MARKETING

It is always advisable that before beginning a market campaign we have to develop a market plan. If the process is adopted accordingly the positive marketing results can be obtained. In this respect cyber marketing is not different than the conventional media. Normally people are very busy trying to get a product out of the door and to devote enough time for planning. This side cyber marketing is changing rapidly and it is really very hard to plan when our marketing vehicle moves so much. First of all the first step is to quickly develop a cyber marketing plan. We can have the information from soap to nuts but it is useful only when we write a comprehensive plan.

To get the objectives of cyber marketing we have to find out what we want to have online. Will you use cyberspace to. Other functions instead of or in addition to try to generate sales such as investor relations, customer service or recruiting new employees. Do you want to market to existing customers; prospects or both. When you answer the above question, you will have your cyber marketing objectives. These objectives should explain which parts of cyber space you use and which tactics are used by you. This is totally electronic/digital marketing which can be done only by educated customers (having the knowledge of computers or cybershops).

Following are some Marketing outline for the development of Cyber Marketing Plan:

(1) Successful cyber-Marketing sites

(2) Cyber marketing information resources

(3) Internet Market research

(4) Internet News Resources

(5) Internet Advertising

(6) Searchable Archieves

(7) Tracking New Commercial Sites

(8) Internet Commerce Organisations

(9) Internet People Demographics

(10) Promoting your electronic storefront

(11) Electronic Payment Systems

(12) Internet Market Makers

(13) Online Shopping & Electronic Commerce

(14) Internet computer Demographics.

No good plan goes without a time line. Different people may have different ideas about how detailed these should be. For example dates for content completion promotion launches, online seminars etc. From the list of your milestones, you can be as detailed with dates and events as you feel it necessary.

After deciding where is cyber space you want to set up shop, determine what kind of information or content will help you achieve your objectives. The technical design and limitations of some parts of cyberspace will determine how your content will look, and so be sure you become familiar with the different elements of cyberspace. What information can you give them about your product or company that they can't get in traditional marketing channels. What information will you provide that will be more reliable to people than typical ads and brouchers. What content can you provide that is not related to your product, you will draw people to your areas. After that decide what you want, who will be responsible for content and in appropriate proportion. Will it be Marketing Sales or ad agency? Can they deliver the materials you need to change you online areas regularly to build repeat traffic? will customer Service or Human Resources develop content? How many people will need to oversee content development and managing your online areas? What outside resources will you need, such as internet providers, website designers writers etc?

The above mentioned tips for cyber marketing plan are dependent for successful implementation of cyber space. This marketing can bedone by the educated customers only. It is proved very costly and beyond the reach of poor customers.

There are seven aspects of traditional marketing that can be effected by cyberspace. Following aspects are considered as tactics for cyber marketing.

1. **Educating Your Market.** It includes giving customers and prospects an in-depth understanding of your product or service, your company or your industry. Many people are more likely to buy a product when they fully understand how it works. This works whether you sell industrial plastics or cakes which are prepared according to an "old family recipe."
2. **Public Relations.** There is a multiple of magazines and newspapers that are publishing online. Work with both the journalists who use cyberspace, and the online publications to get coverage for your company.
3. **Direct Response Promotions.** This may seem like splitting hairs, but there is a difference between promotions that help build brand awareness or loyalty, and promotions that induce people to take a specific action, and preferably right now (buy a product, pick up literature). You may have a greater need for direct response promotions to help you rise above the resulting marketing noise level.
4. **Research and Product Development.** One of the most overlooked benefits of cyberspace is its research potential. Feedback can make the biggest difference in a company's

ability to be profitable. This can be feedback from customers, the market in general, others in your industry, and even your competitiors. Cyberspace can deliver more feedback than you know what to do with.

5. **Product Demonstration and Distribution.** This is an effective way to build people's comfort levels so they'll be more inclined to buy your products or services. Distribution goes hand in hand with demonstrating products because, if you can demonstrate your wares online, prospects should be able to receive them right then when they're highly motivated to buy. It you can't physically deliver products on the Net, at least have a system in place so they can place an order and receive confirmation that the order has shipped.

6. **Service and Support.** If you decide to provide customer service and support online, you should develop tactics to make this happen. You may want to consider activities such as special offers to shift customers from telephone to online support, or incentive programs for customers who regularly volunteer to help others online.

   When developing tactics in this area, consider support for people other than customers. For example, you can support your field sales people or resellers and make sales presentations casier and more effective. Rather than lug around tons of marketing materials, sales people can modem into your online area during a presentation to access the data they need.

7. **Building Brand Awareness and Loyalty.** You want to build a community of customers who are loyal to your product (brand). Besides customers, you want as many surfers as possible to know what your product and company have to offer.

   Your brand marketing tactics may consist of promotions and creative sponsorships, but they can also include aggressive hyperlinking of your Internet information with other sites.

RELATIONSHIP MARKETING

Relationship marketing is the practice of building long-term satisfying relations with key parties-customers, suppliers, distributors—in order to retain their long-term preference and business. Smart marketers try to build up long-term, trusting, "win-win" relationship with valued customers, distributors, dealers, and suppliers. They accomplish this by promising and delivering high quality, good service, and fair prices to the other parties over time. Relationship marketing results in strong economic, technical, and social ties among the parties. It also cuts down on transaction costs and time. In the most successful cases, transactions move from being negotiated each time to being a matter of routine.

The ultimate outcome of relationship marketing is the building of a unique company asset called a marketing network. A marketing network consists of the company and all of its supporting stakeholders: customers, employees, suppliers, distributors, retailers, ad agencies, university scientists, and others with whom it has built mutually profitable business relationships. Increasingly, competition is not between companies but rather between whole networks, with the prize giving to the company that has built the better network. The operating principle is simple. Build a good network of relationships with key stakeholders, and profits will follow.

The basic purpose of marketing is customers delight with permanent customers for the business. In other words, the old customers should repeat orders with the firm. This requires building strong relationship between the seller and the buyer. Philips Kotler has coined the term 'relationship marketing' to signify the need of building good rapport between the business and its customers. The marketer who knows how to build and manage strong relationship with the key customers can secure plenty of future sales from such customers.

Relationship marketing is most appropriate with those customers who can influence the company's future to a great extent. For instance, a small number of customers may, account for 80 per cent of the company's sales. Sales persons working with such customers should build strong relationships by offering personalised attention and service through increased social contacts. Relationship marketing shall pay an important role in future.

Relationship marketing involves the following steps:

1. Identification of key customers who will influence the firm's future prospects.
2. Assignment of a relationship manager to each key customer.
3. Preparation of detailed job descriptions for all relationship managers.
4. Development of annual customer relationship plans.
5. Co-ordination and review of the performance of relationship managers.

Key Principles of Relationship Marketing

To understand customer relationship marketing, we must first examine the process involved in attracting and keeping customers. Figure shows the main steps in the customer-development process. The starting point is suspects, everyone who might conceivably buy the product or service. The company looks hard at the suspects to determine who are the most likely prospects—the people who have a strong potential interest in the product and the ability to pay for it. Disqualified prospects are those whom the company rejects because they have poor credit or would be unprofitable. The company hopes to convert many of its qualified prospects into first-time customers, and then convert those satisfied first-time customers into repeat customers. Both first-time and repeat customers may continue to buy from competitors as well. The company then acts to convert repeat customers into clients—people who buy only from the company in the relevant product categories. The next challenge is to turn clients into advocates, customers who praise the company and encourage others to buy from it. The ultimate challenge is to turn advocates into partners, who the customer and the company work actively together. At the same time, it must be recognized that some customers will inevitably become inactive or drop out, for reasons of bankruptcy, moves to other locations, dissatisfaction, and so on. The company's challenge is to reactivate dissatisfied customers through customer win-back strategies. It is often easier to reattract ex-customers than to find new ones.

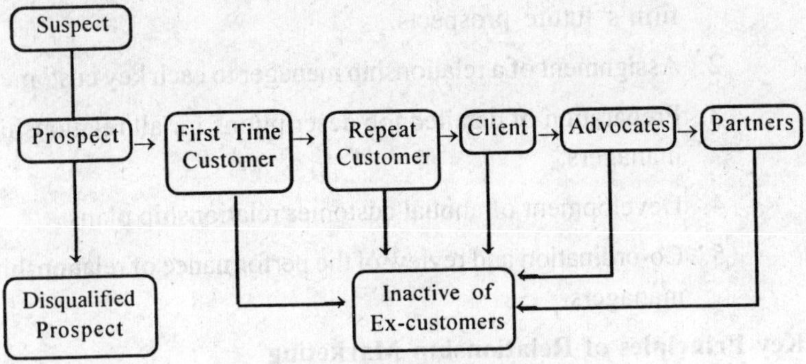

Fig. The customer-Development Process

Source : Philip Kotler, Marketing Management

Developing more loyal customers increases the company's revenue. However, the company has to spend more to build greater customer loyalty. Development of customer loyalty will be more profitable in some business than in others. How much should a company invest in customer-relationship building, so that the costs do not exceed the gains? We need to distinguish five different levels of company investment in customer-relationship building:

(1) **Basic Marketing.** The salesperson simply sells the product.

(2) **Reactive Marketing.** The salesperson sells the product and encourages the customers to call if he or she has any questions, comments, or complaints.

(3) **Accountable Marketing.** The salesperson phones the customer a short time after the sale to check whether the product is meeting the customer's expectations. The salesperson also asks the customer for any product or service improvement suggestions and any specific disapportionments. This information helps the company continuously improve its performance.

(4) **Proactive Marketing.** The company salesperson contacts the customer from time to time with suggestions about improved product uses or helpful new products. (Kraft U.S.A.'s sales reps used to limit their customer efforts to devising promotions in supermarkets, now they are more proactive, offering research and tips for improving a store's profits.)

(5) **Partnership Marketing.** The company works continuously with the customer to discover ways to effect customer savings or help the customer perform better. (General Electric has stationed some of its engineers full time at Paraxair, Inc. to help boost Praxair's productivity.)

❏

12

Case Study Methodology of Business Ethos

Work on individual cases has a long history in the academic study of management and business. However, the methodology behind such work remains opaque. The general aims have always been as transparent as they are laudable: to clarify the use of theoretical techniques by deploying them in 'real life' situations (or at least stimulations thereof). But, the details of just how the process of clarification is supposed to work seem never to have been explicitly mapped out.

Perhaps this simply signals a deliberate pedagogical ploy. After all, an important goal of the learning procedure in business studies of all kinds that are intended to be preparatory for life in the business world is to be able to solve problems for oneself without relying on any rigid, preconceived plan. On that rather charitable understanding of case study work, the undifferentiated material that makes up a typical case study package contains just the kind of haphazard mix of historical data, statistics, value judgements and irrelevancies that business life itself contains. Hence, such cases provide a useful pragmatic test of prospective business acumen. All this may very well be true, and things may pan out perfectly for most practical purposes in areas such as business strategy or financial planning. But in business ethics, something a bit more systematic is required. In this sphere, it is vital to keep a much sharper distinction between:

(A) The kind of 'hands-on' knowledge that would be professional needs to acquire and

(B) The reasoned explanation and justification of business activities.

If the end results are not to be arbitrary, both the analysis of pre-packaged case study material and the initial gathering, preparation and presentation of such material need some preliminary guidance.

In what follows, certain provisional guidelines are proposed that I have found useful in coaching business ethos students for their own investigations of case study material. The ten guidelines have stood the test of time at two universities in the UK (East Anglia and Reading). However, the qualification 'provisional' should not be taken lightly—these suggestions are not intended to provide a methodological analogue of the Ten Commandments!

The guidelines are pragmatically strudy, but theoretically unsophisticated. They may not all apply to good effect in all cases, and they can certainly be supplemented, modified or substantially improved. Perhaps they should best be thought of as constituting a rudimentary 'checklist' to help counter the lack of objective direction that can otherwise creep into case study work in business ethics.

THE GUIDELINES

(1) Classification. A natural first step in either constructing or analysing case study material is to determine what kind of case is involved. The inchoate state of case study methodology in management and business studies is evidenced by the lack of even the most basic taxonomy of cases. There are cases in finance, cases in strategy, and so on, but not much more in terms of subject specific categorisation. In business ethos, a straightforward, threefold classification springs to mind:

(i) Factual cases (which purport to covert real events in the actual Business world).

(ii) Mixed cases (which combine facts about what actually happened with say speculation about either what might have happened or what might be going to happen).

(iii) Fictional cases (which invoke imaginary events).

(2) Aims and Issues. It is important to determine what the goals of a case study are. These should be identified as explicitly as possible so that the case can at least be assessed on its own terms; does it achieve what it sets out to achieve? It is equally important to pin down the moral issues raised by the case study. Since cases can be extremely complex, it is often necessary to be self-consciously selective at this stage: what are the main issues here? Any such selection and/ or interpretation of the issues should be clearly expressed.

(3) The Relevant Facts. If the case study has a factual component then only the facts that are strictly relevant to the 'aims and issues' identified in (2) should be called upon. When presenting a case study, these facts should be stated as clearly and concisely as possible, and in a manner which makes their relevance obvious. When analysing a pre-prepared case study, the irrelevant facts should be culled-but any dependence on irrelevancies should be noted when later assessing the consclusions of the case study.

(4) Selection Principles. The principle behind the selection of the initial facts should be clearly identifiable so that the case study can be checked for verification purposes by others (*i.e.*, the reader needs to know how the facts were obtained).

(5) Options. The options regarding the issues at stake should be reviewed (*e.g.*, what could the company concerned actually do about the ethically problematic circumstances it finds itself in?). These options may need to be narrowed down according to criteria of relevance, practically and so on. If such criteria are brought into play, they need to be made explicit.

(6) Completion Status. It should be established whether the facts are 'complete', and if they are not complete, an explanation should be forthcoming as to the effect this is likely to have on the case study's overall conclusions: are they rendered provisional (because further facts could falsify their claims)?

(7) The Ethical Option. What is the ethically preferable option in the circumstances depicted by the case study material? What, should be done morally speaking?

(8) Justification. The ethically preferable option should be defended: arguments should be produced to show why its recommendations are credible. Here it may be appropriate to draw on the resources of standard moral theories (*e.g.*, the 'option' might be defended on Utilitarian grounds). If such theories are invoked then their authority in the circumstances should be explained rather than simply assumed.

(9) Comparisons. When appropriate, the action that was actually taken should be compared with the ethically commended action (*e.g.*, in what way, if any, did the company involved fall short of the ethically preferable solution to the problems it faced?).

(10) Review. Finally the whole case study should be reviewed. What did it achieve? What conclusions can be drawn from it? Does the case study warrant any general conclusions (*i.e.*, conclusions which go beyond the specific circumstances of the case)?

The Case Method: a Different Style of Learning

"You can lead a person to the university," someone once quipped, "but you can't make him think." What too often passes for learning is the repetition of facts by students during standardised exams. The case method, however, does not allow a student the luxury of memorising a body of accepted wisdom. Rather it forces the student to confront a set of facts that demands analysis and these facts the student soon discovers are not understood by the application of memorized truths.

Thus, a philosophy of education undergirds the case methods namely, that people must be taught to think well in the presence of new situations and to arrive at reasoned courses of action. In this way the method emphasizes judgement as much as understanding. Moreover, it attempts to develop skills of judgement that can be applied to situations in the real world. Although, it varies from practitioner to practitioner, the case method may be defined as a method of instruction that confronts students with descriptions of realistic human events and then requires the students to analyze, evaluate and make recommendations about those events.

What is known today as the case method began at Harvard University in 1908 with the opening of the new business school. The business school's first catalog stated that the problem method would be utilized as far as practicable. After years of struggle and experimentation, the case method reached maturity at Harvard from 1919 to 1942 under the encouragement of the dean of the business school, Wallace Donham. It was during these years that the method became the trademark of the Harvard Business School, a position it retains to this day.

The Role of the Instructor

Just as there is no such thing as a typical case, there is no such thing as a "typical" case-method teaching style. Each instructor develops his or her own questions, responses, and style. Certain pedagogical virtues, however, are obvious, such as approachability, enthusiasm, and articulateness.

The responsibilities of the instructor using a case method approach have been summed up as follows:

1. Assign cases for discussion.
2. Act as a responsible member of the group delegated to provoke argumentative thinking.
3. Guide discussions through remarks and questions toward points of major importance.
4. Take a final position on the viewpoints at the end of the discussion if the instructor chooses.

Sometimes an instructor has a remarkable teaching experience in which it is necessary only to ask an opening question—"Mr. Y. would you begin our discussion?"—and the class is off and running. More frequently the instructor must help the discussion through contributions of his or her own. To accomplish this, the instructor may

1. Ask further questions.
2. Restate and reconstruct what has been said.

3. Voice his or her own opinions and draw upon his or her knowledge of fact.

To open a discussion, an instructor may ask such questions as:

Do you see a problem in this case? If so, what is it?

Would someone volunteer to give us a brief sketch of the facts in the case? (Or simply) What's happening in this case?

Once the discussion is underway, the instructor may invite a student to play the part of one of the managers who has a central role in the case. Thus, the instructor might ask, "What would you do if you were Mr. Jones?" Indeed unless an instructor pushes a student to speak in terms of decisions, the advantage of the case method may be undercut as the discussion regresses into a fragmented series of general observations.

Discussion leader frequently summarize or attempt to interpret a student's remark. Doing so has a double advantage: It helps to confirm what the student actually meant, and it helps to ensure that other students interpreted the remark correctly. In a surprisingly large number of cases the student will want to qualify a remarka once it has been interpreted by the instructor. This has the welcome consequence of encouraging the student to reflect upon both the nature of the view being expressed and the reasons for it.

Professor Andrews has summarized the role of the instructor as follows:

> The instructor provides the impromptu services which any group discussion requires. He keeps the proceedings orderly. He should be able to ask questions which advance group thinking and at the same time reveal the relevance of talk that has gone before.... He needs the sense of timing which tells him that a discussion is not moving fast enough to make good use of available time or is racing away from the comprehension of half the class He exercises control over an essentially "undirected" activity, but at the same time he keeps out of the way Since unpredictable developments

> always distinguish real learning, he examines his class rather than his subject. His workshop is not the study but the classroom He must himself be a student.

An instructor may block a direct question from a student. When a student asks a specific question about the material, the instructor may decide that to answer the question would stiffle the thinking of other students. Hence, the instructor may reply by saying "Well, what does the class think?" or "My opinionis X, but is that really the right opinion?" Here the attempt is to turn the question into a catalyst rather than a retardant of the ongoing discussion.

The following are sample questions asked by case method instructors:

Where does this idea lead?

You said A May I add B?

Do others disagree?

Do you mean A?

Do you have more to say about B?

Do you think that is true in all cases?

How does that apply to the situation in the case?

Is your point related to Mr. B's?

What does that have to do with the bigger question?

An instructor can do more than ask questions. He or she can identify unstated assumptions that one of the participants is making and hold them up to the class for inspection. Or if a discussion is really dragging, the instructor may frankly ask the class what's wrong and attempt to generate discussion about the process of the discussion itself. (Sometimes this will have surprising results). Blackboards can be used to list options, relevant facts, pros and cons, and assumptions.

When a discussion is well under way, it is not unusual for an instructor to retire to an inconspicuous place and simply observe.

The Role of the Student

In the case method, the active cooperation of the student is essential. Previous schooling habituates a student to the role of receiver. In the case method, this previous schooling must be undone; the student must learn the habit of being active, of being a force in the teaching process. Hence, the student must master a number of skills. First he or she must learn to synthesize material on his or her own. Although infrequently an instructor's summary of the main lines of the preceding discussion will help the student to integrate important aspects of the discussion, ordinarily the act of synthesis must be undertaken by the student. Equally important, the student must learn to separate irrelevant from relevant information. Finally, the student must invest sufficient time in preparing a case to make the discussion productive. With other methods, a failure to prepare is problematic; with the case method, it is disastrous.

Sometimes students benefit from discussing a case in a small, preclass group. In such a group they often discover crucial items around which ordinary group discussions will turn; moreover they gain experience in the presentation of ideas.

Discouragement is routine when students begin the case method. They jump to the conclusion that they are making no progress because they are accustomed to defining "progress". After discussing the first case or two, they recognize that not all issues have been resolved and may be left with a sense of incompleteness like hearing a piece of music with no resolving chord. Gradually, however, they will experience a growing confidence in their ability to analyze complex case materials and in turn a growing conviction of the value of the case method. At this stage it is not uncommon for the original skepticism to turn to an uncritical endorsement of the method.

CASE STUDIES IN BUSINESS ETHOS

1. The Use of Cases in the Study of Business Ethos. Business and management education has the purpose of improving business practice. Many other claims are made for it but none is as intuitively or philosophically appealing as this. Employers and practitioners may sometimes take the view that business and management education exists to serve their needs for competent employees who can carry out the tasks necessary for successful operation. Therefore, education should aim to provide people with the requisite skills and appropriate attitudes as well as knowledge of business practice.

We take neither of these positions. Our view is that both business education and business practice are enriched by the synergy of theory and practice. The best practice is theoretically informed. It is based on a clear and firm grasp of concepts and principles. These are not developed as independent, freestanding intellectual products. They are developed within the context of theory. Good theory reflects a sound grasp of practice. Just as it is the case that theory can often be challenged on the basis of non-compliance with reality, so business practice can be criticised because it is not in accordance with the best practice.

Case studies can help students of business ethos to refine theory by refering the application of theory to instances and by illustrating the deficiencies of or inadequacies of theory. One argument against the use of cases might be that since ethical issues are essentially unresolvable dilemmas there is little point in trying to resolve them. An introduction to ethical reasoning would help the student to analyse situations and cases rationally. Furthermore, even if some dilemmas are not totally, resolvable, they may be partially resolvable. Dilemmas may also be avoided or minimised in their force by skilful management. The use of cases can help to sensitise current and future managers to the situation likely to lead to ethical dilemmas and to ways in which they might avoid minimise or otherwise cope with such situations.

2. Aims of the Case Study Approach. Mathews *et al*. (1991) identify three purposes for the study of cases in business and management education. First, it is to develop the sort of understanding, independent thinking, judgement and communication which are needed in the business world. It is the stubborn facts embedded within a chunk of reality which require us to face up to the thorny issues faced by business people. Second, the study of cases develops confidence in the exercise of judgement and the willingness to give regard to other viewpoints. Third, analysing cases in ethos helps to develop moral judgement.

3. Approaches to the Analysis of Cases. There is no one best way of analysing cases. There is however a well established and widely used approach. This is often labelled the rational approach. This approach to analysis owes much to the belief in systematic and positivistic explanations of organisational behaviour. It is a powerful explanatory approach, derived substantially from Benthamite utilitarianism. Jeremy Bentham's felicific calculus was based on the view that the consequences of any social, economic or political action could be divided into pains (costs) or pleasures (benefits) and that it was possible to calculate with some precision the balance of cost and benefit for any such action. It has been developed into the dominant, almost unquestioned method of problem-solving within business.

The rational approach consists of the following five steps:

(a) identify the problem

(b) generate alternative solutions

(c) evaluate the alternatives, using cost benefit approaches

(d) select the solution

(e) implement the chosen solution.

Each step can require detailed investigation and some very hard thinking and the process may become iterative, *i.e.* the analyst may need to think again about an earlier stage as a result of the work carried out in later stages.

It may also be the case that instead of seeking to identify and implement the optional solution, the analyst may be satisfied with a sub-optimal solution. This may be because of pressures of time, lack of analytical capacity, the inability to obtain all the necessary information or basic human faults such as laziness or lack of inerest.

An alternative, less widely used but equally powerful approach, is Aristotelian in origin. Malloy and Lang (1993) present this method as a transrational approach. The transrational approach to analysis is more comprehensive than the merely rational.

In his Metaphysics (1947), Aristotle explores the causes of things in existence. He proposes that things exist because of the First Principles and four causes. The First Principle is the cause of all causes or the prime mover Aristotle's equivalent of the Judeo-Christian God. The Four Causes are the material cause, the formal cause the efficient cause and the final cause. The material cause is that from which something is made. The formal cause is that into which something is made. The efficient cause is that by which something is made. The final cause is that for the sake of which something is made.

The Prime mover in relation to business organisations is the person who creates the organisation. The final cause for an organisation could be described as its raison deire—it is the organisation's philosophy or ideology. It can be seen in mission statements and ethical policies. The formal cause is the organisation's culture or its way of doing what it does. The culture is shaped by the climate of the organisation and this is a product of the leadership process. Leadership is therefore the efficient cause of the organisation. The material cause of the organisation is its membership.

Malloyand Lang offer the following questions, based upon the four causes, as an aide to case analysis:

Final Cause

1. What is the stated purpose of the organisation?
2. What is the unstated purpose of the organisation?
3. What are the organisation's official goals?
4. What are the organisation's operative goals?

5. Is there a stated organisational philosophy?
6. Is there an unstated organisational philosophy?
7. How do employees, management, clientele and society perceive the organisation's purpose, goals and philosophy?

Fonnal Cause

1. How does the organisation socialise new members?
2. What are the organisation's rituals, myths, unique language and slogans?
3. What are the explicit standards of organisational behaviour?

Efficient Cause

1. What is the style of leadership?
2. What is the perceived style of leadership within the organisation? By superiors? By subordinates?
3. What is the preferred style of leadership in the organisation? By superiors? By subordinates?

Material Cause

1. How do employees perceive the organisation?
2. What are the employees value orientations towards work?

Manoy and Lang claim that their approach to the analysis of managerial dilemmas is holistic in nature and they contrast this with the limited perspective on organisational reality provide by the rational approach. A third approach to the analysis of cases is provided by Goodpaster (1983). He begins by describing several frameworks for analysis of ethical issues. First, he distinguishes between issues relating to the external environment of the organisation as a whole and those relating to the internal environment. Within the context of the external environment, the manager sees the organisation as a moral agent in the wider society.

He goes on to distinguish between descriptive ethics, normative ethics and metaethics. Descriptive ethics is aimed at an empirical or neutral description of the values of individuals and groups. Normative ethics seeks to develop and defend judgement of right and wrong, good and bad, virtue and vice-Metaethics is concerned with examining questions, about the meaning and provability of ethical judgements or of comparing one ethical theory with another.

He then divides approaches to ethics into three categories. These are utilitarianism, contractarianism and pluralism. The first asks, what actions or policy maximises the ratio of benefits to costs? The second asks what action or policy most fairly repects rights? The third asks what action or policy reflects the stronger duty?

Goodpaster, on the basis of these frameworks, then offers a list of questions which may be asked in relation to a case study. They are:

1. Are there ethical issues involved in this case? Centrally or peripherally? Is a decision required?
2. If there are ethical issues involved do they relate to the eternal environment or the internal environment? Or are both involved? How? What precisely are the ethical issues involved in each category?
3. From a descriptive ethical perspective, what appear to be the critical ethical assumptions or values shown by the persons or organisations in the case?
4. From the point of view of maximising utility for those affected, what is the best course of action? What facts in the case support this conclusion?
5. From the point of view offairness or individual rights, what is the best course of action? Again, what facts support this conclusion?
6. From the point of view of setting priorities among duties and obligations what should be done? Why?

7. Do the three avenues (utilitarianism, contractarianism and pluralism) converge on a course of action or do they diverge?
8. If they diverge which avenue should override?
9. Are there ethically relevant considerations in the case that are not captured by any of the three avenues? What are they?
10. What is the decision or action plan?

The three approaches to the analysis of cases all offer useful guidance. We suggest that, for cases designed to encourage identification of and deliberation about ethical issues, the approaches of Malloy and Lang or Goodpaster may be more helpful than the rational approach.

Shortcomings of The Case Method

The case method is not foolproof. Like any other method, it is susceptible to the foibles and failings of those who use it and, badly handled, produces classroom disasters. At its worst, the method becomes a boring exposure to the prejudices of others.

Cases necessarily oversimplify business situations. Whereas cases can imitate reality by demanding decisions on the basis of incomplete facts (no realworld decision maker has all the facts) cases are at odds with reality inpresenting a "static" rather than a dynamic decision-making context. A case presents a situation in which the action has already occurred, but everyday situations unfold gradually and every hour brings fresh information to the decision maker.

Essential to a good case discussion is adequate discussion time. A case done hurriedly is an unrewarding experience in which most of the analysis is either superficial or wrong. At first, students may find the discussion of many problems in a short-time stimulating. But soon the frustration of approaching case after case without in depth analysis will bring discouragement with the entire method.

Finally, although the case method is an excellent method for most students, one or two students may benefit little it at all.

However, this is not a characteristic drawback of the case method *per se*, since every approach to teaching misses some students. Indeed, a special advantage of the case method is that it can bring to life a joy in learning for students who have been turned off by traditional methods.

STRUCTURING THE LEARNING EXPERIENCE

The following are suggestions for designing a case discussion process.

Lecturing in Conjunction with Cases

Depending on the style and preference of a given instructor, a lecture may precede or follow a case discussion. Most instructors in busines ethos courses use cases only as one part of their course, with lectures and discussions of theoretical material constituting the remaining parts.

Time. A case may occupy a full class period or, in the instance of exceedingly long and complicated cases, two or more periods. Two or three short cases can sometimes be discussed in an hour. Even the shortest of cases (perhaps a paragraph or two in length) will usually require twenty minutes of discussion time.

Call Lists. Some instructors work entirely with volunteers, but others call on specific students, especially in the beginning, to get things moving. Calling on students increases pressure on them to be prepared, although some instructors and students find such pressure uncomfortable and distracting. Of those who do call on students many use "call lists" containing the names of participants and their frequency of participation. Near the end of a discussion an instructor may stop recognising volunteers and move to call on those who haven't yet participated.

Assigning Additional Work. The usual assignment for students is to read and study the case carefully. With complicated cases, instructors sometimes ask for a brief written analysis to be submitted on the day of the discussion.

Role Playing. Role playing is a device sometimes used to simulate a living situation. Choosing an opportune movement, the instructor invites a student (or students) to assume the role of a participant in the case. In a case dealing with government regulation, for example, one student may remark that the corporation's best option is to stall the regulatory agency. The teacher, knowing that other students do not agree with this strategy, may ask. Does anyone want to play the role of the regulator?" When someone accepts the invitation and responds directly to the student who advocates stalling, the former student has a chance to respond directly to the regulator. Such exchanges can enliven a discussion and reveal difficulties that otherwise might be glossed over.

Concluding Evaluation. At the end of a discussion, some instructors will ask for a vote among various options that have been explored in the discussion. This is not to affirm this correct answers are simple products of democratic vote but to indicate how others have interpreted the points made in the discussion.

Grading. The method of grading of course is the prerogative of the instructor. Most instructors, however, try to form a general impression of a student's performance and then record it either after each class discussion or at one or two points during the semester.

Students may also be given exams that ask them to analyze cases in a written essay. In ethics courses where theoretical material is being covered in addition to cases, it is common to ask students to analyze a case by using concepts drawn from the theoretical readings.

The case method, though not foolproof, offers clear rewards. Socrates insight that moral truth cannot simply "be told" is reflected in the case method's emphasis on analysis, discussion, and decision making. Like any method, it is subject to the failings of its practitioners. Like any method, it must be carefully adapted to the special territory it covers.

❐

13

Ethics and Social Responsibility

According to the classical view, a business was considered to be functioning in a socially responsible way if it strived to utilise as effeciently as possible the resources at its disposal in supplying the goods and services that society wanted and at prices customers willing to pay. If this was done well, business would get maximum profits. It was generally believed that business exists to serve the best interests of the owners of business, namely, the shareholders. This view underwent a change during the 1930s. The view then advanced was that managers of large business houses must make decisions so as to maintain an equitable balance among the claims of shareholders, employees, customers, government and society in general. Managers were considered trustees for these interests. In balancing these interests the profits of the business in the short run may be less than the maximum but in the long run the profit interest of the business would be maximised. Another major break from the older concept is now taking place. It is the view that business must get deeply involved in dealing with major social problems. It must undertake to do things which are not permitted within the traditional boundaries of business decision making. Here too actions may be accepted which do not divertly increase and may actually reduce profits, at least in the short run.

Business exists in the society and uses the resources available in the society. Therefore, there is inseparable relations between the business and society. We can have define the social responsibility of Business as:

According to H.R. Bowen, "Social responsibility is to pursue those policies and decisions or to follow lines of actions which are desirable in terms of the objective and value of our society."

According to George A. Steiner, "In real senses social responsibility implies recognition and understanding of the aspirations of society and determination to contribute towards their achievement."

According to International Seminar on Social Responsibility of Business, "Social responsibility of business can be spelt out as its responsibility to customers, workers, shareholders and to the community."

Social responsibility of business is a universal concept. This concept is applied everywhere, where it is developed, developing or underdeveloped economy. Because every society, the different sections have certain expectations from the business.

Characteristics. The important features of social responsibility concept are:

1. **It is Related with Business Organisations.** This concept applies to business organisations earning profits; and not by any non-profit making organisations.
2. **Social Responsibility is a Two-way Traffic.** The way by which the business fulfills its responsibility towards different sections of the society; in the same way various sections of the society have responsibility towards the business. Both have social responsibility against each.
3. **Supremacy of Public Interest.** Public interest is supreme rather than individual interest. Therefore, the individual interest and public interest both should be integrated while managing and controlling the business operations.
4. **Universal Concept.** Social responsibility concept is universal as it applies to every type of business whether private or public or of capitalist economy of socialist.
5. **Source of Gaining Social Power.** By fulfilling the social responsibility, the business can gain social power and cooperation.

Keith Davis writes that if the business neglects the social responsibility, it loses the social power.

6. Scope of Social Responsibility. The scope of social responsibility is not limited towards consumer, employees, shareholders, government or the suppliers of goods, but it is aimed for the human welfare.

7. Establishment of New Socio-Economic Values. It establishes new economic and social values such as decentralisation of power, equal and justified distribution of resources, business morality, etc.

8. Basis of business Success. It is an important element of business success. It improves the business image and good will.

ASSUMPTION OF SOCIAL RESPONSIBILITIES BY BUSINESS

Since long there has been a controversy whether business should assume social responsibilities, or it has no such obligations to fulfil. It would be worthwhile to analyse the arguments offered both in favour and against assumption of social responsibilities by business. First of all we shall begin with the analysis of arguments in favour.

The Case for Assuming Social Obligations

Three important arguments which are offered in favour of business assuming social responsibilities are as follows:

1. Business is the creation of society; hence it should respond to the demands of the society.
2. The long-term self-interests of business are best served when business assumes social responsibilities; and
3. It is a moral and right thing to do.

Response to Social Demands. It is a wellknown fact that business is set up to earn profit by producing goods or rendering services to the members of the society. Thus, the business is the creation of the society in the sense that its primary objective is to fulfil the needs of the members of the society. In case the business fails to do so, the society through people's representatives in government will either force them to do so through laws or may no longer permit them to survive. A business operates within a set up of cultural norms and restraints and the antennas of the managers of business are tuned to public opinion. They seek to maintain a proper image of their business in the public mind.

Long-term Self-interest of Business. There is a growing realisation on the part of the enlightened businessmen that it is in their self-interest to fulfil the demands and the aspirations of the society because people who have a good environment, education, and opportunity make better employees, customers and neighbours for business than those who are poor, ignorant and oppressed.

Moral Justification. There is a growing feeling among businessmen that if they do not rise to the occasion in meeting the social responsibilities, the government will step in and make them assume such responsibilities through legislation. Such legislative regulation is expensive for business and stand in the way of flexibility and freedom in making decisions and meeting competition. Hence, it would again be in the interest of business community to voluntarily undertake to fulfil the social responsibilities. In doing so the business will retain the needed credibility with the public and will be invited to not restrained from, participating in the political decision making process when new rules of the game for business are being framed.

Criteria for Determining the Social Responsibilities of Business

The problem now arises what business can and should do? This requires laying down certain guidelines for the business to follow. In the light of today's economic realities, the intensity of social problems, society's expectations and goals, the following may be suggested as broad guidelines to be observed by business in discharging its obligation by way of social responsibility.

1. It needs to be remembered that business is predominantly an economic institution with a strong profit motive. As such, business

should not be required to meet noneconomic objectives of society in a big way without financial incentives.

2. Business should be expected to take the long term view and perform socially responsible actions that might primarily reduce profits in the short-run but are in the ultimate interest of the company in the long-run. Helping meet the problems of unemployment, environmental pollution, civil disorders, etc. are some of the obligations which are in the long term interest of business.

3. An individual business has social responsibilities commensurate with its social powers. For instance, Company 'A' is the major employer in a town, and Company 'B' is an employer of only 10% of the working people in the town. Other things being equal Company A should give more thought to its social responsibilities than should Company B. This sort of problem is termed by Keith Davis as a "Sodo-economic Responsibility". He further goes on to say that there are "Sociahuman responsibilities of business" such as maintaining human dignity following loss of a job, and helping employees get selffulfilment from their jobs. This is so because according to Keith Davis, business deals with whole man in a whole socioeconomic structure.

4. Each business firm must think carefully before accepting what it thinks its social responsibilities are—the company should not underestimate the magnitude of the tasks involved in dealing with major social problems.

5. As a firm grows larger, it has an actual and potential influence on more and more people, society takes greater interest in what it does, and the firm, in turn, thinks more carefully about its responsibilities. As companies acquire more power over people there is pressure upon them to install productive policies, rules and actions so that individuals are less likely to be injured unjustly or without due process. Similarly, social responsibilities differ according to the type of the company. The social responsibility of a public utility undertaking is much different from the social responsibility of a company engaged in the manufacture of dry cell batteries.

6. An individual business should choose only those social responsibilities it can best manage. Traditionally business does a better job when the task entails a minimum of political involvement, does not get directly into the democratic political processes, deals with a physical problem that can be quantified and measured and is one in which it has experience.

7. No one should expect a business voluntarily to jeopardize its ability to attract shareholders investment. If a corporation diverts substantial sums of money to social purposes, it will significantly reduce its average return on capital which in turn will bring reduced growth rates, a lower market evaluation of its securities, or both. This sort of thing cannot of course continue in the long-run. A company guilty of serious air and water pollution may be forced to clean up its waste even though the impact may have great profit consequences. On the other hand, a company which has profit levels well above the industry average may find leverage in assuming social responsibilities of greater magnitude than a company much below the industry average.

8. Business should be obliged to internalize most of its external costs. In the past, business enterprises were excused from bearing such costs of production as air and water pollution, scarring hillsides in search of coal and defacing natural beauty. Society then held the economic output of business to be of higher priority. Today, priorities are shifting and business is expected to bear more social costs. This is, however, a complex problem.

As both guides and boundaries, these criteria can justify the assumption of almost no social responsibilities or rather substantial ones. There are, however, a few overriding generalisations that may sharpen the focus.

One area of potential high payoff for little or no cost is informing the public about the operation and social value of the business system. This is an important social responsibility which business has not fulfilled. If people do not know or misunderstand, they are much more likely to be swayed by irresponsible criticism and to expect for more from the business institutions than they should in their own long-range selfinterests.

The shift in the thinking of more and more businessmen is away from short-run to long-run profits. There is also an important philosophical drift from unbridled self-interest to an enlightened social interest. It is a new way of looking at business power, interest and operation. It can accommodate a good bit of what we now speak of as social responsibility without eroding the economic incentive. Indeed, a great deal of the socially responsible action that can be accepted by business will strengthen the profit incentive.

PRINCIPLES UNDERLYING SOCIAL RESPONSIBILITY

Regarding the role of business in a society, there are two broad principles as stated below:

1. The Charity Principle (Business Giving). For many business firms, corporate responsibility means making charitable contributions or what is called 'Corporate philanthropy'. It is considered to be an investment because it benefits business in the long run by improving the community, its labour force, the climate for business etc. For instance, charities to educational institutions is considered to be a means of improving the labour market. Another group of businessmen regards charities as an operating expense *e.g.*, souvenirs distributed at a function may be regarded as a public relations expenses. A third philosophy assumes that a company is a citizen of the community but it has more resources at its command. Expenditure on satisfying community needs is a mark of its concern for the community as well as of its Philanthropic disposition, regardless of whether gifts are considered to be an investment, an expense on philanthropy, most of the costs are probably on to consumers.

2. The Stewardship Principle/Trusteeship Principle. It regards business as agent and trustee for the community, receiving funds and distributing them according to the community needs. In its trusteeship role, business gifts to those whose claims are perceived as being legitimate or capable of threatening business. Professional managers beleive that they have an obligation to see that general public benefits from company's actions. Realisation of this obligation places the managers in a position of public trust. The control by a company of vast resources obliges them to use resources in a way that are good not just for the stockholders but for the society as a whole. In this way, they become the Stewart or trustees of the soceity and hence must use speical care in making business decisions. In discharging this responsibility, they must maintain a harmonious balance among the claims of various interested groups: the stockholders, employees, customers and the public at large. According to this view point, corporate managers must interact skillfully with all groups who have a "sake" in what the corporation does.

Thus, the charity principle requires business to give voluntary aid to society's needy or deprived groups. On the other hand the stewardship principles urges the businessmen to be the trustees of the people and act in the interact of all members of the society who have any stake in its business. Both these principles are the foundation of corporate social responsibility. A firm which looks after both of these could be regarded as socially responsible as well as acting towards the promotion of their long term intersts.

Methods of Discharging Social Responsibility

In translating the theoretical concept of social responsibility into concrete reality, the business firms might undertake any of the following:

1. Adoption of Different Types of Social Programmes. The following areas are attended to by the socially responsible business:

(a) Pursuing the goal of economic growth and efficiency by improving productivity and cooperating with the government.

(b) Helping colleges and universities through grants, donations, funding of research programme, maintenance of interaction, training and placement of students.

(c) Undertaking urban development programmes such as low cost housing, adoption of backward areas.

(d) Retraining and placement of disadvantaged or retiring workers.

(e) Patronising art and culture through and to institutions engaged in such tasks.

(f) Improving management in government.

(g) Pollution and effluent control.

(h) Designing low cost medical care programmes.

2. Substituting Optimum Profits Against Maximum Profits. Maximum profit is the goal of every business undertaking. But some companies may resolve to take optimum profits rather than the maximum. Optimum is lower than what is actually possible but it is higher than the minimum necessary to keep the company in business. Where a company is operating under such voluntarily imposed restraints, it is said to be satisfying rather than maximizing profits.

3. Cooperating with Various Stockholders. *i.e.* undertaking to be responsible to various stockholders for all that the company does. In practice it would cover a vast range of public interests *e.g.* spending in pollution control caused by its vehicles, beautification of the city where the company is located and building hospitals, schools, reading rooms etc. free education of employees' children and so on.

4. Prescription of Social Goals. Social responsibility could find expression in the policy documents of the company wherein a company undertake to discharge certain goals in addition to business goals. There is the blending of two diametrically opposite goals of doing socially useful work and making money. Corporate resources are used to work in cooperation with other sectors of the society to provide major unmet needs such as rural development, poverty alleviation, family plananing, shelters for the homeless, food and clothing for indigents.

ARGUMENTS FOR CORPORATE SOCIAL RESPONSIBILITY

The proponents of social responsibility stress on such things as preservation of environment, protection of consumers as well as of the health and safety of employees, conservation of energy, and other resources, promotion of positive values in the society, promotion of employment etc. The government also endeavours to secure compliance with laws and regulations that protect general public from abusive business practices. Following are the major reasons for requiring corporations to act in socially responsible ways.

1. Need to Balance Power with Responsibility. Modern corporations are powerful bodies some ranking almost at par with the government in terms of the resources and authority. In case a corporation fails to bring about a parity in its power-responsibility equation. It would tend to lose its power in of more responsible competitions. Strong social groups are emerging which react strongly against arrogant companies.

2. Voluntary Actions would Prevent Government Regulation. Where business fails to become alert to its social responsibilities, the government may have to intervene through legal sanctions. It would snatch the freedom of business, restrict flexibility in action and add economic cossts. The spirit of liberalization which is becoming the hallmark of government's business policies is based on reposing of confidence in business firm's sense of morality and responsibility. If business wants to maintain its freedom of action, it must not give a chance to massive, governmental machinery to interpose by means of power and bureaucratic controls.

3. To Promote Long-run Profits. Costs incurred in discharging social responsibility are a kind of investment contributing to long-run business interests. For instance, financial assistance to a management institute may provide a flow of talented workers for a company. Provision of socially useful projects may generate considerable public goodwill for the company. A short-term loss of profit may actually save the way to handsome long run profits.

4. Correction of Business Causes Social Problems. Business is responsible for remedying the social problems that may have been caused by its wrongful actions. Industrial pollution is responsible for damaging the environment. Nobody would question the right of the society to require business to clean up this environmental mess. Congestion, housing and health problems, industrial diseases are the outcome of business actions. The responsibility to launch a corrective action must also be assumed by business.

5. Vastness of Resources and Intricate Social Problems. No other group in the society except business and government commands vast resources. These resources could be used to tackle some of the pressing problems confronting the society. The other institutions may be helpless because of scarcity of funds, lack of know-how and sophisticated planning tools that are normal to a business. However, there are two basic problems connected with deployment of business resources for tackling social problems. Firstly, if it devotes its resources to social problem, its resources may not be sufficient to pursue economic goals. Secondly, those advocating this kind of role for business may have an exaggerated motion of company's available resources.

6. Response to Changing Public Expectations. Business is being relief upon to discharge still higher levels of social performance. The old idea of expecting only economic output is no longer enough. There are forces at work that have changed society's expectations of social outputs from business. In future, only those companies who are capable of grasping these underlying forces of changes will be able to guide destiny to better prospects.

7. Recognition of Moral Obligations by Business. Business is no longer a mere occupation. It is our economic institution operating in a social environment. It calls for the reconciliation of business goals with the demands by the society. It discharging its functions, business must not overlook the moral obligations consistent with prevailing social values. For instance, if social justice demands equal pay for equal work, the company must have equality in pay-scales. According to Thomas Donaldson. "Moral obligation outs tip all other kinds of obligations. Corporate managers may have to consider economic return to stockholders."

CORPORATE SOCIAL RESPONSIBILITY

Corporate social responsibility is neither a clear concept nor a central one for ethical business in a global economy. It is best understood as a modern-day myth, using an approach exemplified by the lae French anthropologist Claude Levi Strauss to explain and analyze it. This does not imply that there is no such thing as corporate social responsibility. The many corporate social responsibility statements, the hundreds of articles, and the numerous textbooks devoted to the topic, all testify to the presence of some reality. But the question is, What is its essence and how can we understand the phenomenon called corporate social responsibility?

Levi-Strauss developed a theory of myths widely applicable both to ancient and contemporary myths, including much of what we call science. For present purposes I shall draw from his account four salient features of myths:

1. A myth is not simply a story, but a story in all its different variations, since it may be told in a number of different ways and in a number of different versions.
2. A myth is not a falsehood, as one common meaning of myth maintains. A myth helps people understand, make sense of, and accept a certain phenomenon or portion of reality.
3. A myth does not stand alone. It is part of a larger whole, either a package of other stories or a way of viewing reality of which it is one part.
4. A myth while not a falsehood, is not a true statement of reality either, for it holds a portion of reality, either through ignorance or through unconscious design.

The story, doctrine, or assertion of social responsibility by business and its critics is a contemporary myth in precisely this sense. It comes in a variety of forms. It is part of a larger package that involves the relationship between business and society: it captures something about the reality of that interaction helping to make sense of it and it hides a portion of that same reality, thus unconsciously serving certain vested interests.

MYTH OF CORPORATE SOCIAL RESPONSIBILITY

First, there is no uniform story or understanding of corporate social responsibility. The term became widely used in the United States only in the 1960s; before that we find only occasional mention of the social responsibility of business. Although the term's meaning remains vague and tenuous, it nevertheless gains currency after 1970. In 1979 Thomas Zenisek, in an article in the Academy of Management Review, discusses various definitions and models of corporate social responsibility and notes that they all lack either empirical and/or theoretical support. He attempts to provide a topology but, in doing so, simply adds one more item to the confusion that the documents on the subject.

There is no definitive or supposedly universal version of social responsibility. The story of social responsibility plays itself out in numerous different contexts and scenarios. We can, in Levi-Strauss's terms, develop the different stories that were and are told about social responsibility or that embody it. All the variations together form part of the myth. Sometimes the term "social responsibility" is used, sometimes "corporate responsibility" or "corporate social responsibility." Among other terms used to express the same idea we find "social responsiveness," social accounting, social audit, social conscience, corporate social policy, and corporate citizenship.

The variant "social responsiveness," to take one example carries with it the implication that business is responding to something that comes from society. The end of the 1960s saw the rise of consumer, environmental and social-action groups. The military-industrial complex became a catchphrase that grew in currency and was used to identify and attack big business in general. Business responded to this and other onslaughts that gained status and stature by being presented as social interest attacks. Groups that had vested interests clothed their demands on business in terms that gave their demands more respectability. By calling them socially interested demands, they disguised the fact that they were often demands not of society as a whole, but of particular groups with special interests, such as themselves. Business countered by responding in a variety of ways. However, rather than saying that they responded to pressure groups either to maintain their corporate image or to preserve their share of the market, they countered by adopting the same strategy as their attackers. They clothed their answers in terms of social responsiveness or social responsibility. No one knew exactly what those terms meant, but that was unimportant. The terms indicated some concern for the social good, the general welfare, or society as a whole. The term "social responsibility" took some of the sting out of the charge that big business was part of a military industrial complex that acted for its own benefit or for the benefit of an elite, rather than for the good of society.

We know what legal responsibility means. Corporations are governed by law. They fulfill their legal responsibilities when they do or refrain from doing what the law requires. We know what moral responsibility means. Individuals fulfill their moral responsibilities when they do or refrain from doing what morality requires. We do not know in some comparable way what corporate social responsibility means. There is no consensus on its meaning, if that meaning goes beyond legal and perhaps also moral responsibility. When individuals or corporations do not fulfill their legal responsibilities, they are liable to state-imposed penalties. When they do not fulfill their moral responsibilities, they are liable to censure. When they do not fulfill their social responsibilities (unless these are also legal or moral), they are open to no sanctions. Firms are neither considered bad nor in any way penalized for not fulfilling social responsibilities. But they are praised for fulfilling them, or at least they can claim praise and lay claim to the rewards of a good reputation. Social responsibility thus turns out to be a very convenient term for business.

Since no one can say definitively what social responsibility means, no one can strictly apply standards to determine if a companay is socially responsible. Hence, different groups may apply different standards, none of which is binding.

The Council on Economic Priorities (CEP) exemplifies one approach to this problem. One ofits publications Shopping for a Better World: A Quick & Easy Guide to Socially Responsible Supermarket Shopping, rates companies according to their charitable giving advancement of women, advancement of minorities, defense contracts, animal testing, social disclosure community outreach, use of nuclear power, and impact on the environment. It also notes if the company makes cigarettes, pesticides, or beer, has misleading ads; engages in clear-cutting, catching dolphins, or union-busting and the like and if it bans chlorofluorocarbons (CFCs), pays 50 per cent day care makes food bank gifts and so on. The CEP provides the information. It makes no judgments except to decide what information to monitor and include. The shoppers are urged to make and apply their own judgments. The result is a vague notion of what it means for a company to be socially responsible.

A no-layoff policy is certainly an employee's ideal. But it has never been an American social policy, even if a few corporations with no such contractual agreement have followed that policy. Laying off employees in times of economic necessity is not illegal and arguably not immoral. Is it a violation of corporate social responsibility? Samuelson seems to think so, but many other disagree.

Similarly, does a company have a social responsibility to make a profit? Certainly that is why most companies are formed, and companies typically do not seek red ink. Society does not look favourably on companies that fail. But do such companies violate a social responsibility? Perhaps many people would be inclined to think that a failing company is not socially responsible. But no one can say so with certainly, because there is no way to determine what is and what is not included in social responsibility. It is not a matter of people arguing about whether or not being profitable follows or does not follow from some principle governing social responsibility. There is no principle governing social responsibility; it is a vague collection of various desiderata framed by various groups for various purposes.

ARGUMENTS AGAINST CORPORATE SOCIAL RESPONSIBILITY

The demand that companies should act in a socially responsible manner has various implications. Utterances in favour of social responsibility by large companies are viewed as public relation exercise aimed at overcoming the public assertions of corporate evil doings. At other times professing to abide by social responsibility may be used as a play to secure government protection or favour. Whatever the compulsions behind allegiance to the doctrine of social responsibility, the general fact remains that business firms have long since discarded the gospel that charity quo charity has no seat at the Boards of Directors. It has freed managers from pursuing the goal of only profits and secured them better sleep at night. The advocates of the opponents of corporate social responsibility have pointed out that the stick of social responsibility would come to be wielded not only to bludgeon individual companies who fail to follow the line indicated by the attacher but also as an invitation to the. government to inerfere more incorporate affairs.

Following are the arguments cited against corporate social responsibility.

1. Unsupported by Logic. There is no underlying theory or philosophy that guides the propondents of social responsibility. Nor is there a consistency in the arguments adduced. The concept of corporate social responsibility is at odds with free market private property system. To begin with the concept extended to community programmers, or mere charities, later the idea was expanded to include support of basic research, scholarships, universities etc. In a still later period, corporations were asked to patronise arts, fine architect and sculpture.

2. Militates Against the Test of Market Place. To the extent a corporation does business in a competitive market, the use of corporate resources for non-productive purpose cannot survive the stringent test of the market place. It is a different matter if the government imposes similar social obligations on all corporate bodies.

For instance, suppose several companies are discharging toxic substance in a water stream. One of the companies actuated by social responsibility decides to take some action to tackle pollution but others just do not care. The chances are that the responsible company would soon find itself in financial difficulties.

3. Cost Burden on Consumers. Irrespective on what item of social responsibility the corporation money is spent the fact is that it remains a nonproductive expenditure and constitutes the cost of doing business. The irony is that these cost will have to be borne by persons whom the advocates of responsibility may not have liked to bear. But there is no such thing as a company itself bearing any cost. These costs are quite likely to be passed to consumers in the form of lower prices or wages.

4. Creation of Ironical Situations. Obsession with social responsibility may lead to several ironical situations. For example, one of the arguments in favour of social responsibility is that it is necessary to prevent further government intervention. However, a voluntary adoption of socially responsible activity may have precisely the opposite effect. Take the case of the company which had decided to take action to prevent pollution of water. Economic forces would compel the company to sooner or later reverse its decision or to find a way to make similar action mandatory for everyone else similarly situated.

5. Non-availability of Social Skills. Business people are oriented to tackle problems connected with finance, marketing production, personnel etc. But they have no training in social problems such as hunger, drug abuse or employee tensions. Compelling them to tackle social problems might lead to blunders. They may end up applying business solutions to social problems.

6. Diversion from the Main Objective. Social involvement of business managers is likely to digrees the company from its main objective. Moreover, it may give wrong signals to the staff who may be confused as to which goal they should concentrate upon. Socially aware managers may dilute the efficiency of their companies. The public would come to have expectations that the business may find difficult to satisfy. Thus social responsibility is a luxury which neither business nor society can afford.

7. Adverse Impact on Economic Efficiency. Principal goal of business is to produce goods and services at optimum cost and sell them at lowest competitive prices. Once this is done, the most efficient firms survive, consumer can have proper quality goods at reasonable prices and profits would be sufficient enough to encourage future economic activity. Attending to social goals would amount to diversion of corporate funds to non-economic activities.

Thus corporate social responsibility places added burden on both business and society without commensurate benefits either in the form of social improvement or lowered costs. It is better left to government initiative.

Social Responsibility and Social Responsiveness

Business management must consider the social and ethical implications of its decisions. Corporate social responsibility is seriously considering the impact of the company's decisions and actions on the environment and the society. Dependence of any business on its social and ecological environment is so complete that the very existence, survival and growth of any enterprise depend upon its acceptance by the society and the environment. If it outlives its utility to the society and the environment it has no place and reason to live.

Today, we also insist on the social responsiveness of management which means the ability and willingness of management to relate the plans and policies to the social environment in such ways that are mutually beneficial to the organisation and to society. The social responsiveness implies actions and the how of the responses of the management. The current trend is in company's involvement in social actions. The mission of a corporation expresses such involvement in social actions to improve the quality of life. Any enterprise must interact with, and live in, as a responsible citizen in the society. In an age of fast changing and turbulent environment proaction on the part of management is demanded to meet the challenges faced by the society.

In today's world, Society is expecting much more from business than in the past. A new attitude towards the managerial role is slowly emerging. Management is required as agent of social change and not merely as agent of economic and technical change. They are called upon to play the role of system regulator in order to keep operations in tune and harmony with the environment. As productivity catalyst, managers have to take into account both economic and social inputs (costs) and the economic and social outputs (benefits) while planning, formulating and evaluation any business project. Managers are now interested in social results alongwith economic results. Society wants its social resources to be used as wisely as its economic resources. Hence, we have to give equal emphasis in utilisation of economic and social resources. Managerial leadership is also called upon to recognise the importance of democratic and participative management in order to satisfy the expectations of modern matured employees, MBO, job enrichment and Organisational Development are implementing the necessary changes in leadership styles. Leadership must evince social awareness and bring about social improvements. Social needs and goals are now compelling managers to work toward high quality of life as well as toward high economic productivity. It has been called the quality of life management. Quantity of life satisfies the hunger of body. Quality of life satisfies the hunger of mind and spirit- higher level human wants and aspirations. Of course, the need for social awareness and social performance is an additional obligation to that of economic performance. Again, we must recognise that economic performance alone enables social performance. In a sense, management has a social responsibility to make a profit.

Social responsibility indicates personal responsibility and obligation of managers and employees, as they act in their own interests, to ensure that rights and legitimate interests of others are in no way sacrificed or prejudiced by their behaviour and actions. Basically, it means that managers should consider the effects of their business decisions (in business planning and developing corporate strategies) upon all stakeholders interested in the enterprise directly or indirectly and who may be adversely affected by those corporate decisions.

Social Responsibility of Business—A Two Way Traffic

Social responsibility is a two way traffic. The way in which the business has responsibility towards different sections of the society also have responsibility towards the business. To understand this facts, the social responsibility may be classified as follows:

(1) Social responsibility of business towards different sections of the society.

(2) Social responsibility of different sections of the society towards the business.

(1) Social Responsibility Towards Different Sections

The social responsibility of business towards different sections are summarised below:

1. ***Towards the Owners of Business.*** Shareholders or the investors are the owners of business and the business has a number of responsibilities towards them; such as to safeguard the capital by investing the capital into profitable schemes, timely payment of dividends, to give notice of meetings in time, to provide with requisitic information asked for, to inform them about the progress made by the business from time to time and to follow the instructions of owners.
2. ***Towards the Business Itself.*** The responsibility of business towards itself are the efficient operation and management of business, optimum use of resources, development and expansion, planned automation and modernisation, maintaining of harmonious relations between employees and customers; and to promote research.
3. ***Towards the Creditors.*** The important responsibility towards the creditors include the following of terms and conditions of loans, proper utilisation of debt capital, regular payment

of interest and advances, and to provide with requisite information; etc.

4. ***Towards the Suppliers of Goods.*** The suppliers of goods may be an individual or an institution. The responsibility towards them include; to pay fair prices reasonable time, make purchases on reasonable terms and conditions, to motivate indigenous suppliers, to provide technical services wherever needed, to inform about the change in demands and preferences, and to promote healthy competition.

5. ***Towards the Employees.*** The business has much responsibility towards the employees. They include providing with a reasonable salary and wages, satisfaction of security needs, providing with good working conditions, assignment of right job for right person, providing opportunity for career development, settlement of grievances and disputes, adopt and execution of welfare plans for the employees, profit sharing and participation in management etc.

6. ***Towards Professional Institutions.*** The professional institutions include the Institute of Chartered Accountants of India, Institute of Cost and Works Accountants of India, Management Institutes, etc. The responsibilities towards them include; to increase the membership of these institutions, regular participation in the seminars and conferences organised by them; preference for the persons qualified from these institutions in giving employment, sanctioning of grants and other assistance, and to follow the code and conduct laid down by these institutions in the conduct of business.

7. ***Towards the Customers.*** The main object of business is to create a customer. Therefore, the business has much responsibilities towards the customers; such as determination of fair prices making available goods and services in time, maintaining of quality of goods, providing

with after sales services, maintaining standard of goods, keeping away from monopolistic and restrictive trade practices, satisfaction and solution to consumer complaints in time, and following the code of conduct in business.

8. ***Towards the World Society.*** The whole world is now formed into one society due to rapid development of communication and transport network. In such a situation, the business has various responsibilities towards the world society; including cooperation with business organisations of other countries in joint production and distribution, use of international technology in production, following of the code of conduct of multinational companies, exporting of goods and services at reasonable terms and conditions, production of goods keeping in view of international standard, maintenance of each others social and cultural values and following of international trade policies, rules and regulations.

9. ***Towards other Business Institutions.*** Responsibilities towards other business institutions include; participation in forming into combinations, following of the code of conduct laid down by trade associations, trusts, pools, etc., do not make effort to find out others business secret and leaks them out; and do not create cut throat competition between them.

10. ***Towards Local Community.*** On moral and ethical ground, the business has many responsibilities towards the local community such as : providing with employment to local people on priority basis, protection of natural environment, construction of social institutions like hospitals, schools, colleges, etc., assistance to poor and unsupported people, providing with scholarship and awards to brilliant boys and girls in their education; providing of suitable assistance at the time of any natural calamity like floods, draught, famine, etc.; protection of the local community from the environmental affects.

11. ***Towards the Government.*** Responsibilities towards the government include: following of government rules and regulations; timely payment of taxes and duties; keeping away from politics of business; participation with the government in fulfilling the national objectives; do not make any business contract with enemy countries; cooperate with the government at the times of emergency, etc.

(2) Responsibilities of Different Sections of Society Towards Business

As in the way a business has its responsibilities towards the different sections of the society, in the same way different sections of the society have responsibilities towards the business. Business has much expectations from the society to which it serves to the satisfaction. The responsibilities by the different sections towards the business may be stated in the following heads:

1. ***Responsibility of Owners.*** The controlling power of business vests in the hands of owners and they formulate policies for the business and implement decisions. It is their responsibility to elect capable and efficient persons in the Board for the efficient management of business.
2. ***Responsibility of Employees.*** It is the employees who execute the policies, plans and programmes of the business enterprise. They should perform their duties with diligence, skill and honest.
3. ***Responsibility of Investors.*** The investors should not withdraw their money from the business all of a sudden. The terms and conditions of loan capital should be simple.
4. ***Responsibility of Professional Institutions.*** The professional institutions like Institutes of Management Studies, Chartered Accountants, Cost Accountants, etc. should inform the business about the latest professional knowledge and techniques developed by them through publications,

organising of seminars and conferences. The business manager may be invited to participate in such programmes.

5. ***Responsibility of Suppliers.*** The suppliers should maintain regularity of the supplies of raw materials, equipment and machinery. The quality of the goods must be maintained.

6. ***Responsibility of Consumers.*** The consumers should make aware to the businessmen about their changing needs and preferences. They should not make a hoarding of goods; but purchase only for the present needs. They should not purchase goods under black marketing.

It is therefore, clear that the social responsibility of business is a two way traffic/activity. The business as well as the different. sections of the society have mutual interest. Such mutual interest will help the growth of the national economically.

Compelsion to Fulfil Social Responsibility

The following compelsions are very effective for controlling and regulating the role of social responsibility of business.

1. ***Increasing Number of Departmental Enquiries.*** In case of neglect of social responsibility by the business enterprises, the government appoints enquiry committees to control such business enterprises. Enquiries or raids are organised by Income-tax/Sales Tax authorities in case of tax evasions by the businessmen. The defaulters are punished under the provisions of respective Acts.

2. ***Change in the Pattern of Investors and Creditors.*** Earlier the shares and debentures are sold and bought by the individuals and the main object was to get dividends. They were not much care about the management and control of companies. At the present time the securities are dealt with by financial institutions, investment trusts, and semi-governmental bodies also. They are not only interested in the dividends, but actively participate in the management

and control of companies and interfere in the matters to fulfill the social responsibilities of business.

3. ***Formation of Code of Conduct.*** The business Associations have formulated code of conduct for the business enterprises and every member is bound to follow the code of conduct. Fair Trade Practices Association formed in 1966 was formulated a nine-point code of conduct and the members were bound to accept it.

4. ***Increasing Labour Union Activities.*** The employees, consumers, shareholders, etc. have now organised to safeguard their interests: The employee unions are now more powerful. Consumer organisations and the provisions under Consumer Protection Act, 1986 give more powers to safeguard the interests and rights of consumers.

All these steps are very essential for controlling and regulating the business for fulfillment of social responsibility. There is need for increasing the quantum of punishment to those who commit breach of the provisions of various Acts. At present the quantum of punishment provided under various Acts needs to be revised. The provision for imprisonment and the fine may be increased at least ten times than provided at present in various Acts like Companies Act, Consumer Protection Act, etc.

ETHICS AND CORPORATE PHILANTHROPY

In an influential essay entitled Social Responsibility of Business, Nobellaureate Milton Friedman argued that the espousal of social responsibilities by the corporate sector was not just bad for business, but was tantamount to a frank and outright advocacy of unadulterated socialism. Friedman's essay was first published in 1970 in The New York TImes Magazine, but it should combatively engage scholars and activists even today. Friedman's argument briefly was that a corporate executives responsibility stopped with the shareholder and went no further. As long as executives make sure that they are functioning within the law, their prime concern should be to promote and protect the interests of those who have invested in the company.

Anything beyond that is a betrayal of trust and rank bad judgment. Friedman however, conceded that corporate executives as individuals, could donate some of their earnings and time to charitable causes. But this should not, on any account, be merged with their responsibilities as managers of shareholders investment, funds and trust.

It is also true that media enriched charity events often deflect attention from the job of running efficient and ruleabiding enterprises. But Friedman's understanding of corporate social responsibility was very narrow as he restricted its meaning to philanthropy and little else. With the arrival of business ethics as an articulated corporate practice, the conception of corporate social responsibility has gone well beyond the donor mentality. Business ethics successfully merges social responsibility with the imperatives of corporate efficiency in a fashion that is hard-nosed, pragmatic, and bottom line oriented. We now know that it is not ehough for business people to stay within the law and make their money—recent studies have shown that business are rewarded when they are ethical as well. What is more, ethical business practices meet social responsibilities much more wholesomely than corporate philanthropy can ever hope to do.

In fact much of the social devastation we see around us is because organisations, both public and private do not work ethically. Ethical practice is under great strain in an unethical environment. In such conditions it is easier to be moral than ethical. Morality is a virtue that lends itself easily to privatisation. Indeed the more unethical the environment the greater the tendency, and scope, for individuals to grandstand as philanthropists. While philanthropy is to be recommended, it cannot take the place of business ethics. It is necessary to recognise, though it may sometimes be distressing, that a philanthropic organisation can often be unethical in terms of how it handles its immediate stakeholders.

This is what makes it imperative to link ethics with principles of functioning that can be immediately operationalised and reproduced across the board. An organisation's philanthropic character can now be mesured on another scale. An ethical enterprise is not concerned so much about beign a do good organisation, but its very internal functioning radiates outward to create a positive impact on social concerns.

Corporate Social

Business ethics further requires a commitment to keep abreast of developments in knowledge and actually put them into operation. This aspect is an intimately linked to the issue of transparency as it is to the cause of advancing corporate social responsibility. Developments in knowledge take place both at the technological and at the human level. Safety regulations have become more stringent and exacting in many engineering and chemical companies simply because technological advances have shown up the dangers of earlier systems of production. Personnel relations, and interactions between levels and functions within companies, have also undergone changes in recent decades. Among other things it has been widely recognised that employee compliance comes more easily when initiatives and enterprise are adequately rewarded. In addition market research and the growth of consumer lobbies have led to a greater degree of awareness of customer attitudes and responses.

An ethical concern can also advance corporate social responsibility by figuring out ways by which the world outside can be linked to its organisational functioning. If an enterprise's underwriting of worthy causes has no import on its functioning then Friedman is probably right in accusing executives of such an organisation of going well beyond their brief. Business ethics, however, aligns itself to larger social issues on a totally different plane. When Lipton India adopted four hundred villages around its Etah dairy it was helping the community and also itself. Excel Industry, an agro-chemical company, puts some of Mumbai's overflowing garbage to productive use. IKEA, the international home furnishing company, started a variety of initiatives to eradicate child labour from units that produce carpets for it.

Though most companies active in this area are multinationals, it needs to be mentioned that their outreach efforts took place in India and in most cases they met with a large measure of success. Can Indian companies learn from this? Indeed, the Tatas have been the traditional pacesetters in this regard. Their efforts for the advancement of the township of Jamshedpur are well known. Other enterprises should likewise think of how they can profitably integrate the logics and compulsions of their organisations with the needs of the broader society. When the corporate sector reaches out in this fashion its positive impact on society is much more lasting than old fashioned philanthropy.

Good corporate citizenship does not emerge from the usual unidirectional philanthropic activities. In fact, many enterprises are turned off by this understanding of corporate social responsibility and thereby undermine it altogether. While everyone is welcome to be a philanthropist, it needs to be recognised that do-gooders are doing good on a highly personalised basis. If corporate social responsibility is identified principally with philanthropy then whenever there is a change of regime at the top, the philanthropic project either abruptly ceases, or changes direction, or becomes lifeless. In fact, the term corporate social responsibility is perhaps a little clumsy. Many IT professionals have pointed out to me that paying taxes and obeying the law are also aspects of corporate social responsibility-as indeed they are. Perhaps the term corporate outreach is a more felicitous one. It best captures the spirit behind which executives strategize to relate themselves to the environment and community.

In the ultimate analysis then it is through strict adherence to business ethics that the corporate sector can best promote social responsibility. There is little point in putting in a drop of charity when an ocean of goodwill is required. There is even less point in donating to philanthropy and being absolutely unethical at home. Business ethics not only adds to the organisation's value, but also provides philanthropy with a sound doctrine and a reliable format within which it can maximize its contributions.

□

14

Administrative and Social Ethics

Every thinker attaches highest priority to integrity in administration. The need for administrative ethics arise from the very foundation of the trust which a government is bestowed with by her people in the democratic countries. Administrative ethics, refers to the moral standards and lies in the honest discharge of administrative work by public officials. According to Stahl, "Government officials and employees are not only committed to loyal and effective performance but are obliged to carry out a public objective which in any nation controlled by the people can mean only such purposes as an arrived at demonstrability. Ethics are truly a part of competence and they are a part of democratically." Those persons who look upon public employment as an opportunity for self aggrandizement and for exercise of authority to favour themselves "their friends obstruct the interest of the commonwill both as to efficiency and as to service to all the people".

The need of integrity at the 'top' of administrative set up is of basic importance for maintaining an honest administrative set up. As it has been pointed out to be sure the most influential public servants, when it comes to ethical performance, are the men at the top, they set the tone of an entire enterprise, and all that is said about administrative ethics, applies to them prominently.

In India, the factor of integrity is administration presents a very bad state of affairs. To quote Nirad C. Chaudhari. There is hardly anyone from a petty clerk to a minister who is not manageable with a proportionate amount of gratification."

In precise terms it may be stated that threats to the administrative morality are "bribery, nepotism, mixture of power or influence, black marketing, profiteering and similar other malpractices commonly associated with administration, politics or business and industry, and also the deliberate or intentional exploitation of one's position, status, or resources, directly or indirectly, for personal aggrandisement, whether it be in terms of material gain or enhancement of power, prestige or influence beyond what is legitimate or sanctioned by commonly accepted norms to the deteriment of the interests of other persons or the community as a whole."

FACTORS AFFECTING ADMINISTRATIVE ETHICS

(1) People's Trust. In the democratic government public service is entrusted to discharge various functions and therefore problems of ethical conduct arise for the public official by virtue of the power and influence he commands and the commitment he undertakes of loyal and disinterested service to the public. In a democracy, authority is derived from the consent of the governed. Therefore Public administration look after the public in a way so as to strengthen the integrity and processes of a democratic society. This fundamental principle writes Stahl, "has at least three implications for performance in a government position, especially as we move up the hierarchy to those of the greatest responsibility. It means *(1)* that all the people must be served, equally and impartially; *(2)* That this must be achieved with full respect for and reliance on representative institutions; *(3)* that internal administration in public agencies must be consistent with these modes of behaviour." It is not easy to define the concept of "public interest". In this regard the safe conclusion is to assert that the civil servant and politician should, above all, think in terms of the total welfare, the overall good, the long range effect and eschew the temptation to please just the individual or group pressing its case before him.

(2) Individual Capabilities. It is strongly believed that "both the specialization of the individual and of the institution' give rise to some risks in the moral level attained by a governmental organization. Since specialization has its advantages and since it is idle to think of dispensing with it in any true sense, it behooves us to understand it and to live with it. But it has its serious limitations.

A public servant, besides relying on his technical judgements must also try to see his whole field in perspective. In attempts to achieve general welfare, there must be care not to confuse one's professional viewpoint, or personal prejudices with the public interest." According to Stahl, "reconciliation of our necessary dependence on experts is government with the realities of public needs and with the inexorable pressure of a change poses a central problem of statesmanship and is therefore at the heart of the civil servant's moral imperatives." Emphasing the limitation of the specialists in administration, Harold. J. Laski who wrote that a political system which fails to keep the expert under control, "will push its private nostrums in disregard of public wants.... It will mistake its technical results for social wisdom and it will fail to see the limits within which its measures are capable of effective application. For the expert, by definition, lacks contact with the plain man. At another point, he observed: The expert, in fact, simply by reason of his immersion in a routine, tends to lack flexibility of mind once he approaches the margins of his special theme.

(3) Attitude Towards Leadership. Decisions in public agencies are the product of a collective effort and it is seldom a process where individual arriving at a conclusions on some policy issue. It is a long process involving a continuous efforts where ideas and solutions are researched, debated, checked, and weighed sometimes to the point of exasperation for the interested citizen on the outside. According to Stahl, "From the standpoint of making sure that an action truly serves the public interest and is consistent with law a carefully followed procedure is both understandable and praiseworthy in the light of the very principles that have been enunciated here. There are several short falls in the multiple reviews and checks as they consume a lot of time inhibit maximum delegation, of authority down the line—a cardinal principle of good management. Further these checks diffuse responsibility so widely that it becomes difficult to determine who did what.

(4) Conflicts of Interest. A conflict of interest occurs when an individual's private best interest (usually economic) might run counter to serving the public interest to appear to do so. Such situations arise in all the branches of government, *i.e.,* the legislature, the exeoutive and the judiciary. As Stahl has rightly put it, the bigistor who steers through or at least votes for a bill that benefits an enterprise in which he has some monetary investment, the judge who hears a corporation in which he holds stock, and the public executive who has decision-making authority affecting the fortunes of persons or business with which he has economic connections. The latter confrontation of interests is particularly noted in the consideration and decision-making of regulatory commissions, purchasing and contracting officers, tax assessors, inspectors of various kinds, and the like. Thus conflict of interest becomes the spring head of bias in decision making at various levels which seriously affects administrative morality.

(5) Social Conditions and Environment. Practically speaking it is too much to desire that a public service can be expected to rise much above the level of its environment, that it derives most of its temptations for wrong doing from that environment, and that, on top of all this, a double standard is applied to public officials as contrasted with men in private life. But it must be put here the fact that we expect higher standards of condcut from our public servants than we do from businessmen. To explain it further, in business and professions, the principals can buy and sell according to their wish: can disclose or conceal information on their operations can show favours can accept gifts without 'question of impropriety', without any worry about conflicts of interest. But when similar activities are discovered in any branch of the public service, everyone is alarmed. Our admiration goes out to the man who makes good in business even though his methods may be ruthless and he may keep within the letter rather than the spirit of the law. The same admiration does not go to the man who makes a full-time job of politics in an effort to win power and wealth.

This has been termed as following double standards and a subcommittee the United States that was among the first to cite the effects of the double standards:

We...believe that the ethical standards of public officials are probably higher than those prevailing in business and other walks of life. On this point there was persuassive testimony from men of experience in both government and business and from observers of both. Public officials apparently are more conscious of the problem of moral standards. The resentment which public officials sometimes show when subjected to public criticism may be explained in part by their awareness of the fact that some of their critics would be even more vulnerable to criticism if the same standards were applied.

This tendency, as it appears from the observation of a Department of Interior official (U.S.A.) makes blurring errors by ignoring serious charges and focussing attention only small incidents if it involves public servants. The American people wouldn't bat an eye if a real estate syndicate stole one of the Daktoas but no matter how high up in government you are, they'll hound you out of office if you take a deep-freeze or a vicuna coar. That's something they can understand. An oil lease, a grazing permit, a mining license, who cares? If you lean towards larcency, swipe a multimillion dollar government patent or a million acres of government land, but don't ever take a washer-dryer combination. That's fatal.

This situation has further been explained by the following quote. The law's reach is necessarily limited and much of the most dangerous and destinctive corruption of our times is entirely legal. The law itself may be used to reap enoromous rewards at public expense, as through subsidies or manipulation of the tax structure. Silver was once the favoured total of the wild Western radicals; now oil is the magic mineral of the "nouveau riche" Southwestern radicals. In comparison with special-interest legislation of such dimensions, the little fees and favors of the five per centers are trivial enough. At the old English rhyme has it:

The law locks up both man and woman
Who steals the goose from off the common
Yet turns the greater felon loose
Who steals the common from the goose.

This discussion leads to the invariable conclusion that society as a whole must bear the responsibility for ethical conduct in public affairs. It has been opined the those who complain to the general public are the more serious corruptors. "Until the citizen's own moral code prevents him from debasing himself by procuring corruption of public servants, the problem of corruption and morality in public life will remain very real and earnest." According to the Staff director of the Task Force on Personnel of these-cond Hoover Commission: The business executive who thinks only in terms of his corporation, the labour leader who thinks only in terms of his union, the leader of organized agriculture who thinks only in terms of his farm organisation are all a menace to the basic integrity of the nation. In a free society the responsibilities of the statesman fall on everyone, and upon each person in accordance with his power and ability.

IDEA OF SOCIAL CONTRACT

The aim of this topic is to discover a corporation's indirect obligations by attempting to clarify the meaning of business's so called "social contract." The task is challenging. Although people speak frequently of such a contract, few have attempted to specify its meaning. Although business-people, legislators and academics offer examples of supposed infractions of the "contract", few can explain what justifies the contract itself. Consider the assertion that Chisso Corporation violated its "contract" with society when it knowingly dumped toxic mercury into the ocean, or that the Nestle Corporation violated its "contract" when it promoted sales of infant formula in Third World countries. What serves as the ultimate basis for such claims? No contract can be pulled from a drawer and pointed to; no signaturaes can be checked for authenticity. Just what, then, is the social contract?

A good starting point is the so called "social contract" that philosophers have spoken of between society and the state. This political contract has usually been viewed as a theoretical means for justifying the existence of the state. Philosophers have asked, "Why should people let a government exist at all?" in other words, "Why should people prefer to have a government control much of their actions - to impose taxes, raise armies, and punish criminals - instead of having no government at all?" They never doubted for a moment the need for a state, but they believed raising such questions would clarify not only the justification for the state's existence, but also the reciprocal obligations between the state and its citizens. If a government began to abuse its citizenry, to trample on its rights or to diminish social welfare, then according to such philosophers it had broken the tenets of the social contract and could be overthrown.

The political social contract provides a clue for understanding the contract for business. If the political contract serves as a justification for the existence of the state, then the business contract by parity of reasoning should serve as the justification for the existence of the corporation.

Thus, crucial questions are: Why should corporations exist at all? What is the fundamental justification of their activities? How can we measure their performance and say when they have achieved their fundamental purpose? Consider a case involving General Motors and the production of automobiles. The automobiles that General Motors produced during the 1950s and 1960s all had noncollapsible steering wheels (called by Ralph Nader "ram-rodding" steering wheels), and evidence indicated that they contributed to hundreds of thousands of highway deaths. But General Motors and other auto manufacturers kept them on the cars anyway, claiming the added expense of collapsible steering wheels would reduce car sales and profits. Their claim may well have been true. However, by refusing to install safer steering wheels, had they failed to achieve a fundamental corporate mission? Had they violated a tenet of an implied social contract between them and society? Or had they jsut attended to business- although in a way which had unfortunate consequences for society? To answer the questions, we must first know what justifies General Motors' existence.

It is reasonable to look for a fundamental purpose, or set of purposes, that justifies corporate existence. Doing so makes conceptual sense, despite the fact one would never look for what justifies say, human existence. We choose to create corporations and we might choose either not to create them or to create different entities. Corporations thus are like political states in their need for justification.

One might attempt to justify corporate existence by appealing simply to corporate productivity: to the automobiles, irons, tools, clothing, and medical equipment corporations create. Because society demands such items, it seemingly also requires the corporations that produce them. Adam Smith, the eighteenth-century Scottish philosopher, emphasizes productivity when he justifies a set of economic practices through their contribution to the wealth of nations. But although productivity is surely a crucial piece in the puzzle of corporate justification, it fails to provide a full solution. To say that an organization produces wealth for society is not sufficient to justify it from a moral perspective, since morality encompasses the entire range of human welfare. To say something produces wealth is to say something morally good about it—assuming that wealth is counted as a human good—but it fails to tell us what else the thing does, or how its process of creation affects society. Consider the example of a nuclear power reactor. To say that a nuclear reactor generates electricity is to say something good about it, but it fails to consider the reactor in the context of the possibility of melt-downs, the storage of nuclear waste, the costs of alternative production, and so forth. And this is true even if we suppose that ultimately nuclear reactors are fully justified. The logic of the problem of corporate justification is similar. To achieve a complete moral picture of a corporation's existence, we must consider not just its capacity to produce wealth, but rather the full range of its effects upon society: its tendencies to pollute or to harm workers, or, alternatively, its tendencies to help employees by providing jobs and other benefits for society.

Suppose, on the other hand, that one tried to justify corporate existence simply through the inherent "right" of corporations to exist.

We remember that one of the two rival interpretations of the corporation sees it as a product of free human association: people freely come together for the purpose of conducting business, and they constitute the corporation. And we remember that in the United States since the midnineteenth century corporate status has been regarded as a right, not a privilege.

Again, this line of reasoning falls short of providing a complete justification. Granted the act of incorporation does not happen in a vacuum; at a minimum there must be a petitioning group of persons. But even granting that individuals, by virtue of their freedom, are allowed to create these superpersonal entities, and even granting that the entities themselves should possess unlimited longevity and limited liability, these facts by themselves say nothing about why people ought to do such a thing. An analogy reveals the distinction: people may, by virtue of their freedom, be allowed to become drunk nightly; but it is abundantly clear that their right to do so fails to justify their nightly drunkenness. Similarly, even if their were a right to incorporate, it would fail to justify corporate existence in the sense of showing why corporations ought to exist.

HISTORY OF THE SOCIAL CONTRACT

Because neither method of justification appears satisfactory, let us return to the idea of a social contract. Other methods, such as traditional utilitarianism, are available and promising, and should not be ruled out. But the focus of this chapter's efforts will be upon the method of social contract. The aim will be to determine what a social contract for business might look like. Since none has been constructed, the best strategy will be to look again at its counterpart, the political social contract. Perhaps if we discover the inner workings of the contract between citizens and the state, a blueprint will emerge for constructing the contract between society and corporations.

In the hands of political philosophers the term "social contract" has referred not to an item, but to a method for justifying and explaining the state. The most renowned classical philosophers adopting it were the English philosophers, Thomas Hobbes (1588-

1679) and John Locke (1632-1704), and the French philosopher Jean-Jacques Rousseau (1712-78). Each first imagined society without a civil state (without, that is, any government), and then society with it. The strategy was to highlight the benefits that society should expect to receive from the state. Yet, despite similarity of method, each reached different conclusions. Hobbes argued that people must obey the king, or sovereign, because the social contract itself is a contract between sovereign and people. Without such a contract, *i.e.* in the state without government which Hobbes called a "state of nature," only a condition of "war" could exist, with each person being pitted against his or her fellow human, and no power or authority to make peace among them.

John Locke, writing after Hobbes, repudiated such pessimism. The state of nature preceding the contract, Locke contended, was not one of war, but rather a tolerable, though mildly unruly situation in which people possessed natural rights, such as the right to property and freedom. Indeed they lacked only an efficient means to arbitrate their disputes and protect their rights. To remedy these drawbacks, society must construct the social contract. However, the agreement is not, as Hobbes thought, between the people and a sovereign. Instead, people first establish "civil society," and afterwards civil society negotiates an agreement (a fiduciary trust) to establish a legislative power, or government that will protect society's rights. If the government fails to protect society's rights, then the trust is broken and revolution is justified. Locke is more wary of government abuses than Hobbes. For Locke, the relationship between people and legislative power is not one of contract rather it is the same kind that exists between employer and employee, that is, a "trust" between principal and agent. "This conception," J.W. Gough remarks, "fitted Locke's intention admirably, for unlike the contract of government, in which rights and duties were reciprocal, it left the duties on the side of the government, and the rights on the side of the people."

Rousseau's version of the social contract differs from the earlier two. According to him, the contract is created when rights are surrendered in toto by individuals to the whole community. As he puts it paradoxically, "Each, giving himself to all, gives himself to nobody." With this, the state is born. The state's desire for its own welfare, dubbed by Rousseau the "general will" thus becomes the yardstick by which all government actions are to be measured.

This cannot do full justice to the arguments of the social contract philosophers; instead, a few general observations about their methods must suffice. First, the tradition of social contract theory is a tradition of social change and reform. This holds not only for the arguments of Hobbes, Locke, and Rousseau, but for ones less wellknown. The Huguenots, a apersecuted Protestant group in France, used a social contract argument in the sixteenth century to defend religious tolerance and the English Whigs, a political group, used it in the seventeenth century to bolster the cause of civil liberty. Consider Robert Ferguson's remark in his Brief Justification of the Prince of Orange's Descent into England: "No government is lawful," Ferguson writes, "but what is founded upon compact and agreement between those chosen to govern and those who condescend to be governed." Social contract arguments have unsettled the clergy, shaken monarchies, and brought on revolution.

The contract has been used as a moral ideal, as a law higher even than the state, against which the state must be evaluated. It is not unlike the "higher law" invoked by the Greeks and Romans. We are reminded of Sophocles' play, Antigone, in which a grief-stricken woman learns that her brother's body has been condemned to rot outside the city's walls, stripped even of the honour of a burial. She defies the orders of the king and risks her own life to bury her brother. When asked why she disobeys, she tells the king that his laws have less authority than the ones she obeys: the eternal, unwritten laws of the gods.

Second, two basic forms of the contract can be distinguished. The first postulates people as being in a "state of nature," and agreeing to create an organized society. By "state of nature" is meant a situation prior to the emergence of government, prior, that is, to legislatures, courts of law, police and public officials. The government is seen as a creation of the people; it emerges from the people and owes its very existence to them. The second approach does not imagine people creating government, but rather defining the terms of an implied contract between them and an existing government. This implied contract imposes obligations upon both parties: upon the government and the people. In the seventeenth century, for example, the people of England who wished to overthrow James II claimed that he had violated an implied contract: although this contract was not understood to explain the structure and formation of James' government, it was viewed as setting down certain conditions which he and the people were bound to follows.

Third, amid the various versions of the social contract theory a common strand exists: an emphasis on the consent of the parties. Most versions invite one to imagine the situation in which rational people, outside ordinary society, must consent to a proposal about the structure of social institutions. The characteristics of the situation—for example, what information people are presumed to have, what interests they bring to the decision, or what issues they are to decide—vary from theory to theory.

Critics have repeatedly attacked the social contract for its failure to represent historical fact. No one, the critics charge, could seriously believe that people once gathered in the woods to establish a contract for the world's first governments. Marx and other theorists (sch as Paley, Maine, and Blackstone) have made this very point. What is more, modern anthropology appears to confirm their suspicions.

But perhaps such criticism misses the mark, since, as was noticed already, social control theories have typically been used to analyze existing institutions rather than to create new ones. Locke wanted to discover the moral foundation for English government, not dig up the historical causes of the Sumerian or Egyptian kingdoms. Even if no pen and ink contracts ever existed, many would argue that an abstract contract exists, not unlike the invisible laws of the gods, which obliges governments to serve the social welfare. Even if no pen and ink contract ever existed, they would argue that the point of the social contract is to clarify the logical presuppositions, not the historical antecedents, of political power.

Terms of the Contract

Two principal classes of people stand to benefit or be harmed by the introduction of productive organizations: *(1)* people who consume the organizations' products, *i.e.* consumers; and *(2)* people who work in such organizations, *i.e.*, employees. The two classes are broadly defined and not mutually exclusive. "Consumer" refers to anyone who is economically interested; hence virtually anyone qualifies as a consumer. "Employee" refers to anyone who contributes labour to the productive process of a productive organization, including managers, laborers, part-time support personnel, and (in corporations) members of the board of directors.

Benefits for Consumers

From the standpoint of our hypothetical consumers, productive organizations promise to enhance the satisfaction of economic interests. That is to say, people could hope for the introduction of productive organizations to better satisfy their interests for shelter, food, entertainment, transportation, health care and clothing. The primq facie benefits for consumers include:

1. Improving efficiency through:
   - (a) Maximizing advantages of specialization.
   - (b) Improving decision-making resources.
   - (c) Increasing the capacity to use or acquire expensive technology and resources.
2. Stabilizing levels of output and channels of distribution.
3. Increasing liability resources.

Each benefit, of course, needs explanation.

The first benefit, improving efficiency, is the special excellence of productive organizations. Productive organizations tend to generate products that are equal or better in quality and price, with lower expenditures of human labour, than is possible in the state of individual production. Let us examine a few of the reasons for this remarkable capacity.

(A) Maximizing the Advantages of Specialization. Adam Smith's wellknown thought-experiment in the Wealth of Nations provides ready evidence for the truth that two can often be more efficient than one. He showed that in the production of pins, one person working alone could account for a mere handful of pins, whereas in a system of first-order specialization-where one cuts the wire, another points the wire, and so on-the proportionate share of pins per worker increases dramatically. The same is true today. To produce clocks, erasers, and antibiotics efficiently, an enormous degree of cooperative specialization is required: the mere existence of products like the space shuttle owes itself to such specialization. Economists agree that many products are further subject to economies of scale; that is, their efficient production is dependent not only upon cooperative specialization, but on a certain level of it. Because of this factor, a company like American Motors may be too small to compete successfully with General Motors in the production of automobiles.

The greater efficiency which derives from productive organizations is partially dependent upon the level of technology. At minimal levels it may be less efficient to have such system. One person working alone with stone implements may be able to clean and prepare vegetables as efficiently as three working in concert. At higher levels of technology this would not be true. The reverse is also possible: advanced technology may allow one person to be efficient in a situation where, minus the technology, he or she would not be Equipped with a mechanical combine, one individual may be efficient at harvesting wheat, whereas without it six or more would be required. But no matter what the level of technology, some tasks benefit from cooperative specialization. Even in a futuristic, thoroughly technological society, a group of scientists who cooperate to perfect an additional piece of technology should, all other things being equal, be more efficient than an aggregate of individual scientists working without contact among themselves.

(B) Improving Decision-making Resources. Productive organizations share with individual persons the tendency to err in decision-making. Despite this, such organizations have decision-making advantages. First, they can utilize the ongoing talents of people with different backgrounds. Thus, a decision by Westinghouse, Inc., to manufacture a new appliance may call on the knowledge of chemists, accountants, engineers, and marketing specialists. One person could never possess such knowledge.

Second, they can increase information storage. In the same way a person can collect and remember information on a small scale, organizations do so on a large scale. Productive organizations can have super human memories: some corporations have libraries larger than those in universities, where all their information bears either directly or indirectly upon productive success.

(C) Increasing the Capacity to Use and Acquire Expensive Technology and Resources. This advantage is nearly self-evident. All other things being equal, two or more people will have greater financial resources than one; hence productive organizations can make capital expenditure on a larger scale than single individuals. Often the use of large, expensive equipment is important not only for increasing production, but for generating higher quality production, since expensive equipment is frequently necessary to improve productive efficiency. An individual who intends to produce bread cannot compete in today's world without mechanical ovens, assembly lines, and mechanical bread-slicers. Yet few individuals can afford such items, much less attempt to operate them singlehandedly. By combining their energies and resources in a productive organization, people can increase the cost effectiveness of production.

Stabilizing Levels of Output and Channels of Distribution

The imaginary inhabitants of our state of individual production stand to benefit by the merging of individual craftsmen into organizations which are relatively stable, and whose level of output and pattern of distribution are relatively constant. Individual craftsmen are subject to illness, psychological problems, and the need for rest.

For example, to rely on an individual mail carrier for the delivery of one's mail is riskier than depending on a large postal organization. Individuals must sleep, eat, and rest, but a large postal organization never sleeps, never eats—it even grows larger at Christmas. In general, then, productive organizations promise to stabilize the market for the benefit of the consumer.

Increasing Liability Resources

Under this heading are grouped the benefits that consumers reap because organizations, in contrast to individuals, have "deep pockets." In short, they are better able to compensate injured consumers. In the late 1970's Ford Motor Company was forced by the courts to compensate victims of the Ford Pinto's exploding gas tank. Because of design defects, the Pinto's tank was prone to ignite when hit from behind. The money paid by Ford to victims (and relatives of victims) was astounding; it ran into the millions of dollars. Although few productive organizations are as large as Ford, it remains true that organizations are better able to back their products with financial resources than individuals. Contrast the capacity of any automobile company in this regard with the capacity of the individual person who builds an auto in his or her backyard.

ADVANTAGES TO EMPLOYEES

These, then, are the *prima facie* from introducing productive organizations for consumers. But productive organizations should also be viewed from the standpoint of their effects on people as workers, that is, from the standpoint of their effects upon individual laborers and craftsmen in the state of individual production who opt to work for productive organizations.

It is not difficult to discover certain *prima facie* benefits such as the following:

(1) Increasing Income Potential. This benefit follows immediately from the earlier fact that cooperative specialization increases productive efficiency. The person, like Smith's hypothetical pinmaker, who joins others in the production of pins is able to make many times more pins than he would alone. This increase also represents an increase in his chance to receive a higher income.

It also increases, if he is so inclined, his overall capacity to contribute to society. For if he feels some personal obligation to contribute productively to society, or if he merely wishes to be benevolent, his increased productivity increases his power of doing so. Two options are available: he can either accept lower than normal personal remuneration, thus increasing his net contribution; or he can accept normal remuneration and give some of it away. An example of the former would be those who work in voluntary organizations, *e.g.*, the Women's Service League or the Peace Corps. An example of the latter is the person who works for a major company, but who donates some of his salary to charity. In any case, the person who increases his productivity by joining a productive organization thereby increases, all other things being equal, both his income potential and his capacity for contribution. Of course, ambitious owners or unjust economic arrangements may deprive workers of the additional income which they (the workers) have generated. But this is a by-product of the particular owners or of particular economic systems, and not a feature of productive organizations *per se*.

(2) Diffusing Personal liabiality. A second *prima facie* benefit from the standpoint of workers lies in the capacity of an organization to diffuse liability, or in short, to insure the individual against the risk of massive compensation demands. A worker in the state of individual production who sells faulty, dangerous products is morally liable for the damages her product causes. If she negligently drops poison in the medicine she manufactures, then she is ethically bound to compensate the victim. But the extent of this liability can exceed her capacity to pay.

(3) Adjusting Personal Income Allocation. The increased resources of the productive organization allow the worker to participate in an income-allocation scheme which is detached from the vicissitudes of his capacity to produce, and which is more closely tied to his actual needs. The vicissitudes of the worker's capacity include occasional illness, disabling accidents, and a tendency to lose speed and strength as he ages. Yet his needs persist and sometimes even increase in the face of these vicissitudes. The employee can work harder when he is healthy; but he needs as much money, and sometimes more, when he is ill. The worker may not be able to produce more when he is 50 than when he was 20, but if he marries and has a family his need for income may be greater at 50. When the worker joins a productive organization, the organization can allocate personal income according to a scheme more equitable for him and everyone else. Income may, for example, be raised in accordance with length of service, even in a proportion greater than the individual's productivity, and it can continue to be distributed to workers even when they are ill and disabled.

These *prima facie* benefits to the worker may be added to the prima facie consumer benefits discussed earlier. Together they constitute a set of reasons which rational people living in a state of individual production might use to justify the introduction of productive organizations. Indeed, if some such set of *prima facie* benefits did not exist, then people would be foolish to introduce such organizations; there would be nothing to gain.

It now becomes possible in light of this analysis to begin the task of specifying the general character of a hypothetical social contract. From the standpoint of society, the goal of a productive organization may be said to be to enhance the welfare of society through a satisfaction of consumer and worker interests. In turn, each of the prima facie benefits that we have discussed can be construed as specific terms of the social contract. Productive organizations should attempt to satisfy consumer interests through enhancing efficiency, stabilizing output, and augmenting liability, and they should attempt to satisfy employee interests through increasing income potential, diffusing personal liability, and adjusting income allocation.

Drawbacks for Consumers and Employees

An obvious question arises. If people in the state of individual production must agree upon the terms of the social contract, and if these terms directly relate to the task of enhancing society's welfare, then why stop with maximizing *prima facie* benefits? Why not also minimize *prima facie* drawbacks? John Locke employed a similar strategy in structuring his political social contract: he not only specified the positive goals of government, but, recognizing government's tendency to abuse privilege, also saw fit to specify certain pitfalls that government must avoid. Are there *prima facie* drawbacks to introducing productive organizations as well? Are there drawbacks from the standpoint of consumers? Of workers?

Our imaginary consumer stands to benefit because productive organizations, alongwith the technology they encourage, improve productivity and put more shoes, clothing, electricity and automobiles on the market. But there is an unwanted consequence of which twentieth-century consumers are painfully aware: increased production tends to deplete natural resources while increasing pollution. More shoes, clothing, electricity, and automobiles require more leather, cotton, coal, and iron. The world has a finite supply. Moreover the amazing machines so well adapted to productive organisations—the gas engines, the coal furnaces, and the nuclear reactors all generate by-products which render the environment less fit for human life.

The problem of the increased pollution and depletion of natural resources is more obvious than a second problem, which is the diffusion of individual moral responsibility which sometimes occurs in productive organisations. In the state of individual production, the consumers buy their goods from the individual craftsman who stands behind his product, or at least if he does not, the consumers know where to go. When the cobbler sells a pair of shoes to John Doe and the shoes fall apart, he must confront Doe face to face. Contrast this situation with that of productive organizations, in which workers never see the consumer. To the employee, the consumer is faceless, and the employee's level of psychic accountability tends to lower alongwith a rise in consumer anonymity. The employee is responsible for his behaviour, but to his superior, not to the customer; and his superior sometimes is more apathetic than he.

Whlle speaking of potential drawbacks of productive organizations, one must also acknowledge that the political power of productive organisations is sometimes used to enhance individual interets. Such power sometimes is used to secure favors from government which damage both consumer interests and the interests of the general public. Organisations can receive favors which bolster monopoly power and aggravate inefficiency, as when the rail-roads in the United States in the late nineteenth century used government grants and privileges to develop a stranglehold on public transportation. Organisations can also use power to divert government expenditures from consumer items to items that actually harm the consumer's interests. In Germany prior to World Wars I and II, for example, large munitions manufacturers used their political influence to increase taxation, and thus decrease consumers buying power, for massive purchases of cannons, tanks, fighter planes, and warships.

From the perspective of consumers these problems represent potential drawbacks often associated with the introduction of productive organizations. But drawbacks also exist for employees.

Workers in the state of individual production possess a few obvious advantages. For one, they are close to the product and able to take pride in their own creations and the fact that their hands were responsible for the lamp, the soap or the shirt being sold. But workers in productive organizations are typically removed from the product. They are, in the words of Marx, "alienated" in a way that may block their very capacity for self-expression. During World War II the U.S. aircraft manufacturers discovered that alienation was shampering production. Production was shown to increase when the draftsmen, riveters, and sheetmetal workers were taken to see the finished product they had worked on-the airplane itself. In addition to possible alienation and loss of pride, the worker may also suffer from losing control over the design of the product and of his or her work structure. Whereas the individual craftsman can structure her hours and conditions to suit herself, the organisational worker must suit the needs of the overall organisation. A man or woman working on an assembly line is powerless to improve the design of the product, and equally powerless to change the design of the work process. The look of the product, the speed of the conveyor belt, and even the number of steps to perform the task all have been determined by others, who are frequently strangers to the worker.

The increased capacity of productive organizations (over individuals) to use large, expensive technology and massive resources reveals on the other side a decreased capacity of the workers to control their lives. They must adapt to the machines. If a machine operates most efficiently at a certain pace, then the worker must, like the spool boys of the nineteenth-century cotton industry, hurry to meet that pace. In such cases it is as if the machine were controlling the person instead of the person controlling the machine. Similarly, the increased efficiency which results from specialization reveals, on its reverse, the monotony of the simple task repeated thousands of times. The man who knocked the struts into place on the wheels of Henry Ford's Model T was far more efficient than the old craftsman who built a carriage from the bottom up.

These *prima facie* drawbacks may be seen as reasons for not introducing productive organizations. Unless the *prima facie* benefits discussed earlier outweigh these prima facie drawbacks, no contract will be concluded because rational people will not choose a lesser over a greater good. And if the benefits outweigh the drawbacks, it follows that in order maximally to enhance welfare, productive organisations should both pursue positive goals and minimize negative ones. Thus, using our discussion as a basis for this list of negative goals, we have:

From the standpoint of consumers, productive organizations should minimize:

1. Pollution and the depletion of natural resources.
2. The destruction of personal accountability.
3. The misuse of political power.

From the standpoint of workers, productive organizations should minimize:

1. Worker alienation.
2. Lack of worker control over work conditions.
3. Monotony and dehumanization of the worker.

Thus the social contract will specify that these negative consequences be minimized.

Trade Offs

The social contract sketched out requires, then, that productive organisations maximize goods and minimize evils relative to consumer and worker welfare. But how will an organization know how to make the inevitable trade-offs between maximizing and minimizing, and between consumer interests and worker interests? For example, a corporate decision may impair worker interests while at the same time enhancing consumer interests. Consider the age-old trade-off between higher salaries and lower consumer prices. If coffee workers are paid higher salaries, then coffee drinkers pay higher prices. Conversely, if doctors are paid lower salaries, then patients pay lower prices. These trade-offs are common not only in the area of salaries, but in many others as well. Where does one draw the line?

How would the rational inhabitants of our state of individual production answer this question? Because the contract specifies that the function of productive organisations is to enhance the welfare of society, our inhabitants might choose a utilitarian standard for making trade-offs, that is, a standard that would specify that organisational policies or action should aim for the greatest good for the greatest number. On the other hand, they might prefer a non utilitarian, or deontological standard, which would specify that organisational action should accord with general policies or rules which could be universalised for all productive organisations (*i.e.*, which society would want al productive organizations to adopt).

Whatever the standard—and it must be acknowledged that determining the standard is difficult—two things seem certain. First, society does acknowledge that trade-offs often must be made. Society could not reasonably expect productive organisations to maximize worker interests come what may, say by adopting the policy of paying workers the absolute maximum possible at a given time, for to do so would grossly neglect consumers. If General Motors expended every bit of its resources on employees, the result for society would be catastrophic. Similarly, the consumer must not receive all the attention.

Because trade-offs must be made, it remains logically possible that people in the state of individual production would choose to introduce productive organisations and to establish the social contract, even when they expected either workers interests or consumer interests to be less satisfied than in the state of nature—so long as overall welfare were enhanced. In other words, the inhabitants might believe that, on balance, people as workers stand to lose from the introduction of productive organizations, and that potential alienation loss of control, and other drawbacks make the overall condition of the worker worse than before.

Justice

There is a caveat which has application to the overall contract. People would make a trade-off of the kind just discussed only on the condition that it did not violate certain minimum standards of justice, however these are specified. For example, they would refuse to enact the contract if they knew that the existence of productive organizations would systematically reduce a given class of people for an in human existence, subsistence poverty, or enslavement.

This point, in turn, provides a clue to one of the specific tenets of the contract. Although the contract might allow productive organisations to undertake actions requiring welfare trade-offs, it would prohibit organisational acts of injustice. It might allow a corporation to layoff, or reduce the salaries of, thousands of workers in order to block skyrocketing production costs; here worker welfare would be diminished while consumer welfare would be enhanced. But it is another matter when the company commits gross injustices in process—for example, if it lies to workers, telling them that no layoffs are planned merely to keep them on the job until the las minute. Similarly, it is another matter when the organisation follows discriminatory hiring policies, refusing to hire blacks or women, in the name of "consumer advantage". These are clear injustices of the kind that society would want to prohibit as a condition of the social contract. We may infer, then, that a tenet of the social contract will be that productive organizations are to remain within the bounds of the general canons of justice.

Determining what justice requires is a notoriously difficult task. The writings of Plato, Aristotle, and more recently, John Rawls, have shed considerable light on this subject, but unfortunately we must forego a general discussion of justice here. At a minimum, however, the application of the concept of justice to productive organisations appears to imply that productive organizations avoid deception or fraud, that they show respect for their workers as human beings and that they avoid any practice that systematically worsens the situation of a given group in society. Despite the loud controversy over what justice means, most theorists would agree that justice means at least this much for productive organizations.

An Overview of the Contract

Our sketch of a hypothetical social contract is now complete. By utilizing the concept of rational people existing in a state of individual production, we have indicated the terms of a contract which they would require for the introduction of productive organisations. The questions asked in the beginning were: Why should corporations exist at all? What is the fundamental justification for their activities? How can we measure their performance, to say when they have performed poorly or well? A social contract helps to answer these questions. Corporations considered as productive organisations exist to enhance the welfare of society through the satisfaction of consumer and worker interests, in a way which relies on exploiting corporations' special advantages and minimizing disadvantages. This is the moral foundation of the corporation when considered as a productive organisation. The social contract also serves as a tool to measure the performance of productive organisations. That is, when such organizations fulfill the terms of the contract, they have done well. When they do not, then society is morally justified in condemning them.

Productive organisations (whether corporations or not) that produce quality goods at low prices, that reject government favouritism, and that enhance the wellbeing of workers receive high marks by the standards of the social contract. Those that allow inefficiency, charge high prices, sell low-quality products, and fail to enhance the wellbeing of workers receive low marks. The latter organizations have violated the terms of the social contract. They must reform themselves, or lose their moral right to exist.

It is well to notice that such a social contract does not specify additional obligations or rights which corporations have in contrast to productive organisations in general. The social contract justifies corporations as productive organisations, not as corporations. Presumably, then, further reasons remain to be discovered for society's establishing a certain type of productive organisation, such as the corporation—with limited liability, stockholder ownership, and its other characteristics. The important task of discovering those reasons, however, must wait for another occasion. Our development of the social contract has fallen short of a full moral comprehension of corporations, but it has secured a solid footing in an equally important area: comprehending the moral underpinnings of productive organisations.

□

15

Globalisation in Business Ethos

Privatisation, deregulation and liberalisation create more space for firms to pursue their corporate objectives. International agreements give more rights to firms to operate internationally. Should this expansion of action, space and rights be accompanied by an increase in corporate responsibilities? In the international context, this question attracts particular attention because TNCs are one of the principal drivers of globalisatien, They are also seen to be the most important beneficiaries of the liberalisation of investment and trade regimes, with rising influence oh the development of the world economy and its constituent parts. The concept of "social responsibility" captures the search for an answer to this question. It implies that firms have obligations that go beyond what countries require individually, and agreements prescribe internationally. The assumption of greater social responsibility by TNCs would be particularly important in light of the economic and social disruptions that accompany the globalisation process, which if not tackled—could threaten the very framework within which firms build their international production systems.

Social Responsibility of TNC

Corporate social responsibility encompasses an array of meanings and intended applications that have undergone substantial modifications over time. These are important to note and understand because they influence the dialogue between governments, business and other civil society groups. The same term, or its variations may carry different implications among various parties regarding the legitimacy, obligations and impact of corporate social responsibility standards. All societal groups are expected to perform certain roles and functions that can change over time with a society's own evolution. Expectations related to business enterprises, and particularly TNCs, are undergoing unusually rapid change due to the expanded role these enterprises play in a globalising society. Discussions relating to TNC social responsibility standards and performance therefore comprise an important component of efforts to develop a stable, prosperous and just global society.

1. Beyond Compliance with Law

Corporate social responsibility is sometimes mistakenly equated with either corporate philanthropy or simple compliance with law. These two ideas actually stand at opposite extremes to the social responsibility concept whose focus rests centrally on a firm's operational behaviour and its impacts on the surrounding society. Corporate philanthropy involves an activity extraneous to a firm's actual operations: while generally appreciated by social recipients, it does not represent an essential or even necessarily expected business function. By contrast, corporate compliance with law is no more than the mandated minimum necessary to permit the continued existence of any legally-chartered corporate entity.

A confusion between corporate philanthropy and corporate social responsibility can arise from this connection between corporate giving and a firm's business activities. Recipients of corporate gifts are often local communities in which an enterprise maintains its headquarters or significant production sites. Other gifts may seek to improve educational programmes in technical fields connected to corporate operations, or sponsor youth or elderly programmes related to the age groups comprising a firm's main product market. In these cases, philanthropic motivations can blend with marketing or brand-name enhancement objectives, creating a link between "good deeds" and corporate interests. However, such a philanthropic programme is really tangential to how a firm's operational behavior: impacts on society, which is the essence of corporate social responsibility. An external programme of "good deeds" will not protect a firm whose actual operations harm its surrounding society, nor will a society reject productive, well-behaved firms just because they do not engage in philanthropic activities.

Compliance with legal requirements constitutes a mandatory minimum standard for corporate conduct. Corporate entities are legal persons granted the right to exist and operate within a society, subject to the laws of that society. Violations of law subject firms to civil or criminal penalties and can result in revocation of the corporation's licence to operate. Some international instruments include references to a general duty of TNCs to observe the laws of the host country. However, these provisions simply recognise the essential role of national law in setting a mandatory minimum floor for corporate conduct. Corporate social responsibility rises above this required floor to incorporate standards of behaviour that may be expected, but are not required, under a society's legal statutes.

Compliance with law, then, is really nothing more than a minimum standard of conduct legally necessary to the corporation's continued existence. Corporate social responsibility that extends beyond legal mandates can help meet societal expectations in the absence of statutory devices. Such conduct may be particularly important to meeting social needs in developing countries where legal regimes may be absent or underdeveloped in areas related to certain aspects of TNC conduct.

2. Evolving Corporate Social Contracts and Stake Holder Interests

The intellectual foundation for most evolving views of corporate social responsibility lies largely with the notion of a "social contract" between a corporation and its host society. The legal incorporation process results in a formal corporate charter that grants an enterprise the right to operate within the governing society's body of established laws and regulations. From one viewpoint, these legal requirements can be seen to constitute the full extent of a corporation's societal responsibility; for anything else, "the business of business is business". A contrasting philosophy, however, asserts a broader, extra-Legal social contract that encompasses a society's implicit assumptions and expectations regarding the behaviour of corporations to which the society has granted a right of existence. This social contract incorporates a firm's contractual legal obligations but extends beyond them to include additional expectations or responsibilities that are not (currently) mandatory. The contents of a corporation's social contract can evolve more rapidly than its legal charter, reflecting a society's changing social and cultural modes. When governed parties, such as corporations, are slow to comply with new societal values, those norms may then be formulated into legally-binding mandates.

In several respects, social contract theory helps bridge the conceptual gap between the early history of voluntary gifts involving personal or corporate philanthropy and broader, contemporary concepts of corporate social responsibility. The first essential step is to attach a stronger sense of moral duty or obligation to desired corporate activity. If certain norms of behaviour are part of an implicit social contract, then complying corporate actions become a more obligatory response rather than a philanthropic "good deed" whose design and initiation re t entirely unilaterally with the charitable benefactor. A second element arises from the potential relationship between social and legal contracts: to the extent that evolving values encompassed within social contract expectations may become viewed as "moral minimums", the expectation is strong that those norms will be made into legal mandates, unless complied with "voluntarily". This notion corresponds to the implicit (or sometimes explicit) "threat" that some corporations perceive behind "voluntary" codes of conduct, where noncompliance may result in even more restrictive mandatory regulations. The third link ties social responsibility standards more closely to the essential nature of corporate operations. Social contract theory encompasses a broad range of corporate behaviour, certainly including the normal operating standards for a firm's core activities. This operational agenda introduces social responsibility notions into a firm's internal operations whereas self-initiated acts of charitable giving to external constituencies keeps non-legal societal standards at a safe distance from the corporation's inside processes. Hence, corporate social responsibility has come to be associated with standards of performance that are applied to both internal and external corporate activities, addressing societal norms that are not (but may become) legally-required mandates.

Stakeholder analysis represents a companion concept to social contract theory. A stakeholder approach seeks to define corporate social responsibility broadly in relation to the groups or interests that affect, or are affected by, a corporation's actions. A contrasting shareholder view of corporate responsibility focuses more narrowly on an enterprise's need to serve the interests of its owners by pursuing and delivering profitable returns to its investing shareholders. Shareholders are indisputably important stakeholders in business enterptises. But these two concepts carry very different implications about whether shareholder interests should be given exclusive or even relative priority over other stakeholder goals.

No consensus exists on any single list of corporate stakeholders, although most discussions include groups such as shareholders, workers, managers, customers, suppliers, local communities and governments. Affected stakeholder interests can also be conceptualised in such terms as the unknown or as yet unrecognised interests (future generations or unexpected side-effects). To some degree, the number of relevant stakeholders, and the nature of a corporation's social responsibility to them, vary with a corporation's own unique characteristics, including its size, sector, product and operations. In any event, it will comprise all those that for one reason or another—feel that they are affected by a company's operation.

The size, scope and impact of modern TNCs extends their potential takeholder groups beyond the realm defined by the normal activities of national corporations. In all societies, some groups affected by corporate activity will lack the economic or political power to ensure that their interests are represented adequately through market mechanisms or governmental regulations. In a global society, however, the under-representation of developing country needs and concerns presents a challenge of far greater magnitude, with considerably broader consequences. Special concerns arise from TNC interactions with developing countries, where FDI can play a large role especially in a relatively small domestic economy. In countries with weak competitive discipline of efficient markets or lacking "good governance" reflected in effective governmental institutions to represent the public interest, TNC social responsibility requires that the corporation pay special attention to the interests of under-represented stakeholders that could be adversely affected by business operations.

3. The Scope and Content of Corporate Social Responsibility

The scope of corporate social responsibility is conceptually quite unbound at the present time. Although the debate between TNCs, civil society and governments often focuses on a few key issues-notably human rights, the environment and workers' rights—this list is by no means exhaustive. In principle, a company is broadly responsible for the consequences of its operations, including direct impacts as well as unintended side-effects or other externalities that affect third parties. In fact, a more expansive definition of the scope of social responsibility would also cover firms linked to another firm by more or less strong business ties (*e.g.* with supplying firms)—what, in the environment discussion is called the "environmental footprint". Calls for greater corporate social responsibility generally arise from incidents involving negative external effects in areas in which legal responsibilities are-not (yet) clarified. These externalities can occur in a wide range of areas involving various stakeholder groups. Negatively affected groups will ask companies causing these impacts to take measures to prevent, reduce or rectify such consequences, or otherwise to internalise the costs resulting from their activities. External effects can, for example, relate to the social changes produced in a community by a TNC's decision to close down large existing operations. Negative externalities involving environmental impacts are well known.

Although the list of issues that can be included under a comprehensive definition of corporate social responsibility is long (and could include, *e.g.* consumer rights, information disclosure and fiscal and commercial probity), very few issues actually receive levels of public attention that might convince TNCs to include them in their responsibilities. Infact many issues, especially ones that may particularly affect people in developing countries, go often unnoticed by the wider public and are not taken up by TNCs as long as they are not associated with sufficiently influential public pressure. A number of development-related issues—such as technology transfer, training of the local workforce, the importance of backward linkages and the promotion of local entrepreneurship—that are of great interest to developing countries are generally not included when TNCs and civil society in the developed countries engage in debates over corporate social responsibility.

4. Business, Civil Society and Government Perceptions of Corporate Social Responsibility

The relationship between standards of corporate social responsibility and potential legal requirements governing corporate operations lies at the heart of the sometimes adversarial relationship between civil society groups and the business community. For many civil society groups, corporate social responsibility signifies conduct that rises above the minimum required by law but still constitutes a corporate duty to act rather than a more optional norm or charitable "good deed". This view—that corporate social responsibility standards are, in fact, normative obligations—is evident when civil society groups implicitly or explicitly threaten to seek legal mandates should business fail to comply with acceptable voluntary guidelines deriving from the social contract. Private enterprises on the other hand generally prefer the flexibility of self-designed voluntary standards. However, when voluntary guidelines are devised as part of a public process involving governments and/or civil society, corporate executives tend to worry that the content and precise wording of voluntary guidelines may become a precedent for subsequent legal requirements.

The business community's aversion to binding international legal standards governing corporate operations contrasts with its strong advocacy of international law commitments applied to the obligations of governments towards foreign investors. This view is advocated on issues such as expropriation and compensation standards, and guarantees of nondiscriminatory national treatment relative to domestic firms. In these cases, governmental responsibilities are seen as normative duties or obligations, based on fair treatment principles, that should be backed by international legal sanctions.

For governments, the relationship between a social contract and legal regulations governing corporate operations assumes new meaning and complexities when the business concerned is transnational. A mismatch exists between the territorially-bounded-authority of national governments and the transnational reach of a TNC's integrated international production system. Although an individual country may seek to extend its law extra-territorially, its reach may infringe on another country's sovereignty, raising the potential for political conflicts and confrontations. The obvious solution is to devise a common foundation of international law whose reach will match the global span of modem corporate activities; but in a world of diverse nation-states with often divergent goals and priorities, this remedy proves difficult, time- consuming and, in many cases, impossible to achieve as a near-term outcome.

Generalisations about national government perspectives on the concept of TNC legal and social contracts can mask important differences both within and between countries. Conflicting domestic pressures exist in many countries that reflect divergent views on whether outward FOI and trade expansion are in the national interest, and how resulting economic and social adjustment costs should be managed, at home and abroad. Perceiving an incipient backlash against globalisation in some home countries, developing countries may fear that proposals for new TNC social responsibility standards can represent a disguised form of protectionism. Thus, proposals that seek improvements in TNC global operating standards can generate mixed reactions within and among countries based on differing views of how national Finterests may be affected.

5. International Guidelines and Codes of Conduct

A consensus on TNC-related issues capable—of supporting international law formulations was unattainable during the turbulent decade of the 1970s when acrimony, over TNC roles and activities was at its zenith, and debates in international organisations split along a widening North-South divide. Faced with the apparent impossibility of generating international standards backed by legal sanctions, some governments initiated discussions aimed at developing nonbinding codes of corporate conduct. These devices developed into new "soft law" alternatives, somewhat akin to a defined social contract, whereby governments would endorse and promote the agreed standards as embodying the type of conduct expected of "good corporate citizens". These soft law standards were achievable precisely because they did not require intergovernmental consensus on the level of detail necessary for legally-enforceable regulations. Instead, differing points of view and emphases could be accommodated through creatively broad and sometimes deliberately ambiguous language that left room for flexible implementation.

Sometimes, voluntary compliance regimes can provide an alternative that permits public action while shifting the burden somewhat onto corporations to discern, apply and monitor the voluntary standards in a way that will be deemed acceptable to that firm's surrounding society (which, in the case of a TNC, actually comprises numerous and diverse societies whose views, expectations and priorities may differ and perhaps conflict). Governments and other constituent groups can then judge corporate performance case-by-case, with wide latitude to interpret the guidelines and respond to corporate actions as they see fit. This aspect might play a particularly important role in countries with deficits of governance, fed where governments lack (the will or) the means to enforce legal standards.

Regardless of the question whether legally binding standards are superior to voluntary regimes or not, voluntary standards appear to be gaining renewed favour among some governments. One reason may be that legally binding standards prove difficult to negotiate internationally. In other instances some governments find voluntary compliance regimes more efficient and cost-effective to address technically complex and rapidly-changing business operations.

6. International Aspects of Corporate Social Responsibility

The concept of corporate social responsibility embraces standards of good business practice that can apply to all firms, whether they are national or international in their scope and orientation. But to devise international legal regulation of TNC operations can be difficult, because of the multiple sovereign governments involved and the great diversity among their respective countries' perspectives, policies and priorities. These same differences also make it difficult, although somewhat more possible, to forge agreement on non-binding corporate guidelines or codes to conduct. For corporations, the task can be equally daunting, for they must strive to meet or exceed these diverse and sometimes conflicting expectations while operating simultaneously in many sovereign countries around the world. Both the greater number of interested governmental and non-governmental' constituencies, as well as the magnitude of differences among them, magnify the challenge of defining and applying corporate social responsibility concepts to TNCs as opposed to national corporations.

Another unique aspect of corporate social responsibility as applied to TNCs arises from activist pressures generated by civil society groups in a TNC's home country (or even a host country) related to the firm's operations in other countries. Although international trading ties may allow groups in one country to bring pressure to bear against interests based in another country, the locally invested presence of a TNC provides an easier channel with a more proximate array of interests and activities to target. From a different perspective, these same TNC interrelationships mean that host governments can face policy pressures generated by non-citizen groups located in foreign countries, channeled through their influence on locally invested TNC operations. Actions by TNCs, whether on their own initiative or impelled by pressures from constituencies in other countries, can be viewed by a host country as unwelcome and unjustified external interference in its internal affairs. Of course, this result may be the explicit intention of external groups, as was the case with opponents of the former apartheid regime in South Africa.

The main point for this analysis is that a TNC's international investments give it a scope and capacity for social responsibility activities in multiple societies and political jurisdictions that broadens the audience of interested external constituencies while increasing the impact of corporate decisions on how to respond to calls for actions based on social responsibility norms.

A TNC's social responsibility may exert a differential impact on developing countries which are most often the target rather than an initiator of such actions. Much of this difference stems from the practical reality that developing countries are more host than home countries for TNCs, meaning that an enterprise will have matured using operating standards developed under a set of foreign legal and social expectations. Although TNCs can and do adjust to their host societies, where significantly different standards are encountered the invested enterprise must decide how to respond, bringing a potential for introducing change within the host society to cl degree that exceeds impacts arising under traditional commercial trading relationships.

The differential impact arising from FDI is reinforced by the earlier emergence and maturation of civil society groups in the developed countries. Developing country organisations that represent various elements of civil society are growing in both number and capabilities, and are expanding their ties with similar organisations in other countries. Still, developed country civil society groups provide the main impetus and follow-through influence for defining social responsibility standards and selecting the issues and business applications to target. Even where internationally—defined standards have been achieved as on certain environmental and human rights, including labour issues the proposition that local applications by TNCs in host developing countries fall unacceptably short of those standards (even though they may be consistent with local law and practice) is often made by groups from outside the country. Affirmative TNC responses to calls for change will then alter local operations and impacts in response to external rather than internal evaluations of "higher" social values and norms. This outcome may be question by developing countries, especially if the evaluation criteria and methodology for social performance measures are designed and implemented developed countries. In reality developing-country standards and practices may differ from those used in developed countries, and differ sometimes from desirable internationally-agreed narrows as well In these cases, however, it is important to assure that evaluation and performance measures derive primarily from international and not solely developed-country normative standards. The powerful influence of TNCs based in developed countries, and the prominent role played by similarly-located NGOs, may sometimes obscure the proper societal reference points for normative standards of corporate social responsibility.

7. Global Corporate Citizenship

The presence of foreign affiliates in many countries also engenders the notion of "global corporate citizenship". This idea can be conceptualised more broadly than the recent usage of corporate social responsibility that may appear one-sided if only the responsibilities or obligations of corporations to their host societies are discussed. Citizenship involves both rights and responsibilities. The "rights" involve the business community's concerns with standards of treatment in host countries for foreign investors become more complicated because TNCs may operate in societies that may well have different norms and expectations.

The citizenship notion also provides a bridge between legal regulations and broader social contract standards, acknowledging that a citizen's responsibilities to society rise beyond a floor of legally-mandated obligations. The addition of "global" to "corporate citizenship" emphasises that, for TNCs, rights and responsibilities must be reconciled within the global arena that constitutes their "society". This concept suggests that TNCs are not just legal citizens in each country in which they do business, responsible to that... society's standards and mores. TNCs are, in fact, "global citizens" whose international span, involvement and capabilities confront them with challenges, as well as opportunities, not encountered by national corporations.

The terminology of global corporate citizenship is naturally employed more by international organisations than by national governments, and by NGOs when they are addressing applications of corporate social responsibility outside a TNC's home country. Corporations themselves tend to use the term in a broadly ambiguous sense that specifies adherence to all host-country legal norms, without much specification of what standards may be global rather than national in character, or ho'" national norms should be dealt with if they conflict with global citizenship responsibilities. On the other hand, TNCs are usually quite clear that international investor rights should be respected if they conflict with national norms (for sample, when seeking the better of national treatment and the international law standard.

Global corporate citizenship has come to emphasise capability as much as causality, with an accompanying shift to notions of "doing good" rather than just "not doing harm". This broadened concept engenders calls on TNCs based in one country to prevent or rectify disagreeable conditions in other countries, because they have the capacity to influence outcomes, even where the firms may be, at most, distantly connected to the problem's origin. This type of challenge arises most obviously in the realm of political issues where TNCs are called upon to influence a host government's policies, or even press fot a change in the regime itself (for example, as occurred in protests against the former apartheid regime in South Africa). Activists in such cases often seek to demonstrate linkages by positing various types of TNC support for, or beneficiary interests in, an objectionable regime's governance. However, the clear trend over the years has been to incorporate as broad an array of TNC actors as possible, despite widely varying degrees of involvement with a country's political situation, in order to maximise potential capacity to alter outcomes. This historical expansion of corporate social responsibility concepts, particularly for TNCs underlines the need to work towards a consensus in the international community regarding how terms such as global corporate citizenship should be understood, defined and applied.

Overall, the idea of global corporate citizenship rests on the linkage between the rights granted in an enabling national and international regulatory framework that permits global business activities, and an accompanying set of social responsibility commitments accepted by TNCs that operate within, and benefit from, an integrating global community. Modern business activities require the certainty and regularisation provided by international agreements and institutions. Much of the expansion of global commerce over the past decade stems from the extension of liberal policy regimes wherein TNCs can organise their operations to seek optimal business efficiencies. However, maintaining the current investment and trade framework and ensuring its implementation—much less formulating new international economic instruments—may well depend on corollary progress towards the achievement of related societal goals that lack so specific an international legal elaboration.

Growing Importance of TNC Social Responsibility

The increased importance of TNC social responsibility corresponds to the growing scope of activities undertaken by these enterprises in the globalising world economy. Another factor that explains the broadened importance of TNCs in the global economy is the conceptual as well as operational expansion in the definition of TNCs, as they are now—in addition to their traditional FDI mode—increasingly defined by a variety of low- or non- equity investments. For example, large retailers, face calls for action against abusive working conditions in foreign plants that produce clothing for them under sub-contracting arrangements, although the retailer has no equity ownership or even foreign presence in the country in which the abusive labour conditions exist. A similarly broadened scope arises with enterprises whose valuable brand-names reflect many years of significant financial investments in building a product's reputation and image. These firms seek to protect their assets from misappropriation or misuse in foreign markets, establishing contractual obligations and accompanying controls that shape related business activities in those markets, with or without an actual presence by the TNC itself. Other low or non-equity TNC investments are reflected in the rapidly expanding range of international strategic alliances and partnerships that blend the comparative and competitive advantages of firms from several different countries in complex sets of evolving TNC linkages.

The changes in the magnitude and nature of TNC activity increase the relevance and importance of social responsibility in o interrelated ways. First, the impact of TNCs on people around the world has grown exponentially as these agents of economic globalisation reach into the life of domestic societies through both equity and non-equity mechanisms. Reflecting their increased global span and scope, TNCs have become more capable, proximate and aware actors whose activities can create causal links to societal outcomes in multiple countries and cultures. This impact can raise particular concerns for governments if the main TNC purveyor of change does not even have an invested local presence that is susceptible to the country's legal jurisdiction. This situation is most likely to occur in smaller developing countries whose societies may already be among the most vulnerable to the impact of external forces. Second, the rate of societal change in all countries has increased exponentially over the past few decades, affecting nearly every segment of the population and fostering noticeable feelings of anxiety and insecurity about the future. Globalisation brings the potential for more dramatic forms of change, derived from foreign influences, than would have developed more naturally and slowly within a country's own society. When channeled through FDI directly into a country's domestic fabric, these external influences can sometimes bypass or overwhelm a society's traditional adjustment mechanisms, thereby causing unexpected disruption or dislocation in social as well as economic processes.

Evidence of a potential backlash against globalisation is now appearing among societal groups most affected by the adjustment costs or other adverse impacts of rapid changes often associated rightly or wrongly with TNC activities. These pressures are most evident in labour and environmental organisations but are also present among domestically-oriented businesses that worry about increased competition and other societal interests that fear a loss of national autonomy or identity. Considered within a global context, social responsibility thereby takes on immediate practical and political importance for an international business community whose operations are conditioned on continued globalisation. In fact, there is a significant recent expansion of attempts to design newly cooperative ways for TNCs to respond, individually and collectively, to the evolving public expectations of a global social contract.

Recent Developments in Corporate Social Responsibility

Recent developments influencing the application of social responsibility concepts to international business derive from many different sources that comprise the stakeholders of TNCs, as well as from the corporations themselves. The major new development, at least in developed countries, is a proliferation of groups representing general public or specific issue interests that utilise a wide array of public pressure tactics, intermingled with instances of more direct dialogue, to promote an activist view of TNC duties towards an expanding agenda of social responsibility objectives. An expanding number of private enterprises are creating and/or revising individual statements of business principles or codes, although this group would still constitute only a small percentage of the total TNC community. Collective business organisations have adopted a mixed approach. Some sectoral groups actively responded to social responsibility pressures with industry-specific initiatives, while most organisations take a more cautionary approach, with the notable exception of a new statement on environmental principles. Governments continue to use international organisations to promote guidelines or codes of conduct on issues or in sectors in which international consensus is insufficient to support more precise legal standards. Only occasionally do national governments individually endeavour to develop TNC social responsibility initiatives.

1. Increased Activities by Civil Society Groups

A major development, particularly evident over the past decade, is the expanding number, range, coordination and activism among parts of civil society on issues relating to TNC social responsibility. Although some groups organise around very specific products, such as tobacco or nuclear energy,' most activism focuses on a relatively small set of major issue themes that are then exemplified and addressed in terms of specific products, companies or events. The issues mostprevalent over the past decade involve labour rights and working conditions, the environment and human rights, reflecting primarily a developed country perspective on TNC social responsibility. Some groups choose to focus principally on one of these areas, such as Greenpeace on the environment to Amnesty International on human rights. Others, such as religious organisations or other socially-directed institutional investors, may be active across a spectrum of social issues. Although most groups originate in the developed countries and draw their most involved membership from that base, an increasing number of organisations is emerging in developing countries as well. Where interests and perspectives are shared, groups may forge ties internationally through affiliated networks, conferences, newsletters and an exponential growth in relatively inexpensive Internet linkages. In fact, the emergence of the Internet is virtually unparall led in its impact, both on increasing international communication among elements of civil society and on facilitating these groups outreach to media channels that can focus instant attention on TNC activities worldwide.

2. Business Responses

The business community remains generally cautious regarding international initiatives that call for expansive new commitments to TNC social responsibility obligations. However, the diverse membership of general business organisations makes it difficult to reach a consensus among various industries on a common position that reflects the interests and needs of the full business community. As with some intergovernmental institutions comprised of diverse country members, organisational dynamics can either stall action or drive it towards a lowest common denominator position.

Many individual companies adopt their own codes of conduct that address social responsibility issues, sometimes drawing on an industry code or a set of international business principles. These codes of conduct have been adopted for a variety of reasons, ranging from the personal interest and beliefs of the chief executive officer to explicit expectations voiced by important governmental or other public interest groups. Often TNC code development is reactive, sparked by instances at perceived misconduct by a firm or others in its industry. Sometimes firms are proactive yet still defensive, formulating codes designed to head off possible public criticism. Among the most common factors that impel TNCs to promulgate individual codes are the following: firms, or their business associates, have received criticism for their practices; the industry is "high risk" in terms of exposure to or involvement with recognised social responsibility issues; the company has a "high-profile" name or product brand whose reputation and image is commercially important; and the firm's sales are vulnerable to organised customer boycotts or other commercial sanctions.

Although most corporate codes appear to be associated with past or potential public criticism, backed by possible commercial sanctions for misdeeds, positive inducements can also play a role. For some corporations, proactive corporate social responsibility is perceived as good business. Individual codes can serve to enhance the corporate image and, quite possibly, bottom-line profitability as well. Corporations may explicitly advertise their compliance with evolving social responsibility standards to gain favourable public recognition, particularly on environmental issues.

The increased activities of civil society groups require changes in the way business responds to the expectations stakeholders put forward regarding the companies' behaviour. In fact, companies see themselves confronted with increasing demands as to their accountability to, and interaction with, groups of civil society. For many years, corporations were generally trusted to be good corporate citizens without any particular activities required to prove this proposition right. Over the past 20 to 30 years however, companies have been increasingly confronted with demands from NGOs in many (especially developed) countries to provide evidence on their activities and impacts in different social responsibility areas. Some companies responded to this charge by drafting codes of conduct, others by preparing special reports on issues pertaining to social responsibility (including environmental or social reports). But this is no longer enough: companies are now more and more asked to establish systematic and independent monitoring and auditing processes to demonstrate how corporate principles and policies are implemented in daily business practices. In a further step, some companies are intensifying their interaction with stakeholders on social responsibility issues by actively soliciting stakeholders views on issues over which conflicts may arise or have already occurred. This process can be encapsulated in a four-step sequence:

(i) the "trust me"—phase, in which companies did not face any expectations going beyond the respect of law and order;

(ii) the "tell me"—phase in which companies were asked to give an account of their companies principles and impacts regarding certain social responsibility issues;

(iii) the" show me"—phase, in which companies are asked by civil society to actually demonstrate that they adhere to their principles and standards; and

(iv) the "join me"—phase, in which companies are asked to involve actively and interact with, stakeholders in the process of solving problems pertaining to social responsibility.

At present, companies can be found at different stages of the model. Many have not paid much attention to social responsibility issues, however. Those that have, do not necessarily respond in the same way to civil society expectations as individual companies find themselves under different pressures and, accordingly, respond differently. Still, there appears to be an overall trend that indicates that companies are putting more resources into responding to social responsibility demands and into interacting with civil society groups on issues pertaining to social responsibility.

3. Government Actions

Recent government actions on TNC social responsibility themes centre around renewed interest and activity on previously formulated international guidelines or codes of conduct. Initiatives in United Nations bodies relating to environment and labour issues, as well as continuing OECD reviews of the 1976 Guidelines for Multinational Enterprises, comprise the primary focus of this activity. The United Nations work on human rights issues is also important and relevant

These developments represent the most active recent government initiatives at the international level that directly address TNC social responsibility issues. Considerably more governmental time and energy has, however, been devoted to formulating legal instruments aimed at improving the international climate for foreign investment. For example, the dramatic proliferation of more than 1,700 bilateral investments treaties creates important rights for TNCs, usually enforceable through binding investment dispute settlement mechanisms. Investment provisions in regional trade arrangements such as NAFTA, which has labour and environmental side agreements, and MERCOSUR—which features a social charter—also aim at complementing the lowering of trade barriers with a parallel liberalisation of regional investment regulations.

Policy Implications

Certain patterns appear to be emerging as a result of these most recent trends in how TNC social responsibility issues are being addressed. First impressions form around the striking growth in both the number of organisations and the proliferation of initiatives that have gained importance in this area. Social responsibility concerns claim increasing attention among both government and business policy-makers, largely due to the stimulus of civil society groups and activities. Although the range of specific issues is quite broad, the vast majority of recent undertakings fall under umbrella categories related to labour, the environment and human rights. Other issues such as technology transfer, competitive practices, consumer protection and community relations have attracted less recent attention or have been addressed in aspects related to the other three categories. However, many of the issues that concern development and, therefore, are of particular interest to developing countries, have attracted little attention. Labour, the environment and human rights also all relate to existing United Nations instruments that furnish some common international ground in identifying core values while providing institutional processes that might help carry forward follow-up activities.

Although efforts continue to elaborate agreed standards to guide TNC social responsibility actions, there is also growing recognition of the importance of designing implementation steps that will give life to the standards' application. Hence, more discussion is occurring related to monitoring mechanisms that might provide for review, evaluation, revision and performance improvements. Crucial monitoring questions regarding "what", "who" and "how" remain unresolved in most cases, although there are clear efforts by civil society groups to encourage the use of management systems techniques and performance measures as well as independent auditors. One difficulty with implementation measures is the large variation among standards in their degree of specificity and applicability to particular industries and business operations. Conversely, the more specifically applicable standards and performance measures are to given products or sectors, the more proliferation occurs among institutional standards and follow-up mechanism, generating attendant time, information and resource demands. Indeed, the growth of activity in this area has been accompanied by an increasing overlap and, at times, seeming competition among proliferating standards arid their sponsoring groups. A plethora of codes may contribute to the risk of inducing a "code fatigue" among corporations, particularly where an enterprise may be engaged in multiple lines of business in countries around the world. TNCs aligned in shifting patterns of multiple international strategic alliances may also find it difficult to meld the various standards and reporting systems adopted by different alliance partners.

A positive pattern emerging from recent social responsibility trends is the increased efforts at improved dialogue between TNCs and social interest groups. Early relationships were often marked by mistrust and misunderstandings that fed a cycle of antagonistic actions and reactions. Harsh public commentaries and revelations of corporate misconduct still serve to focus attention on specific TNCs. While this may be necessary, substantive longer-term improvements often depend on establishing a working dialogue or even partnership with corporate representatives where debates over differences are aimed more at identifying mutually acceptable solutions and practical implementation steps. For their part, TNCs that acknowledge social responsibility commitments in a global context often also recognise that social interest groups can open a window on the world that offers valuable perspectives, insights and access to human resources that can assist an international corporation's search for better operational alternatives. Thus far, this pattern appears to develop more within certain industries and companies than others, often occurring in sectors that have experienced hostile clashes in the past.

A difficulty in this dialogue is to involve the various civil society groups that pursue social responsibility initiatives. Although civil society groups in some areas attempt to forge coalitions, or at least coordinate activities, corporations, business organisations and even governments often confront the task of selecting the most appropriate dialogue partners from among at times overlapping and sometimes competitive civil society groups. Furthermore, the representativeness of a given civil society group in terms of affected TNC constituencies is not always clear, particularly when social activists in developed home countries urge actions on behalf of people and interests located in host countries elsewhere. Although some civil society groups have expanded their international membership and seek to collaborate with local groups in many different countries, the decision-making leadership and institutional resources expended on many TNC social responsibility issues are often still heavily weighted towards the perspectives and priorities of the developed countries, especially institutions based in the United States and Europe. All this not withstanding, civil society groups deserve considerable credit for putting social responsibility on the public agenda.

Trade unions although showing solidarity in the drive to raise labour standards worldwide face a diversity of perspectives and interests among different country organisations, including locations in which effective independent unions do not exist. Human rights organisations pressing TNCs to influence political developments in other countries sometimes confront a particularly complicated challenge to demonstrate that their advocated path towards agreed goals is in line with the preferences and priorities of the most affected foreign population. This dilemma is best exemplified in disputes, even among human rights groups pursuing the same ultimate goal, over whether TNCs should withdraw from a country with significant human rights abuses, or stay and work for change.

An examination of recent TNC social responsibility trends can show where patterns of interaction have emerged, but it can also indicate where they have not developed. The three categories of social responsibility; issues that have in recent years attracted most attention have often been pursued independently of each other in terms of goal priorities. Advocacy groups cooperate and coordinate in efforts to press their agendas with government and business, but the collaboration is sometimes more tactical than substantive, playing off a few readily identifiable areas of overlapping interests, such as trade unions and human rights groups joining forces in supporting freedom of association and collective bargaining. Discussions are important among civil society groups, or with corporations and governments, regarding what trade-offs may exist and where priorities should lie in a practical world where attention, time and resources are allocated among many worthwhile objectives.

Discussion is especially crucial concerning he range of issues that, fall outside the three dominant categories, where desirable goals may go unfulfilled due to lack of attention or devoted resources. Development issues are particularly important here. Also important are potentially detrimental side-effects on other worthy objectives that could result from unforeseen (although potentially discernible) impacts arising from specific actions taken to protect the environment, improve working conditions or alter political circumstances in cm effort to aid human rights. A field in which such trade-offs or impacts may occur relates to a range of development goals, particularly for smaller developing countries and economies in transition.

Placed within the context of development goals and objectives, question regarding TNC social responsibility can involve decisions regarding how the formulation and application of particular standards will affect the distribution of costs and benefits among companies, industries and countries. An illustration of this notion is the differences emerging between developed and developing country 'perspectives on appropriate TNC social responsibility standards relating to employment issues such work hours. Proposals for a minimum "floor" that might substantially narrow the differences between developing and developed countries could significantly affect comparative economic advantages central to a country's development plans, with impacts on inward FOI, export and import levels, and local business development. Many aspects of the demands for improvements may be justified against any cultural background and are believed-unlikely to endanger the comparative advantage of developing countries. Even discrete measures such as the use of certification and labelling methods to signify compliance with labour or environmental standards could unintentionally reinforce the competitive powers of large TNCs, to the detriment of a developing country's smaller national firms that may lack the resources to meet consistently a management system's compliance, reporting and outside auditing requirements.

The fact that a discussion has now begun on some issues related to working conditions may aid in recognising when and which measures may have indirect, unintended, consequences if used to establish globally applied standards without a full prior vetting of interests and impacts on the international level. From the perspective of developing countries, some recent social responsibility initiatives may give the impression that TNCs and civil society groups from developed countries are setting standards that can have major impacts on a country's, development goals, without developing country governments playing a substantial role in determining the standards content, implementation or likely impact. Despite all the best intentions, when backed by the power of consumers in the developed countries, such initiatives could function like non-tariff barriers or significantly raise the cost of competitive entry into global markets. Such fears are exacerbated when standards determined in other countries are transmitted directly through TNC investment channels into the host country. Recent cases show that this influence can even be projected without traditional TNC ownership links through the power wielded by large retailers and other firms that can set contractual conditions all along their global supply chain.

The growing economic interdependence of the world community, to which the liberalisation of international investment and trade regimes has contributed significantly, has great potential for enhancing the living standards of people throughout the world. Greater efforts must be made, however, to manage the adjustment costs and social as well as economic disruption that accompany globalisation. By assuming greater social responsibility, firms can assist in these efforts. This is in their international self-interest. It is precisely the purpose of the global compact to contribute to the emergence of shared values and principles, which will give a human face to the global market, the foundation of a stable global society and economy. Failure to build such a foundation could contribute to a backlash against the liberalisation policies that, in the first place, provide the framework of legal rights within which firms pursue global business strategies. With these expanding global rights, however, come the corresponding responsibilities of "global corporate citizenship", including concern for development, the priority of the vast majority of the world's population. The societal boundaries for TNCs in the twenty-first century will be the global community.

❒

16

Business Concept in Constitution

India became independence with effect from 15th August 1947 and Indian Constitution came into effect from 26th January, 1950. It is a comprehensive one consisting of various provisions that effect every citizen of India. Certain provisions of the Indian Constitution are applicable to the business which are summarised below:

I. The Preamble of Constitution and Business

The socio-economic and political objectives of the Indian Republic and the basic guiding principles of State functioning are clearly stated in the Preamble of the Constitution. It also laid down the economic powers and responsibilities of the Union Government and the State Governments.

Economic Importance of Indian Constitution

The Preamble of the Indian Constitution guarantees to its every citizen:

(1) **Economic Justice.** The Indian Constitution laid down social, economic and political justice to every citizen in the country. It is, therefore, the duty of the business organisations to provide social, economic and political justice to every citizen.

(2) **Liberty of Thought, Expression, Belief, Faith and Worship.** This has been accepted in our Constitution that every citizen has liberty of thought, expression, belief,

faith and worship. According to this concept every business organisation should have liberty of thought, expression, etc. with everyone.

(3) **Equality of Status and of Opportunity.** According to this concept every businessman should believe and give equal opportunity to others. This can be achieved through eradication of poverty. This does not mean widening gap between the poor and rich.

(4) **To Promote Fraternity.** This assures the dignity of the individual and the unity and integrity of the nation. Fraternity or brotherhood in a society can be achieved through national integration. For this purpose, it is necessary to remove untouchability, castism, discrimination of religion, languages, education, removal of regional imbalances, etc. The issue of national integration and economic stability provided in the Constitution develops the spirit of brotherhood and cooperation. It is the duty of the business to work for the dignity of individual and integrity of the country. It should not do any such act which may affect the dignity and integrity.

II. Fundamental Rights and Business

[Economic rights and their economic dimensions]

It has been claimed that the Constitution offers all citizens the best fruit of democracy and of those basic freedom and conditions of life which alone can make life significant and productive. The fundamental rights stated in the Constitution (Part III) cover a wide range of rights; such as:

(1) Right of Equality (Articles 14 to 18)

The right of equality prohibits discrimination against any citizen on grounds of religion, race, caste, sex or place of birth. In public employment it ensures equality of opportunity to all citizens. Similarly for equal wages for similar types of jobs, no discriminatory behaviour with employees, equal opportunity to avail the benefits/advantages provided by the government. According to this concept, the business should provide equality before the law, social equality and economic equality.

(2) Right of Freedom (Articles 19 to 22)

The constitution guarantees the right of freedom to practice any profession, carry on any occupation, trade or business. However, this right is subject to reasonable restrictions in the interest of general public. As per the First Amendment made in the Constitution in 1951, the State is empowered to make laws relating to professional or technical qualifications necessary for practicing any profession or carrying on any trade business, industry or service. This right of freedom may be applied equally in business. The businessmen can express their problems freely to the government and can get a solution to the various problems. Similarly every citizen has the right to choose any business/profession and can form unions, and can call the meetings. Individuals have freedom to travel to any place in the country in connection with his employment or occupation and can settle at any place. Individuals have freedom to acquire property and wealth subject to certain restrictions made in the Constitution in 1951.

(3) Right Against Exploitation (Articles 23 and 24)

This right prohibits traffic in human beings and begar, and other forms of forced labour. Any contravention of this provisions shall be punishable according to law.

The constitutional provision for all types of forced labour purchase and sale of individuals, employing of children under the age of 14, employing of children near to the dangerous machines, dangerous constructive work, employing of women employees in night shifts in factories etc. The State will have powers to declare the public utility services as es ntial services in the interest of the society.

The Economic Importance of Right Against Exploitation are as follows:

(a) The government takes steps to bring an end to the bonded labour.

(b) Provisions are made in the Factories Act to prevent exploitation of women and children employees.

(c) The factory owners are required to appoint labour welfare officers, where in a factory 500 or more workers are employed.

(d) Factory owners have to make provisions for safety and welfare of the workers.

(4) Right to Freedom of Religion (Articles 25-28)

The Indian Constitution has given freedom to its citizens to follow any religion and to publicize it. India follows the policy of secular State. As such it will remain neutral in the religious matters and not interfere in the religious matters. The government is empowered to make certain laws in respect of the following and that are not considered as an interference in the religious matters: *(a)* to control the economic, financial and political activities in relation to religions, and *(b)* steps towards social welfare and social upliftrnent.

The economic/business interests are:

(a) Nobody may be compelled to pay taxes for the welfare of any specific religion.

(b) Killing of animals in the name of religion is prohibited.

(c) The government cannot spend any amount for the development of any religion from the money that has been collected by way of taxes from the citizens.

(d) Nobody shall be forced to give donations for religious conducts or propagation of any particular religion or caste, transfer of property or any agreement of a business nature in the name of a particular religion.

(5) Cultural and Educational Rights (Articles 29-30)

This Right under the Constitutional provisions is an effort to establish secularism in the country. Under this provision each individual and the religions have been given legal protection. Any person can establish his religious, educational and cultural institutions and can seek legal protection for the safety of these establishments.

Economic importance of these provisions are:

(a) The State will not discriminate in giving economic assistance to any educational institutions on the ground that it is managed by an minority community belonging to a particular religion or language.

(b) The aided government institutions cannot refuse admissions to any of the citizens on the ground that he belongs to a particular caste, religion, language or region.

(6) Right to Constitutional Remedies (Articles 32)

Section 32 of the Constitution gives the right to its citizens to make petitions in High Courts or Supreme Court for the enforcement of fundamental rights. These rights are not absolute. They are subject to reasonable restrictions by the State. The 44th Amendment of the Constitution in 1976 has abolished the "right to property" as a fundamental right. It has now been added to Chapter IV (Part XII) of the Constitution in Article 300A which provides that, "no person shall be deprived of his property save by authority of law". Thus, this right now retained as in Constitutional right.

Article 14 has generated equality before the law and equal protection of laws. This is, however, subject to certain limitations, such as the right of state to reserve posts for backward classes who are not adequately represented in services.

Article 19(1) sub-clause (ii) authorises the State to carry on any trade, business, industry etc. Whether to the exclusion complete or partial, of citizens or otherwise. Under this provision the government has nationalised many industries.

Thus, the fundamental rights enumerated in the Constitution guarantee a number of economic and social rights to the citizens. At the same time the State has the power to impose reasonable restrictions on such rights in the interest of the people.

III. The Directive Principles

The Directive Principles of State Policy is a unique feature of our Constitution. These principles are in the nature of directions to the legislature and executive that they should exercise their authority in such a manner so as to ensure due respect for, these principles.

The directive principles that economically or on the business point of view are as follows:

1. The State shall strive to promote the welfare of the citizens by securing and protecting a social order in which justice, socio-economic and political, shall inform all the institutions of national life. [Article 38(1)].

2. The state shall strive to minimise inequalities in income and endeavour to eliminate inequalities in status, facilities and opportunities [Article 38(2)].

3. The State shall, direct its policy towards securing:

   (1) right to an adequate means of livelihood to men and women equally.

   (2) equal distribution of material resources of the community for common good.

   (3) that there is equal pay for equal work for both men and women.

   (4) the operation of the economic system does not result in the concentration of wealth and means of production to the common good.

   (5) that the health and strength of workers (men and women) and the tender age of children are not abused; and

(6) that children are given opportunities and facilities to develop in a healthy manner and be protected against exploitation and against moral and material abandonment. (Article 39).

4. The State shall secure that the operation of the legal system promotes justice ensuring that opportunities for securing justice and are not denied to any citizen by reason of economic or other disabilities. (Article 39-A).

5. The State shall take steps to organize village Panchayat and endow them with necessary authority. (Article 40).

6. The State shall within the limits of its economic capacity make effective provision for securing the right to work, to education and to public assistance in cases of unemployment, old age, sickness and disablement. (Article 41).

7. The State shall make provision for securing just and humane conditions of work and for maternity relief. (Article 42).

8. The State shall endeavour by suitable legislation to secure the participation of workers in the management of undertakings. (Articles 43-A).

9. The State shall endeavour to protect and improve the environment. (Article 48-A).

Article 358 of the Constitution provides that in emergency situations the government shall have the power to deffer the fundamental rights for the time being and after the emergency is over the fundamental rights will be restored. The Government has the right to impose any restrictions on a business which is dangerous in itself or has been operating prejudicial to the public interest. The government shall have the right to impose duties on goods imported from other countries or within States. The Parliament is empowered to make laws to restrict the freedom of the business, commerce and trade in the public interest.

All the above stated provisions of the Constitution guides the government policies towards the business and other economic and social activities. The government has so far enacted a number of Acts and laws, policies and rules keeping in view of the directive principles; which are directly related with the business operations. The various Acts like MRTP Act, FERA, Factories Act, Minimum Wages Act, Payment of Wages Act, Maternity Benefit Act, Industrial (Development and Regulation) Act, Industrial Policy, Licensing policy etc. are based on the directive principles of the Constitution. The government, through these Acts and regulations, protects the interests of working women, men and children; prevents concentration of economic power, and promote and protects the interest of small and cottage industries.

IV. Constitutional Provisions Regarding Trade, Commerce and Intercourse within the Territory of India

The Part 13 of the Constitution dealing with Articles 301 to 307 provide for:

(1) Freedom for undertaking trade, commerce and intercourse within Indian territory.

According to Articles 301 of Part 13 of the Constitution; there will be freedom for every citizen to engage in any trade, commerce or intercourse (exchange) within the territory of India. But one has to observe other provisions of Part 13 of the Constitution.

(2) Powers of the Parliament to exercise restrictions.

Articles 302 of the Constitution provides that the Parliament is empowered to make laws to restrict the freedom of the business, commerce and trade in the public interest.

(3) Restriction on legislative powers of Central or the State Governments, in respect of trade and commerce.

The Central or the State Government will have no powers to make laws in the list provided in seventh schedule relating to trade and commerce by which a state gets seniority over any other State or it creates discrimination between States. [Article 303 (1)]

(4) Powers of the Parliament in case shortages of articles.

The Parliament is empowered to make laws to remove the situation of shortages of materials in any part of the country or may give powers to make laws so that a State gets priority or it creates any discrimination. In such a situation the provisions of Article 303 (1) shall not be applicable.

(5) Restriction of trade and commerce between States.

In spite of the provisions of Articles 301 or 303, the State legislative can impose following restrictions in this respect:

(a) The State Legislatures have the power to enact new regulatory laws or amend old ones so that it shall have right to impose duties on goods imported from other countries or within States. But this cannot be with the intention of discrimination between the States. [Article 304(a)].

(b) Any State can impose restrictions on trade and commerce for the public interest in the State; but such a legislation can only brought in the State Legislature with the prior approval of the President of India. [Articles 304(b)].

(6) The provisions of existing laws or Monopoly Act.

Section 301 and 303 of the Constitution cannot be effected on the provisions of any other existing laws unless the President of India issues any such guidelines on this matter. Similarly, the provisions of Section 301 of the Constitution cannot be effected on any laws passed by the Central of State Government under the provisions of Articles 19(6) (ii), where the Central or the State has monopoly powers in the operation of trade; commerce or service.

(7) Appointment of any Authority. In order to fulfill the objections of Sections 301 to 304 of the Constitution, the Parliament has the right to make any law for appointing an authority. (Article 307).

Thus, the Indian Constitution incorporates a number of provisions that are economically significant in the matters of trade, commerce and industry, and have far reaching implications. A business organisation has to operate keeping in view of these provisions as stated in the Indian Constitution that have been discussed in above paragraphs.

Rights and Duties of Citizen

Just as a citizen enjoys certain rights, he also has to discharge certain duties towards 'Right' and 'Duty' are used as if they are opposed to each other and would exclude each other. The impression is quite wrong because rights and duties are closely connected with each other and they always go together. There are two ways of proving this. Whenever a right is given to one citizen, say 'A', then it becomes the duty of all other citizens 'B', 'C' and so on to respect that right, to allow citizen 'A' to enjoy that right and not to do anything to destroy it. When I am given the right to property, it is the duty of all other citizens not to take away my property, and to allow me to use my property in any way I would like to use it. But is should be remembered that the same rights are given to all citizens and can be enjoyed only if each allows all others to enjoy the same. The right to property is given not only to me but to all other citizens and just as it is their duty to allow me the right of enjoying any property, it is my duty to allow others to enjoy the same right to property, this would mean that I can enjoy my right to property only if I accept at the same time my duty to respect if for other. These rights and duties are so closely related with each other that one cannot exist without the other.

Rights are the claims or privileges enjoyed by a citizen recognized by the State. It is the duty of the State to protect your rights, otherwise rights are meaningless. Your right imposes a two-fold duty on you. You have a duty to see that you do not interfere in any way with the enjoyment of similar rights of others. As you have a right, so have others. It is your duty not to take any action likely to interfere with their rights. Secondly, rights cannot be enjoyed for nothing. You are given certain rights so that you can perform certain duties as a citizen. These rights are necessary to enable you to exercise your civic duties. The State by guaranteeing these rights, imposes on you the duty to act as a responsible citizen of the community. It will be your duty to develop your abilities and to try your utmost to further the common good of the country.

Rights and duties are related in the following way:

1. One's Right is Another's Duty. A right belonging to one person imposes a corresponding duty on the others to respect his right. His right is, therefore, their duty. For instance, an individuals right to property implies that it is the duty of others not to take away or steal his property without his consent or to interfere with his enjoyment of it. In this sense rights and duties are the two sides of the same coin. From the stand point of man who enjoys, it is a right and from the point of view of others who must allow him to enjoy, it is a duty. But it is necessary that every right should carry a corresponding duty with it. For instance, a landlord has only right over his tenants and no duties towards them and that the tenants have only duties and no rights. In fact, in such a case, no right or duty is involved and it is a case of exploitation, not a right or duty. The landlord really has no right over the tenants but only a power backed by the wealth and influence. A right can truly be called a right only if it does not hinder the general welfare of other people.

2. One's Right is One's Duty Also. A right is at the same time a duty. If an individual enjoys a right, it must be remembered that the same right belongs to all other individuals. Therefore, it is his duty not to interfere in the enjoyment of other's rights. For instances, if 'A' has the right to express his opinions freely it is also his duty not to deny the same right to 'B'. Further may right to use public road also implies my duty to admit the fact that others too possess the same right. This right implies one more duty also. If I enjoy liberty of speech, it is my duty not to misuse this right by preaching anything that is against law or that disturbs peace or spreads hatred among different communities.

3. One's Right is One' Duty to Use it in a Right Way. It is the duty of an individual to make proper use of this rights. The improper use of rights proves harmful for others and society can never tolerate it. If an individual is given the freedom of speech and expression, he should not misuse this right by spreading hatred among different communities. He should not instigate the people against the government. He should not spread rumours. Misuse of rights by the citizens of a State leads to disorder and anarchy. I leads to setting up wrong precedents. Public welfare is ignored if people do things of their own accord.

4. One's Right is One's Duty to Use it for Social Good. A right is not only the means for furthering self-interest but it is also a means for promoting the general interests of society. An individual enjoys right only so long as he contributes his best instructed judgement to the common good of the people. In case an individual misuse his rights, and his activities prove harmful to the welfare of the community, his rights are forfeited and he becomes liable to punishment. For example, if an individual uses his right to freedom of speech to spread bitterness between different sections of the community or to preach violence or anarchy, he becomes a hindrance in the way of social development.

5. Duties Towards the State. Rights of an individual imply certain duties towards the State. The State gives us rights and they are also safeguarded by the State. State creates such an atmosphere as is necessary for making full use of rights. Rights have no meaning without the State and hence it is the duty of every individual to respect the laws of the State.

VARIOUS CHARACTERISTICS OF RIGHTS

On the basis of the definitions of rights given above we can say that the following are the essential features of rights:

1. Rights are Available Only in the Society. Rights can be possible only in'the society. The rights cannot be possible outside the society. Whenever an individual lives in society he is to seek the help of others for various,purposes. Outside the society every individual is absolutely free and he makes use of force for achieving his end.

2. Rights Can be Used for Public Good. A right can be used only for social good and not against the interest of the society. Rights can be had in society and are recognized by the soceity. Therefore, it is but natural that they should be exercised in the best interests of society.

3. Right is a Claim of the Individual. Right is a claim of the individual for doing things independently. The individual claims his rights from the society. In other words, rights means demand for certain facilities.

4. Right is Reasonable and Moral. The society recognizes only that claim of the individual which is reasonable and moral. The society recognizes only that claim which concerns the welfare of the individual. A claim which is harmful to society cannot be accepted.

5. Rights are Recognized by Society. Rights are those claims of the individual which are recognized by the society. The claim of the individual takes the form of a right only when it is recognized by society.

6. Rights and Duties go Together. Rights is always accompanied by duties. Rights and duties go side by side. A's right is B's duty and B's right is A's duty. Rights cannot be granted without the performance of certain duties.

7. Rights are Enforced by the State. Another important feature of right is that it is enforced by the State. The rights are also protected by the State. The State grants through laws and those who violate the law are punished by the State. The State is the guardian of the rights of the individuals.

8. Rights Change with the Time. Rights are not static. Rights change with the changed social, economic and political conditions. For example, in the early phase of industrial expansion, the right to unfettered use of one's property was recognised. But in the mid-twentieth century the right to property has been considerably curtailed in almost every country. Hence, no permanent and unchanging catalogue of right can be compiled.

9. Rights are Universal. Rights are given equally to all the people in society. Right is not the claim of a particular individual but it is a claim of all the individuals. A right which is enjoyed by one individual is also enjoyed by other individuals.

HUMAN RIGHTS

There are certain rights of the individuals which are inherent in his personality. Such rights are called as Natural Rights. Man is moral and rational being and this very state entitles him to the enjoyment of certain, rights, which are called as Human Rights. These rights are derived from the inherent dignity of the human person and they should be available to man every where and at all times. These rights are necessary condition for the development of human personality and without them man would really not be man. The ideal of human rights and fundamental freedom is universally accepted and this problem never received so much attention as to day. The Declaration of the Rights of Man following the American and French Revolutions contained fundamental human rights. The Declaration of American Independence, 1776 stated: "We hold these truths to be self-evident, that all men are created equal, that they are endowed by their Creator with certain inalienable rights, that among these are life, liberty and pursuit of happiness." The French Declaration of the Rights of Man, 1789 emphasised the concepts of "liberty, equality and fraternity." In 1941 in his message to American Congress, President Roosevelt laid stress on Four Freedoms, of Man and said, "We look forward to a world founded upon four essential freedoms-freedom of speech and expression, freedom of worship, freedom from want and freedom from fear." Right from the Atlantic Charter till the end of the Second World War in their wartime conferences the Allied Powers laid particulars stress upon the human rights and fundamental freedom. In the Declaration of the United Nations of 1942, the United Nations put on record that complete victory over enemies is essential to defend life, liberty, independence and religions freedom and to preserve human rights and justice in their own lands. But unfortunately, while it is accepted in principle, it seems to be ignored in practice. There are very few states where the human rights and fundamental freedoms are available, otherwise in most of the states people are deprived of it. They are the cases of racial and religious discrimination in general and the problem of apartheid in particular. Again, there is economic and political exploitation. In totalitarian regimes and dictatorships people are deprived of their political rights and freedoms. In 1971 inhuman and barbaric cruelties, and genocide committed on the people of Bangladesh moved the very conscience of making. The policy of Partheid pursued in South Africa has been condemned by all. The General Assembly has repeatedly condemned this policy as a crime against humanity.

THE UNITED NATIONS AND HUMAN RIGHTS

Even before the end of Second World War the Allied Powers expressed the hope that after the victory in the war, efferts would be made for the protection of human rights in every state. In Dumbarton Oaks Conference of 1944 the emphasis was laid on the promotion of human rights and fundamental freedoms. The representatives gathered at the San Francisco Conference demanded that the declaration of human rights should be included in the UN Charter itself. Though a separate declaration of human rights does not find place in the Charter but the specific mention of the human rights has been made in the Charter at various places. The peamble to the United Nations Charter refer to the determination of the United Nation's to affirm faith in fundamental human rights, in the dignity and worth of the human person, in the equal rights of men and women.

Under Article 1, one of the purposes of the United Nations is to achieve international co-operation in promoting and encouraging respect for human rights and for fundamental freedoms for all without distinction as to race, sex, language or religion.

Under Article 13 it is the duty of they General Assembly to assist in the realisation of human rights and fundamental freedoms for all without distinction as to race, sex language or religion.

Under Article 55 it is provided that the United Nations shall promote universal respect for, and observance of, human rights and fundamental freedoms for all without distinction as to race, sex language or religion.

Under Article 62 it is the duty of the Economic and Social Council to make recommendations for purpose of promoting respect for, and observance of human rights fundamental freedoms for all.

According to Article 68 of the Economic and Social Council is required to set up commissions for the promotion of human rights.

It is for the first time that the provision in regard to the protection of human rights and fundamental freedom has been made in the UN Charter. Under the Charter the United Nations is empowered only to encourage the promotion of human rights and fundamental freedom, but has no power to take any binding measure in this regard. The Charter deals with the human rights and the fundamental freedoms but it does not give any precise definition of there rights or a clear acknowledgement of the principle of their observance. In fact, the Charter aims at the voluntary co-operation of the states in achieving this objective. There is no doubt that the provisions of the Charter in regard to human rights have absolutely no binding authority but at the same time the protection of human rights has ceased to be the exclusive jurisdiction of states and has become the concern of the United Nations. According to Oppenheim, "it cannot of the that the provisions of the Charter on the subject signify a full and effective guarantee of the inalienable rights of man on the part of international society. In particular these are absent from the Charter Clauses embodying either a more precise definition of these rights or a clear acknowledgement of the principle of their observance.... Whatever these may be, the observance of fundamental human rights in so far it is the subject matter of local obligations, ceases to be one of exclusive domestic jurisdiction of states and has become a matter of legitimate concern for the United Nations and its members."

UNIVERSAL DECLARATIONS OF HUMAN. RIGHTS

The United Nations Commission on Human Rights was asked to prepare a draft on the general principles governing the human rights. After two and half years of painstaking labour the Commission on Human Rights prepared a draft of the Universal Declaration of Human Rights, as a common standard of achievement for all peoples and all nations. This declaration, the first of its kind in history, was approved by the General Assembly on December 10, 1948. This declaration is the first international definition of the rights of man, It is, therefore, 10th December, commemorated every years as Human Rights day.

The Declaration of Human Rights contains 30 Articles including the preamble. The Preamble stresses the dignity and worth of the human person.

Article 1. All human beings are born free and equal in dignity and rights.

Article 2. Everyone without any distinction is entitled to all the rights and freedoms set forth in this Declaration.

Article 3. Everyone has the right of life, liberty and the security of person.

Article 4. No one shall be held in slavery or servitude; salvery and salve-trade shall be prohibited in all their forms.

Article 5. No one shall be subjected to torture or to cruel, inhuman or degrading treatment or punishment.

Article 6. Everyone has the right to recognition everywhere as a person before the law.

Article 7. All are equal before the law and are emitted to equal protection of the law.

Article 8. Everyone has the right to an effective remedy by the competent national tribunals for acts violative of the fundamental rights granted to him by the constitution or by law.

Article 9. No one shall be subjected to arbitrary arrest, detention or exile.

Article 10. Everyone is entitled in full equality to a fair and public hearing by an independent and impartial tribunal.

Article 11. Everyone charged with a penal offence has the right to be presumed innocent until proved guilty according to law in a public trial. No one shall be held guilty of any penal offence which did not constitute a penal offence at the time when it was committed.

Article 12. No one shall be subjected to arbitrary interference with its privacy, family home or correspondence, nor to attack upon his honour and reputation.

Article 13. Everyone has the right to freedom of movement and residence within the borders of each state.

Article 14. Every one has the right to seek in other countries asylum from persecution.

Article 15. Everyone has right to nationality. No one shall be arbitrarily deprived of his nationality nor denied the right to change his nationality.

Article 16. Men and Women of age, without any limitation due to race nationality to religion, have the right to marry and to found a family.

Article 17. Everyone has the right to own property and no one shall be arbitrarily deprived of his property.

Article 18. Everyone has the right to freedom of thought, conscience and religion.

Article 19. Evenone has the right to freedom of opinion and expression.

Article 20. Everyone has the right to freedom of peaceful assembly and association.

Article 21. Everyone has the right to take part in the government of his country with equal access in public service.

Article 22. Everyone has the right to social security and is entitled to realization of the economic, social and cultural rights indispensible for his dignity and the free development of his personality.

Article 23. Everyone has the right to work, to free choice of employment, to just and favourable conditions of work and to protection against unemployment. Everyone has the right to equal pay for equal work. Every one who works as the right to just and favourable remuneration.

Article 24. Everyone has the right to rest and leisure, including reasonable limitation of working hours and periodic holidays with pay.

Article 25. Everyone has the right to adequate standard of living, including housing, medical care and security in the servant of sickness, widowhood and old age.

Article 26. Everyone has the right to education.

Article 27. Everyone has the right to take part in the cultural life of the community and to share in the scientific advancements and its benefits.

Article 28. Everyone is entitled to social and international order in which the rights and freedoms set forth in this Declaration can be fully realized.

Article 29. Everyone has duties to the community in which alone the free and full development of his personality is possible. In the exercise of his rights and freedoms, everyone shall be subjected to due recognition and respect for the rights and freedoms of others and just requirements of morlity, public order and general welfare.

Article 30. Nothing in this Declaration may be interpreted as implying for any state, group, or person any right to engage in any activity or to perform any act aimed at the distruction of any of the rights and freedoms set forth above.

The Universal Declaration of Human Rights is a historic event of great importance for the mankind. It is an international 'Magna Carta' of all men everywhere. According to Dr. Charles Malik of Lebanon, this Declaration was not simply a resolution but the part of the UN Charter itself. About the Declaration, American representative in the United Nations observed: "In giving our approval to the declaration today, it is of primary importance that we keep clearly in mind the basic character of the document. It is not a treaty, it is not an international agreement. It does not purport to be a statement of law or of legal obligation. It is a declaration of specific principles of human rights and freedoms, to be stamped with the approval of the General Assembly by a formal vote of its members and to serve as a common standard of achievement for all peoples of all nations." According to Palmer and Perkins, "The declaration is merely a statement of principles, not a legally binding instrument; but it has become one of the best known of international documents, and it has often been referred to in resolution of the U.N., the specialized agencies, regional arrangements and other international organisations, and in national constitutions, legislations, and court decisions. It is a beacon light for all mankind, even though it has been honoured more often in the breach than in the observance."

However, it must not he forgotten that no machinery has been provided to enforce the provisions of this Declaration. The states cannot be compelled to enforce this Declaration. Oppenheim remarks. The Declaration is not an instrument which is legally binding either directly or indirectly. In 1948, the Commission on Human Rights tried to make this Declaration binding on the states but this could not be possible as it would have provided an opportunity to the majority states in the U.N. to interfere in the internal affairs of the other states. Although the Declaration is only in the form of a recommendation to the states, yet the U.N. General Assembly has condemned the states which have violated the declaration. The General Assembly has a number of times condemned South Africa for its policies of aparthied.

Lacking in binding and legal force the Declaration, nevertheless, presents a moral ideal before the states in very clear terms. The states can hardly afford to ignore the world organisation and the world public opinion.

International Covenants on Human Rights. The United Nations not only made a Declaration of human rights but it also took steps in the direction that they are effectively implemented by the states. With this view, the General Assembly in 1951, requested the Commission on Human Rights to prepare draft of two covenants, one on Civil and Political Rights and the other on Economic, Social and Cultural rights. The purpose of these covenants is to give more precise definition of the human rights and make necessary provision for their observance. These covenants, after being approved by the General Assembly, were to be submitted to the U.N. members as treaty, and it would be binding upon all states that ratified it. On 16th December, 1966, the General Assembly adopted and opened for signature, ratification and accession three International Covenants on Human Rights *(a)* International Covenant on Civil and Political Rights; *(b)* International Covenant on Economic, Cultural and Social Rights; and *(c)* The Optional Protocol to the International Covenant on Civil and Political Rights.

The principles proclaimed in the Declaration of Human Rights have been embodied in a number of International Conventions, binding upon the states which ratify them; and in some cases the international machinery necessary to ensure the application of the conventions has been established. The important conventions adopted by the General Assembly are Convention on Genocide (1948), Conventation on the Political Rights Political Rights of Women (1952), Convention on Slavery (1956) and Convention on the Elimination of Racial Discrimination (1965). On 20th November, 1959 the General Assembly unanimously approved the Declaration of the Rights of the Child. This Declaration contains a number of human rights and fundamental freedoms that are provided in the Universal Declaratiön of Human Rights of 1948.

The U.N. has been able to do lot for the promotion of human rights and fundamental freedoms. The General Assembly has repeatedly declared that the policies of partheid pursued by the Government of South Africa are a negation of the U.N. Character and constitute a crime against humanity. From 1952 to 1960, the General Assembly made repeated appeals to the South African Government to revise its policy on this question in accordance with the principles of the U.N. Charter. In its resolutions adopted in 1963 and 1964 the Security Council called on all states to implement an arms embargo against South Africa. In 1965 the General Assembly appealed to all states to stop their economic collaboration with South Africa. In 1970, the General Assembly made a General Appeal for contributing moral, political and material assistance to the people of South Africa in their legitimate struggle against apartheild. The General Assembly established the United Nations Trust Fund for South Africa to provide legal assistance, relief and education to the oppressed people of South Africa, March 21, is celebrated as "International Day for the Elimination of Racial Discrimination. "The General Assembly designated 1968 as the "International year for Human Rights." And 1971 as the International year for Action to combat Racism and Racial Discrimination."

ETHICS AS SOCIAL POLICY

For many centuries most Europeans identified morality with the law of God. More recently, more philosophy has turned secular. But much of it retains a central feature of the religious view. Roughly, and most importantly, it reains the view that the term "morality" is a proper name for, a code of conduct that is binding on us by virtue of the sorts of beings we are and that is sufficient for the moral life. That code is knowable and every historical code—the morality of any society—is evaluated by reference to it. This secular view differs from most religious views by holding that the code is accessible to us by reason rather than by faith. But both religionists and the relevant secularists share the view that moral standards are discovered, not devised or invented.

Many philosophers — myself included — deny that "morality" is a proper name for a supercode. There is no supercode. The term "morality" stands to moralitaies as the term "language" stands to languages. Like languages, moralities are human artifacts and are to be evaluated by how well they serve us. These evaluations admit to objectivity. Our choices between standards are not mere matters, of taste. But different standards may be justified for different groups and for the same group at different times.

According to instrumental theories, moral standards are like social policies. The main difference is that policies are established by officially designated bodies, and do not require the allegiance of large numbers of people. Moralities on the other hand, typically evolve and do require allegiance. If most people in a society do not accept a moral standard, that standard is not an element in that society's morality. When moralities are raised to the level of self-consciousness and evaluated, however, they are evaluated in precisely the same way as policies are.

Given the biological similiarities between human beings and the requirements of social life, we can expect certain broad similarities between the reasonable moral codes of various social groups. All such codes will regulate homicide, property exchanges, sexuality, etc. But historically, groups have regulated these activities in very different ways. And given the various conditions of human life, such differences may be reasonable. That is, the specific rules governing homicide, property exchanges, sexuality, etc. may differ from place to place and these differences may be justified.

Moreover, the standards governing these activities may reasonably vary from domain to domain within a given society. Roughly, my own version of instrumentalism differs from other versions by emphasizing this domain sensivity of ethical standards. It also holds that concrete, domain-specific values play important roles in justifying moral standards. Thus, for example, our standards governing family relations are justified in relation to the concreate goods of family life (intimacy, security, etc.). By virtue of the relative concreteness of this approach, disputes about ethical standards resemble disputes about social policy even more than they do on other versions of instrumentalism.

According to the EASP, then, the standards governing homicide, property exchanges, truth-telling and other such activities differ within a society from domain to domain. Many standards, moreover, are specify to particular domains. This is what is meant by "domain, sensitivity." Now is not the time for a rigorous definition of "domain," but the general idea is clear enough. Examples of domains include the family, the educational system, the scientific community, the criminal justice system, the medical system, the economic system etc. Roughly, each domain is characterized by a set of socially recognized goals or purposes and by a set of "structures." Among other things for example, the family is supposed to provide intimacy and love and to nurture children, the scientific community is supposed to deliver truths about nature, and the criminal justice system is supposed to deter crime and otherwise protect our rights as citizens. Unless they can be shown to be unreasonable, these goals count as justificatory values for their respective domains.

As suggested, domains are also structured. A domain structure is a set of related roles or positions. Corresponding to any role or position are: *(1)* some set of qualifying standards (*i.e.* criteria that govern who or what counts as a role occupant): *(2)* some set of rights and duties; *(3)* some system of remuneration and other rewards or penalties; and *(4)* some set of ideals or virtues and vices (*i.e.* characteristics that are admired and condemned in role occupants). Taken together these elements define a role or position. As one can see, various ethical standards are built into roles. Indeed, many of the most important questions of professional ethics are questions about what these elements should be. Most of the standard questions of medical ethics, for example, are questions about what qualifies one to be a patient (*i.e.* to receive various forms of treatment) or a practitioner; what rights and duties one has as an occupant of these roles; what traits we should encourage in people who occupy them; and on what basis people should be rewarded or penalized for role-related conduct.

We are now in a position to see how EASP differs from standard versions of rule utilitarianism and contractarianism. These theories begin with very general accounts of goods and evils and try to justify social moralities in relation to them. They move from the top down. EASP moves from the bottom up. We begin with the goods and evils that play justificatory roles in the various domains of social life. We grant these presumptive status, that is, we assume that they are reasonable unless they can be shown to be unreasonable. And, very roughly, we evaluate the moral structure of a domain in relation to reasonable values for that domain (constrained by impacts on other domains).

Before the development of applied ethics, philosophers paid little attention to role-defined moral standards. In so far as they were interested in normative questions at all, as opposed to questions about moral language, they focused their attention on moral considerations that were supposed to be binding on us merely as persons or human beings. It was widely assumed that we could generate role-related standards by applying these "basic" or "core" percepts to specific circumstances (much as we apply basic principles of physics to solve problems of engineering). Few writers in applied and professional ethics now accept this engineering model. But EASP rejects it in a particularly radical way. For it holds that there is no important difference in kind between "core" standards and role-defined standards. "Core" standards like "don't kill" and "don't steal" seem to be more fundamental than role-defined standards like "don't neglect your children" and "pay workers a living wage" in part because they seem to be perfectly general. But few of them apply in every domain. For example, soldiers are expected to kill during war, and active euthanasia is arguably permissible. Moreover, both the importance of and, in some cases, our criteria for applying core standards vary from domain to domain as well. Other things being equal for example, it is worse to fail to rescue family members than to fail to rescue strangers. And what counts as *x's* stealing from *y* often depends on how *x* and *y* are related to one another. These domain related variations in the weight of moral standards explain why the constancy assumption is false.

HOW TO THINK SYSTEMATICALLY ABOUT THE ECONOMIC DOMAIN

Reflections on the ethics of the economic domain typically occur under two headings; political economy and business ethics. Political economy proceeds at the macro level. To the extent that it is normative, it asks: what set of basic economic institutions serves us best? Here the most basic institution is property. And the question is: what forms or rules or property ownership and exchange serve us best? The traditional candidates are laissez-faire capitalism (unregulated private ownership and exchange), regulated capitalism (private ownership with restrictions on ownership and exchange), and various forms of socialism (public ownership, with varying degrees of central planning or control).

Business ethics is a relatively new area in philosophy and its boundaries are not precise. For the most part it addresses questions that arise within the context of capitalism. Many of these questions are wholly or partly about the degree to which private ownership and exchange should be regulated (*i.e.* about the form of capitalism we should adopt). At a certain point these questions become questions of political economy (the difference is one of degree). But many questions are considerably more specific than that (*e.g.* those concerning whistleblowing, affirmative action, and corporate responsibility). In any case, however we answer the questions of political economy even if we are socialists—those of us who live under capitalism will also need to answer the more specific questions of business ethics. This suggests an important theme, namely the fact that a set of basic institutions is flawed does not by itself entail that those institutions impose no obligations.

EASP employs the same basic strategy for questions of both political economy and business ethics. The difference is that in addressing questions of business ethics it takes capitalist institutions as background conditions. In relation to political economy, the question is roughly: what general set of economic institutions best promotes the goals of the economic domain? In relation to business ethics, the questions are roughly: *(1)* What form of capitalist institutions best promote these goals (*i.e.* to what degree should private ownership and use of property be regulated)? and *(2)* given the institutions currently in place, what more specific distribution of rights, duties, virtues, vices etc. best promotes these goals? These formulations are rough since we also need to take into account the ways in which various answers affect the distribution of goods in other domains. (Some of the most interesting socialist arguments against capitalism contend that capitalism by its nature is corrosive of them.) In any case, EASP holds that disputes about political economy and business ethics are disputes about the ends of economic life and how they are best promoted.

As suggested, the strategy is to assess the wisdom of candidate principles in relation to the goods and evils at stake in the economic domain (and, as appropriate, to a more general class of goods and evils as well). What are these goods and evils? That is, what goods do we, collectively and impartially, want from an economy?

To begin with, other things being equal, we want as much prosperity as we can get, given our resources and technology. Prosperity, of course, is not reducible to the aggregate volume or value of goods and services (*e.g.* to gross national product). A society that produces an enormous volume of goods that very few people want or need, for example pyramids or jetpowered snowmobiles, is not prosperous in the relevant sense. A society is prosperous to the extent that its members enjoy the material basis for a good life. Very roughly, life enhancing goods promote "fits." To provide prosperity, then, an economy must produce the right kinds of goods and distribute them to the appropriate people. The variety and magnitude of these goods will vary with cultural values and environmental conditions. What enhances life in New York may ruin life in Eden.

Production and distribution are not the only dimensions of prosperity. We also need to consider certain "externalities." For example, an economy does less to provide the material basis for a good life to the extent that it poisons its air, food, and water and destroys the beauty of the land. Accordingly, these evils must be subtracted from the goods of productive activity in estimating the life-enhancing value of the whole. This is another reason that the GNP is a bad measure of social prosperity. Ironically, the damages in question may lead to increase in the GNP. When water and air are poisoned, pure water becomes a commodity, and industries devoted to water and air filtration flourish.

The second goal of the economic domain, maximizing the quality of working life, also has several dimensions. Most of us spend more than half our waking time working, so we have a considerable stake in the quality of our job experience. Other things being equal, we want our jobs to be safe, socially useful, secure, and interesting. We also want them to preserve our dignity, that is, we want to eliminate demeaning occupational statuses and demeaning work relationships. In addition, we want our jobs to leave us with sufficient time and energy to enjoy our home life and to develop other interests. Of course, there will be trade-offs among these goals and between them and the goal of prosperity.

Suppose one accepts these as basic economic goods. In that case EASP holds that we can decide basic questions of political economy and business ethics primarily in relation to them. According to EASP, the best set of basic economic institutions is (roughly) the one that advances these goals best while doing the least damage to the goals of other domains. And the best business ethic is the one that satisfies this description within a framework of capitalist institutions. Vague as this is, it is enough to show why minimalism demands too little and those who import principles may demand too much.

Let us begin with the imported principles approach. Moral criticisms of business practices take at least three forms. Practices are said to violate human rights, to violate some principle of commonsense morality, or to violate some abstract principle central to our tradition (*e.g.* that persons should be treated as ends in themselves, or that practices must satisfy rules that promote utility). According to EASP, these criticisms are valid only if the percepts on which they are based can be shown to be relevant to the business domain. And they are only as powerful as those precepts are in that domain. Both issues are decided by determining to what extent adopting these precepts promotes the social goals of business activity (and prevents business activity from undermining other goods).

Consider human rights. According to business ethics Patricia Werhane, free expression and due process are human rights. Accordingly businesses violate human rights if they penalize their employees for exercising their right to free expression or if they penalize employees without due process. Unfortunately, however, Werhane does not provide us with a principled basis for fixing the scope or importance of these rights in the domain of business. Clearly they do not have the same scope or force there as they do, for example, in the political realm. What scope and importance should we grant them?

Let us take the example of free expression. The American courts have ruled that our right to free expression against the state includes the right to dress more or less as we please. Should we have this right against businesses? If we did we could dress as we pleased on the job, that is, there could be no dress codes or uniforms at all. Political expression works differently. The political domain is undermined if employers are allowed to prevent employees from making public speeches, participating in political demonstrations, and so forth. Particular companies may have economic reasons for imposing such restrictions, for example, they might lose customers if highly visible employees take politically controversial stands. But it is not clear that this sort of thing will undermine the goods of the economic domain as a whole. And it is clear that such restrictions on political expression directly and seriously undermine the goods of the political domain (*e.g.* the goods of democracy). According to the minimalist, employees have no rights to free expression against business (*e.g.* one can be fired for expressing political views on or off the job); according to the maximalist, they have the same right to free expression against businesses as they have against the state.

The same holds for due process. According to the minimalist account, employers have no obligation to provide workers with opportunities to appeal dismissals, demotions, and so forth, According to the maximalist, they are obligated to provide them with the same safeguards they enjoy against the state. Again, EASP allows us to take a principled middle position. There are good job-quality reasons for grievance procedures. Workers are protected against the exercise of arbitrary power, job security is enhanced, etc. However we can achieve these without instituting the elaborate range of safeguards maximalism would require (lawyers, juries, etc.).

Moreover, there are good reasons for varying both the grounds and the procedures for grievance from one kind of enterprise to another. Thus, for example other things being equal, corporate managers should not be allowed to make personnel decisions on the basis of personal relationships or likes and dislikes. This is inefficient and creates a low-quality working environment. But personal consideratiqns might be a reasonable basis for hirings, firings, and so forth in small, owneroperated businesses or family business. In small businesses, the quality of the work environment and everyone's job performance may depend heavily on goodwill among the employees and between the owner and her workforce. And, of course, it is hard to know how one could have a family business if one could not hire family members preferentially.

We turn now to the second form of importation, namely criticisms that proceed from some standard of commonsense morality.

Such criticisms are common. They appear in sermons, in editorials and in speeches by business leaders themselves. In his ground breaking book, The Moral Foundations of Professional Ethics, Alan Goldman attempts to provide a theoretical defense of this approach in relation to business (and the professions in general). On Goldman's view, businesspeople (and professionals in general) are sometimes exempt from ordinary moral constraints. But they are exempt only if granting exemptions can be justified in terms of more important moral considerations (or, for him, rights). That is, professionals and businesspeople are exempt from a commonsense, *prima facie* duty *D* in their domains if and only if honoring that precept in that domain violates *D*, a more important *prima facie* duty.

Since Goldman believes that we can make this judgment on a domain by domain basis, his view is domain-sensitive. But since he holds that we make these judgments by making trade-offs between a set of (presumably) constantly weighted duties and obligations, it is not domain sensitive enough.

Consider this account in relation to lying. Golden would condemn lying in business except in contexts where there is an important moral reason to lie (a reason that outweighs the wrong of lying). But consider lying in business bargaining (That's my last offer, if you don't, I'll take all my business elsewhere," etc.). There seems to be no moral reason favouring such lies. But they seem harmless enough. One's last offer can always be sweetened if rejected. And the seller can always accept an offer he had (falsely) described as utterly out of the question. Nothing is lost when business people engage in this common place strategy. Indeed, the game dimension adds interest to the negotiator's job.

We now turn to the third form of criticism based on importation: criticism made on the basis of higher-level principles. Consider Kant's principle that we should never treat another person as a means only. Although it is not entirely clear what this means, at the very least it forbids us to disregard the good or interests of those affected by our actions. Yet business life abounds with cases in which we disregard the interests of others. It is difficult to see how a market economy could function otherwise. If we had to treat everyone as an end in himself, we could not win business from a competitor without considering the impact of our decisions on that competitor's life (will she be driven out of business? Will her income be so reduced that she cannot send her children to college? And so on). Nor could we reject offers from prospective house-buyers or renters merely because we could get a better price elsewhere (where will they end up living or how much benefit would they get from one's house? etc.). In areas in which a market economy is justified, people must be free to meet as buyers and sellers, considering one another merely as means to each other's financial ends. Of course, charity is permitted. But it cannot be obligatory.

But there are also business contexts where we should take the interests of others into account. It is wrong to use high-pressure sales techniques to sell people what they neither need nor want, to underproduce some necessary good in order to keep the price high, to pay starvation wages to people who are desperate for work if one can afford more, etc. These particular ways of treating others as means reard prosperity as have described it. In one way or another they prevent us from getting the right goods to people on a sufficiently large scale. The problem with Kant's principle is vagueness. We need to know when and how we are required to take the good of others into account in our actions. EASP provides us with a principled basis for answering that question.

In sum, many well motivated responses to the minimalism of Milton Friedman and his followers involve importing principles from other areas into the business domain. But no one has yet provided an adequate principled bias for doing this. EASP does. Nonetheless, minimalists will argue that EASP requires too much so we should also review the EASP case against minimalism.

One theoretical foundation of minimalism is libertarian. Property rights are said to be natural rights: and the exercise of those rights is said to be limited only by a very narrow range of moral side constraints (namely, those mentioned earlier). Any transaction, exchange, or strategy that falls outside the range of these constraints is simply the exercise of a right, and is therefore beyond moral criticism.

The main argument against this natural rights approach is that appeals to natural rights are based on appeals to intuition about principles or cases/or to appeals to the natue of persons, and they have no sound theoretical basis. According to EASP, the rules governing acquisition, use, and exchange may differ reasonably from culture to culture, and from historical period to historical period. These rules delimit recognized property rights (and hence define property). And there.is no set of real or true property rights in relation to which they can be evaluated. Rather other things being equal they are justified by how well they satisfy the purposes of economic life.

Even if there were natural property rights, minimalism would not follow. Natural rights provide us with protections against certain sorts of interferences by other persons or the state, but they do not provide us with moral carte blanche. Within those protected boundaries, there are plenty of chances to act immorally. Thus, the right to free association does not morally entitle us socially to exclude someone for petty or malicious reasons. The right to free speech does not morally entitle us to gossip maliciously or say hurtful and insulting things for our own entertainment. And the right to property does not morally entitle us to pay our workers starvation wages whenever the market allows.

The minimalist might respond that minimalist business practices so far outstrip morally constrained practices in producing wealth that they provide everyone with a better prosperity/job quality package even if some job quality is lost. Again, this argument may be empirical, axiological, or some combination of the two. To the degree that it is empirical, the minimalist accepts my account of prosperity (and uses wealth as a synonym for it). To the extent this is so, we differ on whether minimalist practices do a better job than morally constrained practices at producing and distributing life-enhancing goods, where externalities are taken into account. The arguments are economic but the burden of proof is surely on the minimalist. For the straight forward examples are on the other side. Every time a corporation refuses to produce assault rifles, pollute the air, or lower wages to the minimum it refuses to reduce prosperity. The minimalist needs to show that the collective positive impact of unconstrained profit maximization on prosperity is sufficient to compensate for such obvious losses.

❐